WOMEN AND POLITICS

WOMEN AND POLITICS

Editor

KIRAN SAKSENA

GYAN

WOMEN AND POLITICS
(Women)

ISBN : 81-212-0699-5

Reprinted in 2011 in India by
Gyan Publishing House
23, Main Ansari Road, Daryaganj,
New Delhi - 110002
Phone : 23282060, 23261060
Fax : (011) 23285914
e-mail : books@gyanbooks.com
gyanbook@vsnl.com
website : gyanbooks.com

Printed at : Gian Ridhi Offset Printers, Delhi

CONTENTS

PREFACE

This book "Women and Politics" is a compilation of essays, which are contextual as well as theoretical. The fact is that the women have been sidelived in all political systems of the world.

And in reality, it is true that at present democratic politics is unable to establish a democratic society in real sense and the presence of women in the political process, in the most economical, scientific and technological advance countries is almost negligible.

How could this sorry state of affairs be dealt with is a moot question. The chapters in this book make an effort to grapple with theoretical insights and empirical studies.

The feminist movement is not confined, at the present juncture to a small segment of society. More and more people are joining it—women as well as men. Its contours also spreading. As the movement has gained momentum it also has evoked varied responses. Many issues relating to women and socio-political economic set-up have cropped up which led to many discourses. At times it appears that they are incoherent and clash with each other's ideological concerns. There are also confusions in drawing straight-forward goals. The confusion would not be cleared by only wishing. This requires a deep understanding about women's issues. There are some issues which unite women and some divide them. To understand the problematics of women's questions world-wide, the context social relations has to be taken into account. The perspective of women's movement in developed countries would be different from those of the developing countries. The differences reflect inherent contradictions in the established social order of which women are integral part. The entrenched power structures of all the societies, developed and developing look for ways and means to continue their domination. When they confront movements which call for restructuring social and economic relations, they resist with utmost power and construct ideologies to retain their control over the system. These ideologies surrepitiously make inroads in the women's movements to obstruct the radical transformation of society. Unable to turn the tide backward they camouflage as the champion of women's rights. The constitutional political rights in all democracies are a case in point. The democratic constitutional stipulations guarantee equality of sexes in the political field. Women like men can take equal part in political processes and can participate in all political activities, can vote, contest elections, be associated with political parties, be members of legislative bodies, head of executive, be in judicial system, be in bureaucracy and everywhere, they have a right to reach at the top without legal hinderances. However, when this constitutional and legal rights are seen in real life, it becomes clear that women are conspicuous by their absence everywhere and especially at the top. They are supposed to slog in inferior positions by creating an artificial boundary, i.e., private and public. Private domain is for women and public for men. The private domain draws power from public and therefore, women have to depend on men for exercising whatever power, if they have any, very reluctantly bestowed on them, as the benevolence of some great men. The established socio-political order and their economics only perpetuate a facade of equality. Women are all over the world not content with this situation and are exploring the ways to come out from this impose. There are divergence of views, differences in approaches, but there is also the determination to overcome all hurdles to acquire the status of humanity, equality, freedom and friendship and hopes for bright future. This book is an effort in this direction.

Kiran Saksena

LIST OF CONTRIBUTORS

Ms Madhvi Lakshmi
Research Scholar
Centre for Political Studies
Jawaharlal Nehru University
Delhi.

Ms Jinee Lokaneeta
Lecturer Department of Political Science
Kirori Mal College
Delhi University.

Dr Sanghmitra Budhapriya
Assistant Professor
Birla Institute of Management Technology
New Delhi.

Ms Saraswati Haider
Freelanco Journalist and Research Scholar
Centre for Social System
Jawaharlal Nehru University
New Delhi.

Pradeep K. Sharma
Research Scholar Centre for Political Studies
Jawaharlal Nehru University
New Delhi.

Dr Sudha Pai
Associate Professor
Centre for Political Studies
Jawaharlal Nehru University
New Delhi.

Ms Seema P. Salgaonkar
Lecturer, Political Science
Government College
Quepem Goa
American.

Ms Sandhya Gupta
Fulbright Scholar
Princeton University Princeton
New Jersy.

Dr Uma Singh
Associate Professor,
Centre for South Central,
Southeast Asian and South Pacific Studies
Jawaharlal Nehru University
New Delhi.

Prof S.J. Havewalla
Centre for Persian and Central Asian Studies
Jawaharlal Nehru University
New Delhi.

Dr Vijaya Lakshmi
Associate Professor
Centre for American and Weat European Studies
Jawaharlal Nehru University
New Delhi.
Ms Yamini Gupta
University of Burmingham
U.K.

INTRODUCTION

In the following introduction an attempt has been made to take an overview of the various ideas and propositions put forward by the gender scholars and theorists, which would serve as the theoretical framework of the chapters which comprise the present compilation.

The last phase of the previous millenium in the history of human society has been an era of women's march for coming out of oblivion for self-realization of their immense potentialities. The march has not been smooth and the path is arduous with many hurdles. The domination of patriarchy with the advent of civilization left no room for women to allow them freedom to live life of their own choice. The shackles were so strong that very rarely some women of extraordinary calibre could break them and i.e., why very seldom women were visible in social and political life. They were exceptions rather than the rule. It is a fact "that women have been systematically deprived of rights in the past". However, less and less consensus exists on their position in the present time (Figueira, 1987, 19).

The present cannot be snapped from the past. The women all over the world, east-west, north-south have not only been marginalized, but had suffered most cruel and torturous behaviour. Humanists, philanthropists, religious leaders and prophets have advocated a fair and gentle treatment to women, time and again, in spite of misogynist social and political set up of all societies. However, the 'sympathetic' spokesperson of various hues, religious and social leaders of society were not simply hesitant, but vehemently opposed to equality or independent rights of women. Women as silent sufferers made tremendous contribution to society in the past, which remained unrecognized and therefore, history is considered 'his' achievements and 'hers' has been completely blacked out (Figueira, 1987). History records the united struggle of suppressed people who had fought against their oppressors, but no where there is any mention of united women's struggle, before the advent of modern socio-political structures of democracy in the West. More precisely in the 19th century only John Stuart Mill clamoured for political rights of women and drew attention, within his liberal framework, to the consequences of women's deprivation of the right to vote, in his famous book *Subjection of Women*. At the same time Mary Wollstonecraft's strong defence of women's rights in *A Vindication of the Rights of Women*. These two stalwarts of the champions of women's rights gave a push to a sort of movement, which at the end of millenium has taken momentum and now women's issues have become important for social-political thinkers, philosophers and as well as women activists.

The liberal interpretation of women's subjugation has been counteracted as the emphasis of these liberals mainly rested on the arguments for the support of women's rights to vote (Lewis, 1989). This is asserted that the argument that equal political rights have been granted to women through universal suffrage is at best naive. Voting is necessary, but it is not a sufficient condition for gender parity in politics. Two major obstacles stand in the way of such parity. First, given the close relationship between economic and political power, women as a group are at a disadvantage. Second, women as newcomers in overwhelming male institutions have to contend with issues of internal legitimacy (Figueira, 1987, 29).

Women have been marginalized in every walk of life. The nineteenth century liberal thought made great effort to give some space to women in socio-political life, although that space was quite inadequate, has been asserted by the champion of women's rights. They looked toward the problematic that why women are marginalized, the answers are sought in gender questions and feminist interpretations. Feminism is not a unified simple, corpus of thought, but a complex multidimensional, multiple discourse. Rosemarie Tong defines feminism as a struggle to end sexist oppression. Therefore, it is a struggle to eradicate the ideology of domination (Rosemarie, 1984, 25). Its aim is not to benefit solely any specific group of women, any particular race or class of women. It does not give privilege to women over men. It has the power to transform in a meaningful way all our lives. Most importantly, feminism is neither lifestyle nor a ready-made identity or role one can step into. Diverting energy from feminist movement that aims to change society, many women concentrate on the development of a counter culture, a woman centred world, wherein participants have little contact with men (Rosemarie, 1984, 26).

Feminism investigates that why women are marginalized and there are many divergence of views as they look at this very question from their ideological and methodological perspective. In early liberals, who began to question about socio-political injustices done to women and possible rectification hardly mentioned themselves as feminists, but the trend they started put in the brand name as liberal feminists. Liberal feminism is closely associated with the liberal thought emerged on the scene in late eighteenth and nineteenth century, which moved from early thinkers to contemporary times and there are many champions of this strand of thought. For them society remains structured in ways that favour men and disfavours women in the competitive race for the goods with, which our society rewards us power, prestige and money (Rosemarie, 1984, 29). They agree that the single most important goal of women's liberation is sexual equality, or as it is sometimes termed as gender justice. What liberal feminists wish to do is free women from oppressive gender role that have been used as excuses or justification giving women lesser place at all ... (Rosemarie, 1984, 28). The effort of classical liberals to do away discriminatory policies from the law books did not yield much and women's position did not improve and they are not able to achieve the equal status with men. The welfare liberal feminists argue "that society should not only compensate women for past injustices, but also eliminate socio-economic as well as legal impediments to women's progress today (Rosemarie, 1984, 29). The liberal clamour for empowerment of women in all walks of life so that they could take advantages of the legal constitutional equality provided to them by continuous reform process in recent times in democratic society.

Liberalism associated with capitalist system is unable to guarantee the rights of women. The Marxists believe that class ultimately better accounts for women's status and function(s). Under capitalism bourgeois will not experience the same kind of oppression that proletarian women will. What is distinctive about Marxist-Feminism is that it invites every woman, whether proletarian or bourgeois, to understand women's oppression not so much as the result of the intentional actions of the individuals, but as the product of the political, social and economic structures associated with capitalism (Rosemarie, 1984, 39).

The radical feminism asserts that women's oppression is inherent in all societies.

Tong refers to Alison Jagger and Pala Rothenberg's book titled *Feminists Frameworks,* which delineate radical feminism as follows :

1. That women were historically, the first oppressed group.
2. That women's oppression is the most widespread, existing in virtually every known society.
3. That women's oppression is the deepest in that it is the hardest form of oppression to eradicate and cannot be removed by other social changes such as abolition of class society.
4. That women's oppression causes the most suffering to its victims, qualitatively, although the suffering may often go unrecognized because of the sexist prejudices of both oppressors and the victims.
5. The women's oppression ... provides a conceptual model for understanding all other forms of oppression (Tong, 1984, 71).

Regarding gender and sexuality radical feminists have taken the lead not only in articulating the 'highly elaborate' and deeply entrenched nature of sex/ gender system, but also in sketching exit routes out of it. In particular, radical feminists have proposed several ways to liberate women from the cage of femininity. These proposals have ranged from working towards an androgynous culture in which male and female differences are minimized to replacing male culture with female culture. Similarly, radical feminists have proposed several ways to enable women to depend thereselves from the sexual domination of men. These have ranged from transforming institution of heterosexuality so that neither men nor women play a dominant role to rejecting heterosexuality in favour of celibacy, autocraticism or lesbianism. Although much of what they had to say about sex and gender has also been said by non-radical feminists should be credited with detailing the ways in which men rather than 'society' or 'conditions' have forced women into oppressive gender roles and sexual behaviour (Tong, 1984, 95).

Radical feminism became quite popular in the sixties of previous century. Some feminists feel that the questions radical feminism address are one sided and do not explain the complexity of women's subjugation. The socialist feminists make effort to grapple with this question. Socialist feminism is largely the result of Marxist thought. That is with the tendency of Marxist patriarchs to dismiss women's oppression as not merely as important as workers oppression supposedly, what women suffer at the hands of men is slight compared to what proletariat suffers at the hands of bourgeoisie (Tong, 1989, 173). Currently socialist feminists are no longer content with simply fitting capitalism and patriarchy together, whether it be through the use of two concepts or one .... These theorists seek to encompass not only Marxist, but radical and psycho-analytic insights under one conceptual umbrella (Tong, 1989, 193).

This is interesting that Sigmund Freud has been castigated by many feminists for apparently basing his notion of penis envy or the the girls perception of herself and all those like her as inferior. Feminists used him (Freud) productively. During the last two decades, or so, at least four variety of psycho-analytic feminism have been evolved each developing the Freudian corpus in feminist directions. A first variety attempts to cleanse Freudianism of any and all traces of biological determinism; a second pays scant attention to overly discussed Oedipus complex, analyzing instead the pre-Oedipal stage during, which mother infant relationship was most intense; a third focus on the strength rather than the much discussed weakness of woman's morality and a fourth reinterprets the Oedipus complex, giving its non-patriarchal meanings. Together these four varieties of psycho-analytic feminism have shown that Freudian thought may have liberating as well as enslaving potential for women (Tong, 1999, 147).

Simone De Beauvoir, the existentialist philosopher focussed on women's marginalization from existential perspective. She has adopted the ontological and ethical claims to explain the lower position of women in society and says that from the beginning man has named himself and the woman the other .... If the other is a threat to man, if woman wishes to remain free, he must subordianate woman to him. According to existentialist it is not only women are subordinated, there are other categories too, however, they hold that woman's oppression by man is unique for two reasons. First, unlike the oppression of race and class the oppression of women is not a contingent historical fact, an event in dime, which has sometimes been contested or reversed. Women have always been subordinated to men. Second, women have internalized the point of view that man is essential woman inessential (Tong, 1989, 202).

Post-modernism also takes into account women's issues, however, more than any other type of feminist thought—Marxist, liberal, radical, psycho-analytic and post-modern feminism has an uneasy relationship to feminism (Tong, 1989, 217). Their starting point is very similar to that of Beauvoirs 'understanding' that woman is still other, but rather than interpreting this condition as something to be transcendental, post-modern feminists proclaim its advantages. The condition of 'otherness' enables women to stand back and criticize norms, values and practices that the dominant culture (patriarchy) seeks to impose on everyone, including those who live on its perphery-in this case women.

Thus, 'otherness', for all its associations with oppression and inferiority is much more than oppressed, inferior condition. Rather it is a way of being thinking and speaking that allows for openness, plurality, diversity and difference (Tong, 1989, 219). Post-modern feminists ... attempt to criticize the dominant order, particularly its practical aspects and to valorize the feminine, the woman and the other.

The environmentalists feel very close to feminism. For them the women have close affinity with nature. The protection of nature, therefore, integral to feminine personality. The eco-feminism, that therefore, assumes women play a predominant role in activities relating to resources and that degradation of these resources in turn has disproportionate effect on women is considerably well-established by now. There also seems to be a strong line of thought endorsing women's special consciousness of ecological issues, which supposedly makes them better managers of natural resources. But does this hold true for all women? Before we begin to assess the extent of this alleged link, it is essential, therefore, to look more critically at the category of women (Sandhya Venkateswaran, 1992). Eco-feminists believe that "the process of change have actually sharpened gender inequalities where women have remained confined to the domestic sphere with none or reduced access to resources and decreasing control over their labour and knowledge, whereas men have not only gained control over resources and access to technology, but given their orientation and motivations, have derived benefit from most programmes. Of course, this may not hold true for men of all socio-economic groups. Landless labour or artisans for example, men or women may not have such access to resources, but in such cases too, men have found other options, such as migration, or merely transferring their responsibility to women, leaving women in a worse position (Sandhya Venkateswaran, 1992m 165).

'Feminism' this way is not a closed thought process. It has been growing and has become amorphous and cannot be defined in straight terms. However, this cannot be denied that in spite of vast differences in approaches, there is a recognition that virtually across time and place men and women are unequal in the power they have, either in society or over their own lives and the corollary belief that men and women should be equal, the belief that knowledge has been written about, by and for men and the corollary belief that all schools of knowledge must be re-examined and understood to reveal the extent to which they ignore or distort gender (Barbara Arneil, 1999, 3).

There is unanimity amongst all the feminists that women are handicapped because they are bereft of power, therefore, they may be endowed with 'power' in other words they should be empowered. The women's movements all over the world took up cudgels for the development of women and various yardsticks are evolved to measure women's development. The UN agencies take into account development of a country in terms of how much they have achieved in 'human' terms and indeed women are also considered 'human' and their development is also taken into consideration. The fact that in developing countries the general living standards of are extremely low and women lives, a very substandard life. They are even deprived of bare human necessities, the question therefore, revolves around rights and empowerment. The protagonist of 'rights' clamour that women should fight for their rights and they focus attention to political, social and economic rights of women. The participation of women in social and political life should not be only symbolic, but real. The women should struggle against the discriminating social practices, which almost all societies practice. The women's movement in the sixties during last century was reflective of the mood of 'rebellion' against the different kinds of women discriminatory taboos practiced in society. In economic sphere, their labour is under-estimated, they do slog and work, but it is generally unpaid or underpaid and unskilled. They are always in the lower wrung of society and very seldom get opportunities. They are considered only body and therefore confined to 'body oriented' work. Their mental capacities are ignored and are kept at bay where mental calibre is required.

In the sphere of politics at the present juncture, women's position is very contradictory. Generally ... the political rights have been 'bestowed' on her without facilitating her the exercise of these rights. The critical situation has been aptly described by Figueira-Mcdonough De Sarri. "The argument that equal political rights have been granted to women through universal suffrage is at best naive. Voting is necessary, but not a sufficient condition for gender parity in politics. Two major obstacles stand in the way of such parity. First, given the close relationship between economic and political power, women as group are at a disadvantage. Second, women as new comers in overwhelmingly male institutions have to contend with issues of internal legitimacy (Figueora-Sarri, 29).

The sorry state of affairs women's rights group assert could be overcome only by sustained struggle.

The empowerment school of thought tackles this issue differently. It takes cognizance of the fact that women have to be given their due share in economic, social and political life to have capacities to achieve their goal. Therefore, empowerment is necessary, education, health, social awareness, etc., are prime conditions, which women need at the moment, which would give her consciousness for 'rights' too. This is asserted that fundamentally there is not much difference between women's rights movement or women's empowerment. They are complimentary.

Needless to say that political power plays a very important role in the domination of women. Therefore, engendering politics is need of the hour. There are different aspects of politics and almost complete exclusion of women there. The gender discrimination practiced for centuries has incapacitated women that they cannot stand unless a strong system is provided to them. They have been left behind. They have to be brought forward. The task is stupendous and there is a lack of will on the part of the establishment. The end result is aptly described by Barbara Arneil (1999, 1) who discusses the Western societies, which is also applicable to all societies. Pick up any newspaper in any major Western city. In it you will find a daily snap shot of the political world around you. It will be filled almost certainly with images of conflict and people who are trying to resolve these conflicts. It will have the words of politicians and political pundits. And there will be advertisements, editorials and cartoons. And if you pause to consider it, you will find almost universally that the majority of these images, words and their authors will be men. We must ask ourselves 'why'. How do we explain the gender imbalance in nearly every aspect of Western political life? In search of these answers we must go beyond the headlines and front pages of our newspapers to the roots of Western thinking about both politics and gender.

The core of politics is the exercise of power. This exercise of power goes beyond government encompassing instead nearly every human grouping, where individuals conflict over collective goals and means by which they resolve those conflicts.

Politics has many different facets and sociability is one of its important ingredients. Sociability implies duality of existence, public and private. The politics belongs to public sphere, where intrusion of woman is forbidden. They belong to private world only. Now, this is anti-democratic as it is against the principle of equality. It is recognized world over that this gender division of public-private is unjust for both men and women. Politics has to be engendered. This book endeavours to make an effort to take up issues concerning women and politics.

Madhvi Laxmi in her keenly perceptive chapter on "Construction of Gender: Deprivation of Women from Politics in India" looks into the question of gender construction, which is a universal phenomenon. She suggests how biological differences become gender differences in social processes. The author on the authority of some studies emphasizes that gender not only relates to man-woman relationship, but reflects other relationships too, like problem of white feminism vs black feminism, first world feminism vs third world feminism, upper class feminism vs lower class feminism, upper caste feminism vs Dalit feminism lies in the domination of 'one' over the 'other'.

Jinee Lokeneela's essay: "Women Empowerment: Redefining Agenda" is an extension of theoretical issues raised by Madhvi Laxmi. She questions the political agenda of empowerment of women, which has become vogue as method of redressing gender discreimination. She argues that empowerment of women emerges as an extremely limited concept. The fact that empowerment should imply a power to participate in all decision making in all sphere of society, with no separation of the public and private in all social, political, economic and cultural process of the society. However, discourse of women's empowerment in order to nullify the emancipatory potential of the concept has reduced it to signify a demand for political participation defined only in terms of reservation into given set of political institutions. She emphasises her view by pointing to the fact that political parties with no political commitment towards struggle for women's rights not only fail to transcend the state's agenda, but further collaborate with the state in order to keep the patriarchal process intact.

Sanghamitra Budhapriya in her psycho-analytical essay "Fear of Success among Women Managers", an empirical study bordering theoretical issues with empirical evidences analyzes, the psychological role of gender in social, political and professional life of women, opines that organizational roles and statuses have traditionally been gendered: certain positions have been considered appropriate to women and filled by women or men. The gendered aspect is located within a large patriarchal social world, which is hierarchically based with men occupying positions of dominance over women. Sanghmitra with her empirical data analyzes the psychological responses of women, if they ventured to achieve against the gendered categories.

Saraswati Haider in her article "Political Conscienization and Participation of Women in a Squatter Settlement" studies the political attitudes amongst the migrant woman: conscienization is a complex phenomenon, which Haider documents. She focuses on the liberal parliamentary democratic system of India; its processes, issues, its institutions: the role of migrant women are expected to play in the system, their rights and duties within the liberal parliamentary democratic grid as well as the migrant women's conscienization of women politics as charted out by Indian women's movement.

Another important marginalized section of women is Dalit women in India who are at the lowest wrung of society in India. Pradeep Sharma makes an indepth study of the marginalized status and observes that, if politics means power then women must achieve power by themselves and by their own fight and struggle. They must fight for their recognition as an equal partner of social life. Dalit women in particular have to fight against oppression in more active and vocal ways. They have to fight against the caste system and against the male dominated patriarchal social structure. At the first level, they have to associate their movement with the large anti-caste Dalit movements while at the second level they have to align themselves with the feminist movements.

The women's movement in India, while facing great difficulties is able to achieve some gains regarding the invisibility of women in politics. The 73 Constitutional Amendment passed in April 1993, by the Indian Parliament and ratified by all the State Governments by April 1994, which gives women 33 per cent reservation of the seats at all levels of panchayat system, is a significant measure. The experience of women's participation in grassroot politics is very important as this will pave the way for further development. This book records the experiences of three studies of different parts of India, viz., Meerut in Uttar Pradesh, Goa and Kalva village from Andhra Pradesh. Sudha Pai's study deals with office bearers of *Gram* Panchayats in her essay "Pradhans in the New Panchayat: A Study of Three Villages of Uttar Pradesh". The essay touches the social milieu of Uttar Pradesh and rampant gender inequality that exists there, which, nevertheless, would have strong bearing on the functioning of officials of panchayat such as *Pradhans*. Against Sudha Pai's observation Seema P. Salgaonkar's study of women in "Panchayat Raj Institutions: A Case Study in Goa", gives an optimistic picture, as in Goa trends show that women have been able to assert themselves in village panchayat politics. They also have started taking interest in their work. Salgaonkar gives very constructive suggestions on how the participation of women at village level be more affective. Sandhya Gupta, a Fullbright Scholar wants that women should learn some lessons from Kalva village of Andhra Pradesh for political participation. Her article on "Transforming Women's Participation in the Panchayat from the Bottom UP: Lessons from Kalva Village", draws the point that there is perceptible change in the participation of women in panchayat activities, which was earlier passively dependent on husband and family and was dismissed by much of the village. There are three things, which should be kept in mind: the motivation of women, networking involvement of the village and redefining (thereby transforming) the panchayats in the mind of the villagers.

This compilation has not only focussed on India, but also covers the experiences of other countries. Uma Singh's essay "Islamic Fundamentalism and Women in Pakistan", analyzes the role of religion in Pakistan politics and how Islamic fundamentalism is throttling the rights of women in the name of religion. Successive rulers have repeatedly used religion in an attempt to win political legitimacy and mobilize public support. But such moves have never worked. Now in recent past Nawaz Sharif, like a true successor of Zia was pursuing the same retrogressive course in the name of Islam. (The essay was written before the coupd'etat by the military in Pakistan). J.J. Havewalla's observations about religious fundamentalism are slightly different from those of Uma Singh. Havewalla thinks that women in Iran are enjoying their rights very well within religious edicts. Her article "The Status of Women in Islamic Republic of Iran", says that Iranian women, mentally, physically and politically seem to be more independent than many other women behind the veil anywhere else in the world.

Yamini Gupta in her essay "The Political Socialization of South Asian Women in British Politics", draws the conclusion that political socialization plays an important role in assisting a woman to achieve her political ambitions. Vijay Laxmi's study, "Gender Gap and American Election", analyzes the changing women's vote in 1980 and 1990s and brings out the startling facts about that in spite of affluence, opportunity for education health care, etc., women in the USA are as 'behind the scene' as in any of the poor developing country.

This book *Women and Politics* focuses on issues concerning women is the result of workshop held under the auspices of the Research Committee "Women Politics and Developing Nations International Political Science Association". Some of the contributions were not presented in the workshop and were written to make this book more comprehensive. I thank to Dr. Hemlata Swarup, former Vice-Chancellor, Kanpur University, Kanpur and Dr. Pam Rajput, who extended their cooperation and inspired me to hold the workshop. I also thank the Indian Council of Social Science Research (ICSSR) for generous financial assistance for organizing this workshop.

1

CONSTRUCTION OF GENDER: DEPRIVATION OF WOMEN FROM POLITICS IN INDIA

Madhavi Lakshmi Kondreddy

Whenever the question of Indian politics arises, the last issue that is discussed, is the issue of women. Women, constituting half of the humanity, are being marginalized all over and one of those 'mainstream' marginalized areas for women is the area of electoral politics. Before understanding the deprivation of women from Indian politics, it is necessary to understand some of the theoretical aspects on gender. Hence, this chapter is divided into three parts. The first part deals with some theoretical aspects on gender, the second part discusses the deprivation of women from Indian politics and the third part comprises of the strategies for engendering politics.

I

The term 'gender' is a very complex one and hence, it needs a systematic examination. Generally terms like 'gender' and 'sex' are taken for granted as mere biological categories. It is very important to understand that these are socially constructed categories and not natural ones. In order to understand gender, one has to go through some of the diverse perspectives on it. Joan W. Scott's definition of gender contains two parts. According to her "gender is a constitutive element of social relationships based on perceived differences between the sexes and gender is a primary way of signifying the relationships of power."[1]

Gender is seen as one of the foundations of every existing social order. From the social construction perspective of gender, women and men are compared as gender categories (female-male, feminine- masculine, girls-boys, women-men) and this perspective analyzes how different social groups define them in everyday life and in major institutions such as the family and economy.[2] Gender denotes not only the sexual difference, but also the power and sexual hierarchy.[3] By these definitions, it is evident that the social relations between the sexes determine gender and gender is a socially constructed, internalized category by which the subordination and oppression of women is constructed and constantly reconstructed. Another important thing to be noticed is that the concepts of masculinity and femininity that emerge in the discourse of gender are not completely separate categories. In this connection Irene Visser points out that, "femininity and masculinity, as abstract non-biological concepts are very difficult to define, and moreover, being culturally and socially induced, they are subject to drastic change over time. Although it seems relatively safe to analyze and assess the construction and meaning of gender during earlier historical periods and within cultures other than our own, yet, currently held notions of gender distinctions appear to be increasingly slippery and fragile".[4]

In the initial stages of theoretical expansion regarding gender, social scientists used to recognize women as the single largest oppressed group. But the emergence of post-structuralism abandoned the beliefs in grand theories of global oppression. Post-structuralism deconstructed the universal theories and gave a scope to discuss different types of oppression. This paved way to discuss the suppression of different sections of women, instead of taking 'women' as a homogenized category.

For example, in the US white feminism has emerged as 'the feminism' and entered other countries and dominated other cultures regarding women. The problem of White feminism vs Black feminism, First world feminism vs Third world feminism, Upper class feminism vs Lower class feminism, Upper caste feminism vs Dalit feminism lies in the domination of 'one' over the 'other'. It is not just the oppression of Women by Men, but the oppression of Lower classes by Upper classes, oppression of Dalits by Upper castes, oppression of the Third world by the First world, oppression of Blacks by Whites, oppression of Homosexuals by heterosexuals and there is no end for it.

Analyzing the oppression of black women, bell hooks says that, "in the United States all men are oppressors and all whites are oppressors, white men oppress white women and men and women of colour, white women oppress men and women of colour, and men of colour oppress women of colour. In this way, in the daily actions and experiences, the systems of domination are constructed and reinforced."[5]

Black women could not relate themselves with the issues of White women. According to bell hooks, "the white middle class and upper class women have dominated every women's movement in the US". She further says that, black feminists initially have approached the women's movement that was organized by white women. She stresses that they were disappointed and disillusioned when they discovered that white women in the movement had little knowledge about the problems of lower class and poor women and also about the particular problems of non-white women from all classes.[6] This paved way for the emergence of black feminism in order to counter the dominant white middle class feminism.

Asserting the specific economic, social and political contexts and countering the dominant notion that, the First world women's experiences are universal experiences, the Third world academicians activists started emphasizing the feminisms of the Third world. Most of the Third world countries have a common feature, i.e., colonialism. The colonial and post-colonial dimensions of these countries have seriously targeted the gender question.

In order to counter the general myth that, feminism was imposed on the Third world by the West, Third world feminists like Kumari Jayawardena focused on bringing out the hidden histories of women in the Third world countries. In her opinion, feminism is not imposed on the Third world by the West, but rather historical circumstances produced important material and ideological changes that affected women. At the same time, she recognizes the impact of imperialism and western thought to be among the significant elements in these historical circumstances.[7] In this connection, Bina Agarwal raises some serious questions about First world feminists. She asks whether the First world feminists have embraced the Third world women's struggles as a part of their own history. She stresses on the need for the First world feminists to recognize their privileged position within the international division of economic and intellectual labour and the sources of that privilege.[8]

In spite of the differences between the First world and the Third world, one should not either globalize or completely localize theories. According to Ania Loomba, one should be careful not to homogenize either the First world or third world women. She says, that, in each case considerations of class, colour, religion, location, sexuality and politics have divided the women's movements and their dominant concerns. She emphasizes the need to recognize the Third world women and the women of colour as the most exploited of the world workers today.[9]

Apart from the above complexities, one of the major problems that arises with the gender question is that of equality vs difference. Very often the discussions regarding gender will be ending with two arguments on opposite sides. On one, there is the argument that men and women are equal and on the other, the argument that men and women are different and hence, they have different goals to pursue. One tends to see these as binary oppositions of equality vs difference. Joan W. Scott opines that, if equality and difference are paired dichotomously they structure an impossible choice. If one opts for equality, one is forced to accept the notion that difference is antithetical to it, if one opts for difference, one admits that equality is unattainable.[10]

According to Scott, by subsuming women into a general 'human identity', we lose the specificity of female diversity and women's experiences. By doing this we will be back to everyone's story. When women were hidden from history, when the feminine served as a negative counterpart, for the 'other' employed in the formation of positive masculine identity. At the same time, the idea of difference draws a line between the genders and invests it with biological explanations, and then treats each side of the opposition as a category (male/female) assumed to be the same, hence, differences within either category are suppressed.[11] For these reasons it should be recognized that a debate on the question of equality vs difference regarding gender is not going to be useful.

After analyzing certain theoretical aspects on gender in general, it is interesting to analyze different dimensions of gender like class, caste, religion and the colonial experience in the Indian context.

In the period of colonialism, the colonialist masters and the nationalist natives in India were seriously engaged with the question of gender. The constant construction of gender by colonialists as well as nationalists has got serious consequences. The colonialists tried to justify their role by criticizing the 'low status' of women in India, whereas, the nationalists countered it with the concept of 'Indian Womanhood' and its' past glory. In this whole discourse the upper caste Hindu woman represented the Indian woman.[12] Their concern was with the upper caste Hindu women, but not with the different sections of the 'other ' women. There is a conscious neglect of the histories of Dalit women, histories of lower class women, histories of women belonging to the religions in minority. In this connection, it is important to recognize that homogenizing women as an analytical category does not hold ground in the Indian context. As Sharmila Rege points out, "A feminist standpoint of interlocking oppressions that would recognize the complex mediations between caste, class, ethnic and gender oppression would be more connected to the living and the concrete".[13] It is a fact that in India, neither the Dalit movement nor the women's movement has concentrated on the issues of each other's. This indicates the need to explore a theory regarding gender and caste and the interconnections between the two in the Indian context.

Another important factor with, which gender is related, is class. The problem with Marxist approach is that, it believes that women's oppression lies in their exclusion from the control over the means of production and their confinement to the family and society. This approach pays much attention to the larger structures which are responsible for women's subordination but does not discuss the oppression at a micro level.[14]

To discuss the impact of religion on gender, the two issues in post-colonial India, viz., Shabano's case and the issue of Sati are considered here which show the gender oppression in communal forms. These two issues are the marks of Hindu and Muslim fundamentalism and support of the state to the communal patriarchies. In the first issue, a 75 years old Muslim woman Shabano was deprived of her right to maintenance and Supreme Court had given a verdict for changes in Muslim personal law. Muslim fundamentalists opposed the changes and mounted pressure on then Rajiv Gandhi Government and thus a bill was introduced in the parliament, which took away the Muslim women's right to maintenance from their husbands.[15] Another issue, where the support of the state to the fundamentalists can be seen is the agitation regarding 'sati-daha' in 1987-88. Roop Kanwar's sati (widow-immolation) in Deorala, Rajasthan and the aftermath incidents explicitly showed the patriarchal attitudes of the state as well as the civil society.[16] For the state, it was more of a question of vote banks than a question of gender oppression. In both the issues the question of gender was seriously linked with religious sentiments.

All these indicate the need to explore the relationship between class, caste, religion and gender in the Indian context. This also reveals the complexity of theorizing gender in the Indian context. In this connection it is very important to discuss the deprivation of women from Indian politics and how different factors like class, caste and religion are related with gender when the issue of Indian politics comes up.

II

In order to achieve gender equality, United Nations adopted a convention on the Political Rights of Women in 1952. In 1985, at Copenhagen it took drastic steps, towards promoting international cooperation and to strengthen peace through women's participation. UN stressed in the declaration of Nairobi that women by virtue of their gender, experience discrimination in terms of denial of equal access to the power structure that controls society and determines development issues and peace initiative. UN asserted that for women the sharing of power on equal terms with men must be a major strategy for achieving equality.[17]

In the same way Indian Constitution guarantees the rights of equality, liberty, safety and dignity to all its citizens irrespective of their class, caste, race, religion and sex. But the reality is far from these resolutions. Women in Indian politics continue to be marginally represented.

If one examines the political participation and political representation of women in India, one can find that it is very ironical. Voting percentage of women was always lagged behind that of men except in 1984. Their representation is also in a low rate. 23 women were elected to the first Lok Sabha, i.e., only 4.7 per cent. In the subsequent years, their number has been fluctuating. The highest percentage of women elected to the Lok Sabha is 8.27 per cent, i.e., in 1984. In the same way women's strength is marginal in comparison to men in the Rajya Sabha also. Their strength in Rajya Sabha was highest in 1980, i.e., 29. After that there has been a diminishing trend in the number of women members in the Rajya Sabha.[18] In State assemblies their representation is a dismal 4 per cent. All these numbers show that women's participation and representation in major decision-making bodies is very marginal. Apart from this one has to observe the participation and representation of different sections of women. From the times of Nationalist Movement, it is upper/middle class and upper caste women who are dominating the political scenario. Even if Gandhi has got the fame of bringing women into the public sphere, their roles remain unchanged; and it was upper/middle class and upper caste women who had the accessibility to participate.

An observation regarding women's representation in different political parties also reveals surprising and shocking details. There was not a single woman member in CPM's politburo and CPI's secretariat in 1996, which parties are supposedly progressive and gender-sensitive. Janata Dal and United Front followed the left parties, where as BJP with one woman member and Congress with two women members were in leading (?) position.[19] Interestingly all these parties claim that they support the reservation bill for women. In this connection Sudhir Varma points out that,"looking through the manifestos of the various national parties, it comes out clearly that except for promises to takeup programmes for women's welfare, no political party has looked into the actual issue of empowerment of women in spite of the pressure exerted by the national and international movements of women and the various pledges made by the governments in the United Nations and other such fora". He explains that crucial areas like education, health, employment and violence against women have been left almost untouched by the political parties and that no one has ever promised the formation of a national policy on women in its manifesto.[20]

After analyzing the attitudes of different political parties towards women, here are few examples to show the patriarchal attitudes of men, who are in so-called responsible positions.

Former chief justice of the Supreme Court Ranganath Mishra's advice to women is that, women should sit at home and should not work outside their domestic sphere. This shows the patriarchal bias of Judicary and legal machinery.[21]

Sharad Yadav targeted women supporters of the reservation bill as *parkatis*, which is a derogatory reference to women with short hair. He told the National Council of Women that, "*Mahila vote bhi koi cheez hai* ? You must be joking".

Referring to the Kozhikode call-girl racket in Kerala in which politicians were allegedly involved, E.K. Nayanar said that, as long as there were women, there would be sex scandals.[22]

All these examples show not only the internalised gender discriminatory attitudes of men, but also their egoism.

Apart from this, women, who are in the field of politics, constantly face different kind of problems and harassment. Women decision-makers, politicians and activists not only face character assassination and threats, but also become the targets of violence. There are several instances of physical assaults, rape and murder of women decision-makers in India.[23] This indicates the need for strategies towards engendering politics.

III

Any kind of simplistic conclusion regarding the strategies for engendering politics can make the issue much more problematic. For example, to take the issue of women's reservation bill, many activists and scholars opine that there is a need for the implementation of the bill. At the same time, equal number of people are opposing it in the name of tokenism. Some of them are afraid of women being co-opted by the power structures. A doubt remains that even if women enter into politics how many of them will be conscious of their oppression? In this connection it is also important to recognize the inter-links between caste, class and gender structures. One should be able to recognize the problem with homogenization of women. To take the example of caste structure, the suppression differs from an upper caste woman to a lower caste woman. If we apply bell hooks' analysis of the suppression of Black Women to the Dalit Women, it can be recognized that an uppercaste man is always in the oppressor's position, whereas a Dalit Woman is always in the oppressed position. Upper caste men suppress upper caste women and Dalit men and women; upper caste women suppress Dalit men and women; and Dalit men suppress Dalit women. Here upper caste women and Dalit men are suppressors and suppressed at the same time.[24] Generally upper caste women are not recognized as the suppressors and women are categorized as a single oppressed category. For example, the oppression of upper caste women over the Dalit men can be seen in the issue of violence on Dalits in Chunduru (Andhra Pradesh), where the upper caste women helped upper caste men in suppressing Dalit men.[25] This specifies the need for reservations within the reservation system. In this connection Vasantha Kannabiran and Kalpana Kannabiran say; "if women manage to push the 81st amendment bill through the Parliament, it will topple all current assumptions about hierarchies of caste, class and gender". They observe that, it would also create the possibility for a woman to represent not only men of her own caste, but also upper caste men and women as well, if she is from a non-upper caste background.[26]

On the other side, one has to recognize the fact that those women who are contesting, are gaining their candidature by their relationships with already established party leaders.[27] In this connection Madhu Kishwar warns that by this Bill *Biwi-Beti* brigades might occupy the power structures. To put it in her words "political socialization of such women legislators into the parties, required for being an effective member of state assemblies and

Parliament cannot take place smoothly when women members remain filially attached to and politically dependent on the male party leaders".[28]

The problem of *Biwi-Beti* brigades and the domination of upper caste women have to be taken seriously. There is a need to avoid these kind of major loopholes of the reservation bill. All political parties should start thinking towards the implementation of reservations within the parties. They should also include a national policy on women in their manifestos.

There is a strong need for gender sensitization. Women have to be educated in order to make use of reservations. Apart from the interlinks between gender and caste, the interlinks between gender and religion and gender and class also have to be taken seriously. As earlier stated Shabano's issue and the issue of sati-daha are the marks of religious fundamentalism. For all the political parties it was the issue of vote banks but not of the women's basic rights. To take another example for the attitudes of male members of the Parliament, in the discussions regarding the Hindu Code Bill in 1950's, certain male Hindu members of Parliament opposed the Bill because it denies the right of Hindu man to have more than one wife and does not deny the right of Muslim man to have four wives.[29] Here women became mere objects to be discussed. It was the question for Hindu men whether to have one wife or 'four wives'. It was the question for them to 'give' rights to women or not to 'give'. This itself shows the need of women who are conscious of their oppression to be there in the Parliament to stand and demand their rights.

One has to recognize the facts that the change only in the state is not sufficient. It should come from both the state and the civil society. The institutions of civil society like family, religion, massmedia, etc., constantly legitimize the subordination of women. Hence, change in these institutions is essential. The academia which is limited to the discussions and criticisms should go beyond that and should try to bridge the gap between theory and practice. To conclude, different, struggles like caste, class and gender should go together towards moving a gender sensitive politics.

REFERENCES

1. Joan W. Scott, "Gender a useful category of Historical Analysis", in *Gender and the Politics of History,* Columbia University Press, 1988, p. 42.
2. Judith Lorber and Susan A. Farrel (ed.), *The Social Construction of Gender,* Sage Publications, London, 1991, p. 1.
3. Elaine Showalter's cited in Irene Visser, "The Prototypicality of Gender, Contemporary Notions of Masculine and Feminine", *Women's Studies Journal,* Vol. 19, No. 6, November-December 1996, p. 589.
4. Irene Visser, "The Prototypicality of Gender, Contemporary Notions of Masculine and Feminine", *ibid.,* p. 589.
5. Lorber and Farrel (ed.), *op. cit.,* p. 9.
6. bell hooks, *Ain't I A Woman, Black Women and Feminism,* South End Press, Boston MA, 1981, p.188.
7. Kumari Jayawardena, *Feminism and Nationalism in the Third World,* ASR Publications, Lahore, 1986. p. 2.
8. Bina Agarwal, "Positioning the Western Feminist Agenda: A Comment", in *Indian Journal of Gender Studies,* Vol. 1, No. 2, July-December, 1994, p. 250.
9. Ania Loomba, *Colonalism/Post-Colonialism,* Routledge, London and New York, 1998, p. 228.
10. Joan W. Scott, "Deconstructing of Equality Versus Difference or the Uses of Post-Structuralist Theory for Feminism," in *Feminist Studies,* Vol. 14, No. 1, 1988, (33-50), p. 43.
11. *Ibid.,* p. 46.
12. Uma Chakravarti, "Whatever Happened to Vedic Dasi?" in Kumkum Sangari and Sudesh Vaid (ed.), *Recasting Women: Essays in Colonial History,* Kali for Women, New Delhi,1989, p. 34.
13. Sharmila Rege, "Feminist Pedagogy and Sociology for Emancipation in India", *Sociological Bulletin,* 44 (2), September, 1995, p. 224-25.
14. Patricia Loveridge, "Approaches to Change: The All India Democratic Women's Association and A Marxist Approach to the Woman Question in India", in *Indian Journal of Gender Studies,* Vol. 1, No. 2, July-December, 1994, p. 226.
15. Radha Kumar, "Identity Politics and the Contemporary Indian Feminist Movement", in M. Valentine Moghadam's *Identity*

Politics of Women: Cultural Reassertions and Feminisms in International Perspective, Westview Press, USA, 1994, p. 280.

16. Indu Agnihotri and Rajni Palriwala, "Tradition, the Family and the State Politics of the Contemporary Women's Movement", Research in progress papers on *History and Society,* 2nd series No. Lxxxv, N.M.L. New Delhi, December, 1993, p. 38.

17. Ranjana Kumari, "Introduction" in *Women in Politics: Forms and Processes,* Har-Anand Publications, New Delhi, 1993, p. 1.

18. Bhawana Jharta, *Women and Politics in India: Impact of Family and Education on Women Political Activists,* Deep and Deep Publications, New Delhi,1996, p. 62-65.

19. Saraswati Haider," All Women's Political Party Launched in UP", *Economic and Political Weekly,* Vol. 33, No. 8, Feb. 21, 1998, p. 386.

20. Sudhir Varma, *Women's Struggle for Political Space: From Enfranchisement to Participation,* Rawat Publications, Jaipur and New Delhi, 1997, p. 151.

21. Vibhuti Patel, "Women's Participation in Policy and Decision Making Process: Need for a Network", in *Women in Politics: Forms and Processes,* Har-Ananad Publications, New Delhi, 1993, p. 22.

22. Ishan Joshi and Bhavbeep Kang, "The Female Principle 98", *Outlook,* January 19, 1998.

23. Vibhuti Patel, *op. cit.,* p. 32.

24. bell hooks, *Feminist Theory: From Margin to Center,* South End Press, Boston MA, 1984, p. 14-15.

25. Susie Tharu and Tejaswini Niranjana, "Problems for a Contemporary Theory of Gender", *Social Scientist,* Vol. 22, No. 3-4, March-April 1994, p. 100.

26. Vasantha Kannabiran and Kalpana Kannabiran, "From Social Action to Political Action: Women and the 81st Amendment" *Economic and Political Weekly* 32, (5), 1-7 Feb. 97, p. 196.

27. Susheela Kaushik, "Women and Political Participation", in *Women in Politics: Forms and Processes* Har-Anand Publications, New Delhi, 1993, p. 49.

28. Madhu Kishwar, "Out of the Zenana Dabba: Strategies For Enhancing Women's Political Representation", *Manushi,* No. 96, September-October, p. 26.

29. Kumkum Sangari, "Politics and Diversity: Religious Communities and Multiple Patriarchies", *Economic and Political Weekly,* December 23, 1995, p. 3295.

BIBLIOGRAPHY

1. Crompton, Rosemary and Mann, Michael (ed.) *Gender and Stratification*, Polity Press, Cambridge, 1986.
2. De Beauvoir, Simone, *The Second Sex*, translated and edited by H.M. Parshley, Picador Classics, Pan Books, 1949.
3. Figes, Eva, *Patriarchal Attitudes*, Fawcett Publications, Greenwich, 1970.
4. Hooks Bell, *Ain't I a Woman: Black Woman and Feminism*, Southend Press, Boston MA, 1981.
5. Hooks Bell, *Feminist Theory: From Margin to Center*, Southend Press, Boston MA, 1984.
6. Jaggar, Alison M., *Feminist Politics and Human Nature*, Rowman and Littlefield Publications, New Jersey, 1983.
7. Jayawardena, Kumari, *Feminism and Nationalism in the Third World*, ASR Publications, Lahore, Pakistan, 1986.
8. Jharta, Bhawana, *Women and Politics in India*, Deep and Deep Publications, New Delhi, 1996.
9. Kaushik, Susheela, *Women and Panchayati Raj*, Har-Anand Publications, New Delhi, 1993.
10. Kaushik, Susheela (ed.), *Women's Participation in Politics*, Vikas Publishing House Pvt. Ltd., New Delhi, 1993.
11. Loomba, Ania, *Colonialism/Post-colonialism*, Routledge, London, 1998.
12. Lorber, Judith and Farrel A. Susan (ed.), *The Social Construction of Gender*, Sage Publications, London, 1991.
13. Mitchell, Juliet and Oakley, Ann (ed.), *What is Feminism?* Pantheon Book, New York, 1986.
14. Moghadam, M. Valentine (ed.), *Identity Politics and Women: Cultural Reassertions and Feminisms in International Perspective*, Westview Press, USA, 1994.
15. Moghadam, M. Valentine (ed.), *Patriarchy and Economic Development: Women's Positions at the end of the Twentieth Century*, Clarendon Press, Oxford, 1996.
16. Dr. Ramachander M. and Dr. Lakshmi K., *Women and Politics: A Study in Political Participation*, Booklinks Corporation, Hyderabad, 1993.
17. Sangari, Kumkum and Vaid, Sudesh (ed.), *Recasting Women: Essays in Colonial History*, Kali for Women, New Delhi, 1989.

18. Varma, Sudhir, *Women's Struggle for Political Space: From Enfranchisement to Partcipation*, Rawat Publications, Jaipur and New Delhi, 1997.

19. *Women in Politics: Forms and Processes*, Har-Anand Publications, New Delhi, 1993.

ARTICLES

1. Agarwal, Bina, "Positioning the Western Feminist Agenda: A Comment", *Indian Journal of Gender Studies*, Vol. 1, No. 2, July-December, 1994, pp. 249-56.

2. Agnihotri, Indu and Palriwala, Rajni, "Tradition, the Family and The State Politics of Contemporary Women's Movement", *Research in Progress Papers on History and Society*, 2nd series, No. Lxxxv, Nehru Memorial Museum and Library, New Delhi, December 1993.

3. Haider, Saraswati, "All Women's Political Party Launched in UP", *Economic and Political Weekly*, Vol. 33, No. 8, February 21, 1998, pp. 385-88.

4. Kannabiran, Vasantha and Kannabiran, Kalpana, "Caste and Gender: Understanding Dynamics of Power and Violence", *Economic and Political Weekly*, Vol. 26, No. 37, 14 September, 1991, pp. 2130-33.

5. Kannabiran Vasantha and Kannabiran Kalpana, "From Social Action to Political Action: Women and 81st Amendment", *Economic and Political Weekly*, Vol. 32, No. 5, 1-7 February 1997, pp. 196-97.

6. Kishwar Madhu, "Out of the Zenana Dabba: Strategies for Enhancing Women's Political Representation", *Manushi, No. 96, September-October, 1996, pp. 21-30.*

7. Kishwar Madhu, "Women's Marginal Role in Politics", *Manushi, No. 97, November-December, 1996, pp. 9-21.*

8. Loveridge, Partricia, "Approaches to Change: The All India Democratic Women's Association and a Marxist Approach to the Woman Question in India", *Indian Journal of Gender Studies*, Vol. 1, No. 2, November-December, 1994, pp. 215-42.

9. Sangari Kumkum, "Politics of Diversity: Religious Communities and Multiple Patiarchies", Economic and Political Weekly, Vol. 30, December 23, 1995, pp. 3287-309, and December 30, 1995, pp. 3381-390.

10. Scott. Joan W., "Gender: A Useful Category of Historical Analysis", American historical Review, 91 December, 1986, pp. 1053-75.

11. Scott, Joan, W., "Deconstructing Equality-Versus-Difference or the Uses of post-structuralist theory of feminism", *Feminist Studies*, Vol. 14, No. 1, 1988, pp. 33-50.

12. Tharu, Susie and Niranjana Tejaswini, "Problems for a Contemporary Theory of Gender", *Social Scientist*, Vol. 22, Nos. 304, March-April, 1994, pp. 92-117.

13. Visser, Irene, "The Prototypicality of Gender, Contemporary Notions of Masculine and Feminine", *Women's Studies Journal*, Vol. 19, No. 6, November-December, 1996, pp. 589-600.

14. Young, Marion, Iris, "Gender as Seriality: Thinking about Women as a Social Collective", *Signs*, Vol. 19, 31, Spring 1994, pp. 713-38.

15. Joshi Ishan and Kang Bhavdeep, "The Female Principle 98", *Outlook*, January, 19, 1998.

2

WOMEN EMPOWERMENT: REDEFINING AGENDA

Jinee Lokaneeta

The concept of Women Empowerment has predominantly become a focus on political participation. The latter in turn in the context of the debate on the 81st Constitutional Amendment bill Regarding reservation for women in Parliament, has become a restricted discourse on the role of women in formal representative institutions of decisions making, whether it is Panchayati Raj institution or Parliament. In the process, empowerment of women emerges as an extremely limited concept. The fact that empowerment should imply a power to participate in the decision-making in all spheres of society, with no separation of the public and private and in all social, political, economic and cultural processes in society is completely obfuscated. This study seeks to argue that the state has appropriated the discourse of women's empowerment in order to nullify the emancipatory potential of the concept and reduced it to signify a demand for political participation defined only in terms of reservations into given set of political institutions. Hence, the arena of political participation itself is in practice clearly demarcated by the state. The article further argues that the political parties with no political commitment towards the struggle women's rights not only fail to transcend the state agenda, but further collaborate with the state in order to keep the patriarchal processes intact. Finally, in the role of the women's movement in the sphere of political participation is analyzed as a necessary step to redefine the agenda of women's empowerment.

State Appropriation of Empowerment

The State response to any articulation of demands by apprised sections of society has been in the form of appropriation of their agenda and compartmentalizing it within the mainstream partiarchal, upper caste/class discourse. Hence, even, while using the average of 'empowerment' or 'rights' the attempts is to limit the scope of those terms such that they are unable to challenge the dominant structures and processes in society. Their politics of struggle against unequal power relations is sought to be replaced by a limited concept of 'empowerment', which may be restricted to say, even a demand for reservations. The fact that empowerment should imply a struggle at various levels of society against the structural basis of appression is completely obliterated in the process.

The concept of women's empowerment has been a victim of this very appropriation by the state. Not only has it reduced its scope by focusing it only on political participation, but it has infact, made political participation almost synonymous with a demand for women's reservations. That political participation may mean a democratization's of various political process and groups in society and could be linked with the various struggles for women's empowerment, is obviously ignored by the state. The politics of struggle of the women's empowerment, is obviously ignored by the state. The politics of struggle of the women's movement is sought to be undermined not only in terms of reducing its scope, but the state is also attempting to take away the agency of the struggling women by acting as the providers of the empowerment.

Political Parties and Women's Empowerment

The right of political participation came as a result of the struggle of women within the national movement the fact that despite about 53 years of independence women still remain a marginalized force in representative institutions, which is one parameter of political participation is reflective of not only the patriarchal nature of the state, but the political parties of today. Reservations then become one form of increasing political participation in the sphere of representative institutions. All political parties have committed themselves to reservation for women in their imposed struggle for gender equality. But the hollowness of their commitment is clearly exposed, infact that they have never allowed women to participate in decision-making within their own party structures. This is true for all parties, whether it is CPI, CPI(M) or JD, Congress, or BJP. One looks at the figures show that the percentage of participation in party decision making committees has ranged from 0 and 7 in CPM politburo and central committee to not more than 11 per cent or 12 per cent in Congress waving committee and BJP election committee respectively (*Source-Mahishi(96), September 19*). It is also significant to note that despite the higher success rate of women in winning elections, the percentage of women candidates filed by each party has been extremely low. The CSDS Data Unit figures show that in the 1996 Lok Sabha elections, the Congress fielded only 9 per cent women, while BJP and UF fielded 5 per cent women candidate each. It is, therefore, not very surprising that the highest percentage of women representation in the Lok Sabha has only been 8.1 per cent in 1984, which came down to 7.2 per cent in 1996.

This dismal scenario in the sphere of women participation in political parties and representative institutions clearly reflect that the continuing patriarchal values on the part of all political parties towards the question of women empowerment. It is also significant to see that women of political parties have not directed there challenge towards their own parties. Infact, they too have uncritically accepted their party's theoretical commitment to women's political participation despite the party's inability in increasing women's participation within its structures of decision-making. The women of these parties seem content in restricting their struggle to the parliamentary arena and equating political participation with reservations for women.

Role of the Autonomous Women's Movement

In India, the Autonomous Women's Movement emerged as a critique to the mainstream, left parties and other progressive movements, which had failed to articulate the specificity of the women's appression. It was also under the influence of these autonomous women's groups that the political parties and women movements is a heterogeneous movement. Here, I am referring to the autonomous women's movement as distinct from the women's wing of parties set-up separate women's wings to mobilize and organize women. If the discourse on political participation and reservations has been appropriated and distorted by the state and the political parties the role of the women's movements acquires special significance.

The autonomous movements have been organizing national conferences, on the issues concerning the women's movement at different points of time. Hence, since the 1980's, when the issue of rape was taken up in the context of the Anti-Rape Campaign and communalism in 1993, it had different themes in accordance with the issues concerning women and other oppressed sections. The issues have been always reflective of the turbulence in society. But interestingly, the issue of political participation has never been accorded much importance in the themes of the conference. Infact the issue of reservations has never been addressed, even to place it within a broader context of political participation. Some empowerment autonomous groups feel that reservation would not lead to any substantial change in the political processes. A numerical increase of women in the representative institutions may not necessarily lead to a progressive nation of women's rights, since women are not a homogenous category divided by castes, class, religion as well as differing ideologies.

Although one shares these apprehension regarding reservations one also feels that it is only by interacting with the formal and informal political institutions, that the women's movement can constantly reiterate the limited scope of reservations and broaden the agenda to link it up with other forms of political participation. Even, while becoming the nature of the state and its strategy of appropriation it is only the women's movement, which can subvert a limited tool by linking it up with its agenda of women's empowerment in spheres. Since, it has a close relationship with mass movement of fulfil their commitment to gender equality. The nation of political participation can be given a new direction by linking it up with the simultaneous struggles in other spheres of society. The women's movement has to reiterate the agency of women, even in the sphere of political participation and intervene in the processes of democracy and representative institution despite its mistrust of the state.

3

ARE WOMEN REALLY AFRAID OF SUCCESS? —AN EMPIRICAL ENQUIRY

Sanghamitra Buddhapriya

Women constitute more than half of the world's population, yet, their representation in management has been significantly low in comparison to men. However, the recent trend suggests an assuring rise in the number of women in managerial positions. Today's high profile executive women have acquired the same credibility accorded to their senior male colleagues. They have performed turnaround management tasks. Naisbitt and Aurdene (1990) in their book *Megatrend 2000*, called 1990's, "The Decade of Women in Leadership." In their view, women have reached a critical mass in virtually all white-collar professions, especially in business. They are, no longer, a token minority. Their values, their management styles are closer to the standard norm. These women have broken the glass ceiling to be recognized as successful, talented and practising executives.

Yet, because of their late arrival on the management scene, their stark minority position, which makes them subject to high visibility and stereotyping and because the work organizations are embedded in a cultural milieu which still upholds, in ways, subtle and obvious, the superiority of men over women, the social reality of work organizations for women managers is often different from that of the male managers. Organizational roles and statuses have traditionally been gendered; i,e., certain positions have been considered appropriate to, and filled by, women or men. This gendered aspect is located within a large patriarchal social world which is hierarchically based, with men occupying positions of dominance over women. Male domination of the organizational world in the form ownership control positions of status and authority in cultural values and hegemony has not permitted women into the managerial positions.

Common Features

Until the late 1970s, women remained virtually invisible as managers and their absence was generally considered a non-issue (Berthoin Antal and Izraeli, 1993)[2]. Since then women managers have been becoming increasingly visible in many countries. Each country produces a growing number of the qualified women seeking managerial positions, as well as, an emerging cadre of women performing every possible managerial task with zeal and fervour.

An analysis of the status of women managers reveals that women managers of different countries share certain common features. These are:

Gradual increase in the number of (women) in the managerial profession. Increase in their education, changing socio-cultural values, increasing awareness and consciousness about their rights and the need for supplementary income are some of the reasons. However, there is still an under-representation of women in managerial jobs. Most of them hold lower and middle management positions and the number of women remain extremely small in top management positions.

Major barriers which restrict women's entry into managerial jobs are stereotypical attitude towards women managers, geographical immobility of women, conflict between career and family responsibilities. The stereotypical perspectives of women's traits as inferior, hence, unsuitable for leadership, restrict women's entry into management. The cultural constraints on women's access to managerial positions can be traced to the deep-rooted images of traditional women's role. Gender differences appear more deeply embedded in Asian Countries than in Western Societies.

Factors that confine women managers to reach the top echelon of management are: blocked opportunity, lack of support of employers, limited access to information, restricted access to training, fear of success, marriage and motherhood, prioritization of family over career, stereotyped perceptions.

Discrimination against women managers exists, relating to remuneration, job allocation, performance appraisal, promotion, training opportunities and reward structure. The exclusion of women from policy formulation and decision-making relegates them to peripheral, supportive activities. Women are better represented in departments like, personnel, human resource management, marketing, public relations and training and there is a dearth of women in engineering and finance.

Women managers face a dual problem—work and family—which creates a lot of stress, strain and role conflict. Patriarchal division of labour consign household tasks, childcare, etc., to women and women's domestic roles are viewed as equal to or more important than their careers. This affects the career perspective and prospects of women directly. The dual burden is further enhanced, because, lack of arrangement of flexible working arrangement, lack of childcare benefits, acute shortage of creches and daycare facilities and re-entry policies.

Changes are taking place, as a result of which more number of women are recruited, for managerial jobs. The major changes are Equal Remuneration Act (equal pay for equal work irrespective of sex), removal of discriminatory clauses in labour legislation, changes in legal status of women, initiatives taken by NGOs, (Non-Governmental Organizations) business women clubs and media, training programmes conducted by organizations, greater availability of educational opportunities, delay in marriage and having few children, and greater awareness of women relating to their career development. But, these changes are, yet, to provide a discrimination-free work environment.

From the common features it is revealed that gender disparity owes its origin to gender discrimination, which is a worldwide phenomenon. Its persistence over the years has prompted the UNDP to introduce the Gender Related Index (GDI) in the year 1995, in its *Human Development Report* to compare the levels of gender disparity among different countries across the world, for the *Human Development Report,* the GDI been calculated for 137 countries in 1996. The five top ranking countries are:—Sweden (1), Canada (28), Norway (3), United States (4) and Finland (5). Several developing countries and areas also do quite well in the GDI ranking: Barbados (16), Bahamas (18), Hong Kong (25), Uruguay (26), Singapore (29), the Republic of Korea (31), Costa Rica (32), and Thailand (33). These countries have succeeded in building the basic human capabilities of both women and men, without substantial gender disparity. India ranks 103 among the 137 countries. The bottom five places are occupied by Niger, Sierra Leone, Afghanistan, Burkina Faso and Mali in ascending order.

Women in these countries face a double deprivation: overall human development achievement is low in these societies and women's achievement is lower than that of men's. Several conclusions can be drawn from the GDI rankings. First, no society treats its women as well as its men. Second, comparing the GDI ranks of countries with their income levels confirms that removing gender inequalities is not dependent on having a high income. Third, gender equality is not necessarily associated with high economic growth.

So, the most persistent and rising disparities within nation and between nations has been gender disparity, despite a relentless struggle to equalize opportunities between women and men and also visible in the management. Women occupy only 14 per cent of managerial and administrative jobs (*Human Development Report, 1996*)[3]. The table below highlights the economic participation of women in different countries.

TABLE 1

Economic Participation of Women in Different Countries

Name of Countries	*Administrators and Managers*	*Professionals and Technical Workers*	*Clerical and Sales Workers*	*Services Workers*
Japan	9	42	50	54
China	12	45	39	52
Malaysia	12	45	—	—
UK	33	44	—	—
France	9	41	—	—
Israel	19	54	55	57
South Africa	17	47	—	66
US	42	53	—	60
India	2	21	—	—

Source: Human Development Report, 1996, UNDP.

Status of Women Managers in India

While analyzing the status of women managers in India, it is important to discuss the status of Indian women in general. The social status of women in India is comparatively lower than many other countries of the world. Though, the Constitution of India guarantees, 'Equality of Status' to Women; they do not enjoy full equality in the society. The vast majority of women are illiterate, underpaid, deprived and disadvantaged. Some of our religious and social practices have steeped women in a morass of backwardness, illiteracy and ignorance, condemning them to inferior positions in society, completely dominated by men. But in urban areas, with the spread of education and the increase in number of working women outside their homes, the situation is gradually changing. Women have risen above socio-cultural traditions to take a serious look at themselves, their potentials and capabilities. The traditional and well-defined role of a housewife has gradually evolved into the dual and more self- fulfilling role of a working woman and a housewife. Some of the factors responsible for this change are better education, changing socio-cultural values and the need for supplementary income caused by inflation.

Despite these changes Indian society remains 'male dominated'. Though women have entered various jobs and professions, they are not yet recognized as sincere professional workers. They are regarded as women first, and as workers afterwards. Through the generations, Indian men have dominated women and therefore, they feel humiliated while being ordered by a woman superior. Even women are prejudiced against each other, the reason being that women are net used to taking orders from other women. Throughout their lives they are conditioned to identify authority with male persons such as fathers, husbands and sons.

The status of women can also be analyzed in terms of the sex-ratio, education and women's political and economic stand. The sex-ratio of the population of India has been generally adverse to women, i.e., the number of women per 1000 men has generally been less than 1000. Apart from being contrary to women the sex-ratio has also declined over the decades from 946 in 1951 to 929 in 1991.

The reasons for the general disparity in the sex-ratio and the declining trend over the years are mainly because of preference for male children resulting in neglect of female babies in the form of foeticide (through aminocentesis) and infanticide, the relative gap in the health conditions between males and females and certain types of morality which are sex selective. The adverse sex-ratio is also due to the lower expectation of life at birth for females in the past compared to males, part of which is due to high maternal mortality. It is, however, difficult to pinpoint any particular. reason for the declining sex-ratio which requires a detailed analysis.

With regard to education, even though there is a gradual increase in the number of female students in different types of education (as shown in table 1.2), their proportion in professional faculties is much lower than that of the male students. In spite of increasing parental awareness of girls' education and conducive government policies, stereotypical attitudes towards professional faculties still prevail. However, in recent years a large number of management schools and business administration departments, producing professionally trained management graduates, have emerged. As a result the number of women students in Management Studies is gradually increasing.

Coming to the political status, though Indian women constitute 24.3 crores out of a total of 51.4 crores of the electorate, their participation rate in the political process is very low. Many women, especially in the rural areas do not exercise their franchise during elections and even if they do, they act as 'rubber stamps' of their husbands, brothers or fathers. Also the representation of women in Parliament and State Legislatures is not satisfactory. In the 11th Lok Sabha election (1996), out of 538 members elected there were only 36 women constituting less than 7 per cent of the total membership.

A review of the economic role played by women in India reveals that, Indian women have played a distinctive and significant role in the process of earning a livelihood for the family, putting in sometimes more, sometime less and often an equal amount of labour compared to men. In India, one third of the labour force consists of women. Working women constitute only 16.43 per cent of the female population of the country. Traditional village women are engaged as agricultural labourers, artisans, producer of handicrafts and also perform menial services. The cultural norms that influence women engaged in manual labour outside the home vary according to their position in social hierarchy.

However, developments in the economic field, with increasing stress on an Industrial mode of production, has opened some avenues for women. Modernization, social change and education have enabled some women to enter new professions, and new occupations which were totally closed to them earlier (Vidya Rani, 1990)[4]. For example, the presence of women in the pubic, private services and other jobs in the tertiary sector is now an accepted one. In both public and private sector the employment of women is gradually ascending.

Women have entered into the managerial profession for almost three decades. But it is surprising to note that, there has been no systematic government sponsored data gathering exercise to ascertain the number of women in management in India. Women in public Sector (WIPS), a *Forum of Women in Public Sector,* discovered that the most of the undertakings do not maintain separate data for women and hence, it is not possible for them to give detailed information. So, a study was conducted by WIPS to ascertain the number of women employees working in different levels, their qualification and the training imparted to them during 1980, 1985 and 1990. Though the questionnaire was circulated to all the Chief Executives of Public Sector Undertakings, the data was received from 75 undertakings only. But the data is enough to give an idea about the general trends of women working in public sector undertakings. The data (table 1.5) has been given by the Personnel and Administration Departments of the respective Public Sector Units (P5U).

TABLE 2
Data of Women in Public Sector Undertaking

Level	*Year*	*Total Employees*	*No. of Women*	*No. of Men*	*Per cent of Women*	*Per cent of Men*
Total	1985 1991	738035 879539	62720 76757	675315 802782	8.5 8.7	91.5 91.3
Top Mgt	1985 1991	747 1575	16 51	731 1524	2.1 3.2	97.9 96.8
Middle Mgt	1985 1991	31693 55773	1101 1964	30592 53809	3.5 3.5	96.5 96.5
Lower Mgt	1985 1991	50900 72921	1695 3465	49205 69456	3.3 4.8	96.7 95.2
Super-visor	1985 1991	55790 78270	2181 3751	53609 74519	3.9 4.8	96.1 95.2
Work-man	1985 1991	587405 671000	57726 67526	529679 603474	9.8 10.1	90.2 89.9

Source: Data Base, Women in Public Sector (WIPS), 1993.

The table (2) shows that the percentage of women (taking the total number of women in these PSUs) in 1985, in executive (top, middle and lower), supervisory, and workman category are 4.5 per cent, 3.5 per cent and 92 per cent respectively. Out of 4.5 per cent of women executives 0.6 per cent are in top management level, 39.1 per cent are in middle management level and 60.3 per cent are in lower management level. It is observed that as per the Census

Report of 1991, the literacy rate of females has increased by 9.6 per cent in the last decade and male literacy rate has increased by a mere 7.4 per cent. In spite of this, the share of women in Public Sector Undertakings has increased by a mere 0.23 per cent during the last 5 years. The number of women has increased in the executive categories, even though the overall percentage of women remains the same. This could, of course, be directly linked to the fact that more women are professionally qualified today as compared to the situation in 1985.

The representation of women in 1991, is 7.1 per cent in executive cadre, out of which 0.93 per cent is in top management, 35.8 per cent is in middle management and 63.3 per cent in lower management level. This confirms the fact that the number of women has increased at the entry level. However, it is disheartening to note that the share has decreased in the middle management category, possibly because women at that level have already moved up without a proportionate movement of women from lower to the middle level. And at the senior management level they are highly underrepresented. This may be due to the fact that, women's promotion into senior positions appear to be related to their access to the channels from which, firms recruit executives and they have a very limited access to these channels.

The low proportion of women in the higher ranks may also be a reflection of either prejudices and discriminatory recruitment policies, or lack of career orientation and lack of career commitment on the part of women in general. Committee on the Status of Women had brought into notice a case where one of the nationalized undertakings refused to appoint women in administrative positions on the ground that they lack of efficiency, discipline, administrative ability and hard work (*Towards Equality*, 1974, p. 214)[5].

The (International Labour Organization) report on "Women Workers in a Changing World", noted that while formal discrimination in employment based on sex in tending to disappear, informal policies and practices still persist. The residual forms of discrimination, tend to operate formally and informally at a higher level in the occupational pyramid after blocking the advancement of women on the ground of their individual merit irrespective of sex (*Towards Equality*, 1974, p. 215)[6].

The paucity of women in management is never coincidental. There is no systematic evidence indicating ineffectiveness of women as managers. In different countries where the entry and middle level management positions are held by a sizeable number of women, experience confirms their effectiveness. In upper level also women managers have proved their mettle. If ineffectiveness is not the reason, why then are there so few female managers worldwide. This can be explained as a consequence of 'sex-role stereotypes' about women which are widely shared within our culture.

Sex-role Stereotypes

The term 'sex-role stereotype' refers to the belief that a set of traits and abilities is more likely to b found among one sex than the other (Pleck, 1971)[7]. Studies reveal that the stereotyped notion regarding women, that they lack in the abilities and personality traits required of managers, is widely held and has contributed much to the lack of progress of women in employment. The structure of management hierarchies in organizations has been seen as a reflection of power structure in society which is dominated by men (Kruse and Whitermental, 1986)[8]. Thus, studies suggest that, even jobs themselves are gendered (Webb, 1991)[9]. The sex-typing of management as a male occupation requiring male traits, poses a major obstacle to women, who would otherwise qualify and excel in positions of leadership. Much of the stereotyping is based on myths.

To be specific, at least five stereotypes cited below, which are commonly presented as arguments against women in management, appear to be fallacious.

- Men are intellectually superior
- Men are emotionally more stable than women
- Men value achievement, promotion and meaningful work more than Women
- Men are inherently more assertive than Women
- The successful manager possesses masculine attributes.

The Present Study

In this study an attempt is being made to examine the impact of managerial level and sex-role orientation on fear of success of women managers. The sample includes 160 women managers (16 from senior level, 48 from middle management level and 96 from junior management level) from 10 major Public Sector Undertakings (PSUs)*, whose offices are located in Delhi. Bem's sex-role inventory (BSRI, 1974) and Kirtida Surti's fear of success scale, 1982, are used to measure sex-role orientation and fear of success respectively. The basic objectives of the study are:

- To explore the sex-role orientation pattern and fear of success of women managers
- To study the influence of managerial level and sex-role orientation on fear of success of women managers.

Now we will discuss the concepts, i.e., sex-role orientation and fear of success.

Sex-role Orientation

The process of sex-role orientation describes the ways in which biological gender and associated cultural differentials are incorporated into an individual's self-perception and behaviour. In other words, it is the process by which the culture transforms male and female into masculine and feminine adults. The term 'sex-role' and 'gender-role' can be used as synonyms, though 'sex' basically indicates biological and physical differences between members of the same species, whereas 'gender' is socially constructed perception of an individual based on expected behaviour and specific roles assigned to her/him by the society.

Females as well as males are conditioned by societal and cultural pressures to accept behavioural patterns consonant with society's expectations of how they should behave. Most cultures attribute dominant, aggressive and masculine qualities to males and passive, dependent and feminine qualities to females which in turn affect gender identity as well as behaviour. Gender roles are taught and learnt within a complex set of relationship in the family and are reinforced through the socialization process in every

---

*The PSUs include SAIL, MMTC, HUDCO, STC, IOC, EIL, ONGC, NTPC, BHEL and BALCO.

society, and thus, right since childhood one is socialized to pick up one gender identity with socially ascribed roles and duties as per the norms of the particular society (Chakravarti, 1995)[9].

Sex-role identity refers to one's perception that one is masculine or feminine according to a personal definition of masculinity and femininity. Femininity and masculinity have long been conceptualized as opposite ends of a single bipolar dimension. But scholars in a number of disciplines have begun to concern themselves with the concept of psychological *androgyny*, a term that denotes the integration of femininity and masculinity within a single individual. The term androgyny comes from the Greek words *andr* (man) and *gyne* (woman). The concept of psychological androgyny implies that it is possible for an individual to be both compassionate and assertive, both expressive and instrumental, both feminine and masculine, depending upon the situational appropriateness of these various modalities. And it further implies that an individual may even blend these complementary modalities in a single act.

With the emergence of a new set of organizational values and a new work-force comprising more and more women whose needs require different management skills, and with the growing need to reduce work related stress, it is becoming necessary that traditional and ineffective ways of conducting the management process must be replaced. Traditionally, cultural norms have been categorized into organizational (male) and family (female) norms. Changing social values and increasing pressures for efficiency have now created the need for managers to be more androgynous, who can combine both the norms.

So the concept of 'Androgyny' has been gaining increasing popularity. Since the term is designed to express a transcendence of traditional conceptions of masculinity and femininity, it offers the vision of a future society, where people would be free to pursue their own interests and develop their own talents regardless of sex. Traditional theories of psychological well- being which prescribed masculinity for men and femininity for women were being put to question, when more and more studies began reporting that rather than only stereotypic sex appropriate traits, it was the presence of both desirable masculine and feminine characteristics (androgyny) within an individual's sex-role repertory which seemed to make for social competence and superior adaptability. So, sex-role orientation has a significant influence on the female as well as male managers. Now, researches have begun shifting their focus from biological sex to sex-role orientation as a better predictor variable. But, further research is needed to settle the dispute over the relative utility of being androgynous and thereby displaying a combination of masculine and feminine characteristics or simply being confirming to a particular sex-role.

Fear of Success

There have been many attempts to explain why women, who despite contributing in ever greater numbers to the work-force, continue to occupy lower status positions. One of the much quoted study is Horner's (1968)[11]. Assessment of Women's Achievement Motivation; She strove to provide explanations for the findings that despite apparent increases in educational and career openings for women, they still seem to show reluctance to match men in competitive situations. Horner argued that most competent and achievement motivated women, when faced with a conflict between their feminine image and expressing their competencies or developing their abilities and interests, adjust their behaviours to their internalized sex-role stereotypes. This is because the anticipation of success among women is anxiety-provoking and as such inhibits otherwise positive achievement, directed motivation and behaviour. In order to feel or appear more feminine, women especially those high in fear of success disguise their abilities and withdraw from the mainstream of thought, activism and achievement in our society.

Fear of success is defined as a specific motive to avoid success, because of the negative consequences that results from success. It seems to be a major problem of women managers and more particularly those occupying top positions. Fear of success received a great deal of attention in the late 1960's and 1970's, as a personality characteristic that was supposed to distinguish women's and men's responses to task-oriented situations. The concept is originally postulated and operationalized by Horner (1972)[12].

Horner's model of 'Fear of Success' is derived from her observation that highly competent females, when confronted with standard achievement tasks or when on threshold of culturally desirable attainments, appear to face both anxiety and decrement in performance. According to her, most of the women have a motive to avoid success arising from fear of success, i.e., a disposition to become anxious about achieving success, because a person expects negative consequences as a result of succeeding. Negative consequences are social disapproval, rejection and a feeling of being unfeminine. Thus, fear of success is more a characteristic of high achievement oriented and high ability women than of low achievement oriented women, who neither aspire to nor can achieve success.

She further suggests that there exists a fundamental difference between males and females in the structure of their achievement motivation. Her first clue came from the one consistent finding on women: they get higher test anxiety scores than do men. Maccoby has suggested that the girl who is motivated to achieve is defying contentions regarding what girls should do. As a result, the intellectual woman pays a price in anxiety. Mead concurs, noting that intense intellectual striving can be viewed as "competitively aggressive behaviour". Even, Freud thought that the whole essence of femininity lay in repressing aggressiveness (and hence intellectuality). Thus, consciously or unconsciously the girl equates intellectual achievement with loss of femininity.

Thus, Horner argues that there is basic difference between the sexes in their orientation to success. Where males univalently value success, females are ambivalent about achieving success. This led her to the assumption that along with possessing motives to approach success and avoid failure, females also possess a motive to avoid success. She observed that this motive is unconscious and is issued by a female specific socialization process which leads them to anticipate a loss of femininity, and contingent about traditional success in our culture. This anticipation leads females to become anxious when they approach success.

In another study, Horner (1972)[13], viewed this female specific fear of success motive as originating from sex-role socialization process, as an instance of anxiety or strain generated by role conflict. That is, the demands imposed by an achieving competent society on its competent members, conflict with implicit sex-role demands that direct them to be compliant, non-competitive and nurturant. As a consequence, achievement circumstances, particularly competitive ones, have the potential for activating both success approaching and success avoiding tendencies in women. Horner suggests that, in order to understand female achievement behaviour, it is necessary to consider both these orientations towards success.

In the words of the famous anthropologist Margaret Mead, "each step forward as a successful American regardless of sex means, a step back as a woman". The failure of women was observed as a conflict between marriage and profession and women who were successful thus, preferred to be single. The notion that achievement could be realized only at the expenses of marriage and family, was accepted by many anthropologists. A number of women found a socially acceptable solution in teaching, nursing and social work areas, where the generally accepted traits of women like nurturance, protection, and fostering of growth in others could be realized. Society has fostered an image of femininity that emphasizes tenderness and compassion at the expense of other valuable talents and emotions. Women thus, have fallen into *compassion traps*. Horner's research demonstrates that, women still tend to view competition, independence, intellectual achievement and leadership as basically in conflict with femininity. Evidence indicates that women who seek independence and intellectual mastery pay a high personal price for their defiance of prescribed sex-role, a price in anxiety.

This idea is already encompasses in the motive to avoid success. Achievement in the outside world is at present not a viable choice for women, because of psychological barriers like the motive to avoid success. Either consciously or unconsciously, a woman accepts the society's judgment that intellectual or professional achievement for a woman signifies her loss of femaleness. In Horner's words, "A bright woman is caught in a double bind. In achievement oriented situations, she not only worries about failure, but also about success. If she fails, she is not living up to her standards of performance, if she succeeds she is not living up to societal expectation of female role".

Empirical Findings

Sex-role Orientation of the Women Managers

As seen in Table 3, given below, a large number of respondents fall in the androgynous sex-role type followed by feminine, masculine and undifferentiated categories. Results of the undifferentiated group are given in the tables, but they are not analayzed, because of their negligible number.

TABLE 3
Sex-role Orientation of the Women Managers

Sex-role Orientations	*No. of Respondents*	*Percentage*
Androgynous	71	44.38
Feminine	41	25.63
Masculine	35	21.88
Undifferentiated	13	8.13
Total	160	100.00

The study shows that out of 160 women managers, 71 (44.38 per cent) are *androgynous,* 41 (25.63 per cent) are *feminine* and 35 (21.88 per cent) are *masculine.* Only 13 (8.13 per cent) respondents are in *undifferentiated* category and they have not been included in the analysis because of their insignificant number.

Thus, our analysis reveals that a large number of women managers are androgynous. There can be several explanations for it. Firstly, androgyny presents a desired means for individuals to move beyond the rigid constraints of sex-roles (Bem, 1974)[14]. When women managers adhere to the usual gender stereotypes they face problems in their functioning, because often behaviours specific to sex-roles limit the development of effective management styles in a particular situation. Secondly, androgynous individuals whose self-image and behaviour are less narrowly restricted along sex-role lines, are more ready to meet the complex demands of the society (Lenny, 1979)[15], and thus, they are more flexible. So, androgynous women managers who perceive themselves as having high levels of both stereotypical masculine and feminine behaviours, have access to a wider repertoire of possible behaviours to meet various situations, because of greater psychological flexibility.

Women managers are required to manage two separate fronts: family and profession. In Indian society, usually, household work, child rearing, maintenance of family, etc., rest primarily with the female partner which require qualities like patience, sensitivity and nurturance, which are considered as basically feminine qualities. In the professional sphere, she has to work on equal terms and even, sometimes more to prove herself. Sometimes, she is required to be tough, task oriented and more assertive, which in turn are considered as stereotypically male traits. So, to maintain a perfect balance between home and profession, women managers are required to carry both the feminine as well as masculine qualities. In other words, in order to be successful on both the fronts, they try to be androgynous.

Another explanation can be that, while dealing with the subordinates, sometimes situation warrants them to be tough, dominant, assertive and task-oriented, while at other times, situations require them to be tolerant, sensitive, gentle, participative and nurturant. So, instead of sticking to a particular style, they adopt different styles according to different situations. A recent finding shows that managers perceived by their subordinates as being androgynous are considered to be better handlers of conflict situations than their masculine or feminine peers (Jurma and Powell, 1994)[16].

Again, women in managerial positions usually prefer to have high occupation attainment, self-esteem and job satisfaction. Androgynous subjects having high level of occupational attainment are found to have higher level of self-esteem and greater degree of work satisfaction than those with other types of sex-role identity (Chow, 1987)[17]. So, this may be one of the reasons why women managers prefer to be androgynous. Androgynous individuals are also found to exhibit better health-related behaviors than masculine, feminine and undifferentiated individual (Shifren Bauserman and Carter, 1993)[18] and this may be one factor which motivates women managers to be androgynous.

The second largest group of women managers are of feminine sex-role type. They valued the feminine traits more. They try to adhere to the traditional gender roles prescribed by the society Males and females are expected to have different personality traits which are supposedly consistent with their biological sex. When they adhere to the traditional gender roles, they easily get social approval and acceptance (Buddhapriya and Khandelwal, 1995)[19]. But, when they violate the traditional gender roles they are criticized. So, to get social acceptance, the women managers might be adhering to the traditional gender roles and prefer to be feminine in their sex-role orientation. Society's differential expectations from males and females are also affect their identity as well as behaviour. Girls tend to be socialized to grow and possess expressive qualities such as sensitivity, passivity and conformity (Kleinplatz, Mc Carrey and Kateb, 1992)[20]. This is often accompanied by the fear that if they violate the traditional gender roles, they will be criticized, which may eventually lead to social rejection and isolation.

Another reason for the feminine sex-role orientation may be that adaptability, sensitivity, generosity, participativeness, and relationship orientation, which are considered feminine qualities, are well accepted by management for success. Apart from this, feminine individuals are also found to be more confident in professional ability and in dealing with personal problems (Johnson, 1988)[21].

An analysis of the sex-role orientation of women managers reveals that management of profession and family, changing social values, attitudinal changes might be some of the factors in influencing the sex-role orientation of women managers. With the emergence of a set of new roles (family role as well as professional role) women managers are trying to adjust themselves by becoming more androgynous.

Fear of Success of Women Managers

In this chapter, one of our objectives is to measure the extent of fear of success experienced by women managers. A perusal of Table 4 reveals that the respondents' average score on fear of success is low, the mean value being 139.18 as against the possible range of 20-320. The subjects' fear of success actually varied between a very low value of 72 to a high of 247 showing a very high degree of standard deviation (33.25), which, in turn, is also indicative of wide dispersal of the subjects on the normal distribution curve. Maximum respondents fall in 107-141, and 147-177 scoring divisions. Very few respondents score very high.

TABLE 4
Respondents' Scoring on Fear of Success

		Scoring Divisions	*No. of Respondents falling in each category*
Total Respondents	160	72-106	27 (16.88%)
Mean	139.18	107-141	62 (38.75%)
Standard Deviation	33.26	142-177	53 (33.13%)
Highest Score	247	178-212	12 (7.5%)
Lowest Score	72	213-247	6 (3.75%)

But the result shows that the women managers exhibited generally low fear success. Such low fear or success exhibited by the respondents could be indicative of lesser career-mindedness, achievement motivation and low success anxiety. Certain other factors may also be responsible for this. Firstly, in a metropolitan city like Delhi the social values, patterns and attitudes are rapidly changing and roles are becoming less narrowly restricted to a particular sex. Society has started accepting women as professionals. In due course of time, women managers have also started adjusting themselves to the demands of job as well as family responsibilities. So the fear of social disapproval, and rejection is gradually becoming less. Some other factors like, large number of androgynous respondents, higher education, high income, less number of children, parental education and nuclear family system may have influenced them in scoring low in the fear of success measurement. Surti (1982)[22] has found that women having low education and low income have high fear of success than highly educated income group, indicating that the concept of fear of success is more applicable to women living in traditional society than women having modern environment. Fear of success is also positively and significantly related with the number of children and women in nuclear families, were found to have low fear of success.

Managerial Level and Fear of Success

Fear of success seems to be a major problem of women managers and more particularly those occupying top positions. Because, there is an apprehension that as women moveup the ladder, they will have to devote increasing amount of time to their work responsibilities, thereby, jeopardizing their family obligations. Thus, women who are faced with a choice between two, tend to allow family responsibilities to take precedence over work obligations. This is also supported by our interview result where most of the respondents give priority to their family life. Moreover, fear of success is more a characteristic of high achievement-oriented, high ability women than of low achievement oriented women (Horner, 1969)[23]. Usually fear of success springs from role-conflict and role-conflict is more in case of women occupying top positions. The demands imposed by an achieving competent society, conflict with implicit sex-role demands that direct them to be compliant, non-competitive and nurturant.

Taking the managerial level and fear of success with consideration this hypothesis was formulated, i.e., 'Senior level women managers would score high fear of success as compared to middle and junior level women manager'. But contrary to the expectation, senior level managers scored less compared to middle and junior level managers, who usually are more concerned with their career development and may not be able to pay enough attention towards their husbands, children and other family members. So, women's pursuit of their careers is often in conflict with their family demands. Again, women who are more concerned with their career development do not get social approval. This is shown in Table 5.

TABLE 5
Mean and Standard Deviation of Fear of Success in Different Levels of Management

	Total	*Managerial Level*		
		Senior	*Middle*	*Junior*
Mean	139.18	133.0	137.6	141.0
Standard Deviation	33.26	40.77	33.34	32.06

TABLE 6
Analysis of Variance of Fear of Success

Source of Variation	*Sum of Squares*	*Degree of Freedom*	*Mean Square*	*F*
Main Effects	58340.32	4	14585.08	19.85**
Managerial Level	490.67	2	245.33	.33
Sex-role Orientation	57295.69	2	28647.85	38.99**
2-Way Interactions (MTL × SRO)	5842.59	3	1947.53	2.65*
Explained	64182.91	7	9168.99	12.48**
Residual	111682.19	152	734.7	
Total	175865.10	159	1106.07	

*significant at .01 level,

**significant at .05 level.

MTL—Managerial Level, SRO—Sex-role Orientation.

From the ANOVA result Table 6, it is found that management level does not have any significant influence on fear of success. If we analyze the mean score of fear of success in different managerial levels, then women managers do not differ significantly in their mean score, though the senior managers' score was less than the middle and junior level managers. This result is supported by Savage, Stearns and Friedman's (1979)[24], study in which they found no significant mean difference between freshmen and senior black women so far as fear of success was concerned. Freshmen who were high in fear of success, experienced anxiety about beginning their college careers which was quite analogous to senior's anxiety about beginning other experiences. Hence, the hypothesis is not supported by the result.

Sex-role Orientation and Fear of Success

Female-specific fear of success-motive originates from sex-role socialization process. Many studies have been conducted relating to sex-role orientation and fear of success. The hypothesis which has been formulated taking these two variables is that: 'Women managers having androgynous and masculine sex-role orientation would experience less fear of success as compared to those having feminine sex-role orientation'.

TABLE 7
Mean and Standard Deviation of Fear of Success in Different Sex-role Orientations

	Total	*Sex-role Orientations*			
		Androgynous	*Feminine*	*Masculine*	*Undifferentiated*
Mean	139.18	123.01	170.02	127.14	162.54
SD	33.26	24.00	26.09	32.26	17.00

The analysis of variance result Table 6 shows that sex-role orientation has significant influence on the fear of success of women managers. In other words, the androgynous, masculine, feminine subjects vary significantly in their score on fear of success. When we analyze the mean score Table 7 of fear of success across different sex-role orientations, it has been seen that androgynous and masculine sex-role type women managers experienced much less fear of success than the feminine managers. The feminine group's mean score was much higher than these two groups. From this it can be inferred that women managers having feminine sex-role orientation have high fear of success as compared to androgynous and masculine groups. The androgynous group's fear of success is the least, followed by masculine and feminine groups.

Thus, the hypothesis is fully supported by the results. The study conducted by Laine et al. (1984)[25], also indicates that androgynous and masculine subjects reported less fear of success than feminine or undifferentiated subjects regardless of their sex in fear of success. So, our results support Laine's (1964)[26], findings.

The relationship between sex-role orientation and fear of success is interesting. One possible reason why androgynous and masculine subjects have less fear of success, because of the fact that these two groups may be more successful in balancing their work as well as family obligations. The conflict between family and profession seems to be manageable. Secondly, the androgynous individuals are high both in masculine as well as feminine traits. So, combining the roles of a woman and a manager may not appear to be incompatible. Thirdly, the fear of social rejection, and social disapproval may be less in case of androgynous and masculine subjects.

Subjects having feminine sex-role orientation have high fear of success. Throughout history, society has viewed femininity and achievement as incompatible goals. (Horner, 1970)[27]. At work, where these women find themselves in environments largely dominated by masculine values like, competitiveness, achievement orientation and individualism, they may experience anxieties about their abilities, showing a lack of confidence and having a sense of emotional splitting.

One of the reasons why feminine subjects scored high fear of success was, because of the fact that the conflict between family and profession which is a major cause of fear of success might be more in case of feminine sex-role orientation. The feminine subjects may think that if they are more involved in their profession, they would not be able to pay enough attention to the needs of their family. They may have a high degree of conflict between the behaviour they expected of themselves as women and as a managers.

Those who have feminine sex-role orientation, probably, attach more importance to their commitment towards family responsibilities. They may try to carryout the traditional duties and responsibilities at home along with liabilities towards their professions. Their fear of success increases which is closely associated with striving to develop career interests compatible with their strong commitment to have husband and children.

Feminine women managers must be giving high importance to family and accordingly, their social relation and fear of social rejection, disapproval, unpopularity and loss of femaleness must be quite high too. They may disguise their abilities and withdraw from competitive situations in order to be more feminine.

Implications of the Findings

The above findings lead to certain implications for the women managers, organizations and society at large. The results reveal that public sector women managers having androgynous sex-role orientation tend to have lower fear of success and organizational role stress compared to masculine and feminine sex-role types. This indicates that androgynous respondents are more likely to be effective in managerial positions. On the contrary, feminine sex-role oriented women managers experienced significantly high amount of fear of success as well as organizational role stress, which could impinge upon their effectiveness as managers.

Androgynous rather than masculine orientation should be taken into account while seeking to orient women managers towards successful managerial careers. Androgyny, which is taken as a favoured sex-role orientation, is associated with high self-esteem and a tendency to adopt more flexible approach to situations, as it combines the best of both masculine and feminine qualities. As the women managers are required (and often feel compelled) to manage both the fronts, i.e., profession and family, a combination of feminine and masculine qualities could help them immensely in balancing their dual roles and accompanying responsibilities. They should not restrict their self-image and behaviour to any particular sex-role, as the nature of their functioning warrants greater psychological flexibility to meet the complex demands of profession and family.

The study seeks to suggest here that a significant effort in this direction can be taken up at the organizational level by imparting training to its employees to recognize their sex-role identity and to help them in developing an androgynous sex-role orientation. If the trend of the past decade persists, we would have more women entering into managerial professions in the years ahead, occupying top positions. This may go a long way in dispelling the existing gender-biases and in disposing women managers favourably towards their job without any inhibitions. People's expectation would undergo a seachange then. Indeed, research suggests that the prevalent/conventional tendency to define leadership and management in masculine terms is on the wane and it will soon bury itself, as women gain access to higher level of management and successfully handle their jobs. Thus, the entry of a substantial proportion of women into managerial roles may itself change the perception of these roles in an androgynous direction.

Fear of success, which is usually found in highly competent, achievement-oriented and ambitious women professionals, is comparatively low in case of the respondents of the study. Such low fear of success exhibited by the respondents could be indicative of career-mindedness, low achievement motivation and low success anxiety of public sector women employees. Hence, it is worthwhile to examine the level of fear of success of private sector women managers as they operate in a different work environment marked by higher degree of competitiveness and efficiency.

Even though the effect of managerial level on fear of success was found to be insignificant from the ANOVA results, still at the junior level the amount of fear of success is comparatively high. This could be because of the possibility that fear of success, which arouses success anxiety in women managers, inhibits their role performance and compels them to compromise their job roles making them less career-minded. In addition to that, factors like dual burden (family and profession), multiple and incompatible roles, over-expectation and demands from various quarters could be some of the common reasons for raising the levels of fear of success.

Hence, it is the responsibility of the organization to provide adequate training for appropriate career planning of women managers, where they can rise to the needs of the job fully and excel through competence. On the other hand, to reduce the conflict between family and profession, flexible time arrangement, creche facility, re-entry policies, longer maternity leave, paternity leave etc., could be arranged by the organizations too. But, none of the organizations covered by the study had any such facility.

REFERENCES

1. Bem, S.L., (1974), "The Measurement of Psychological Androgyny", *Journal of Consulting and Clinical Psychology*, pp. 42, 155-62

2. Berthoin Antal, A., and Izraeli, D.N., (1993), "A Global Comparison of Women in Management: Women Managers in their Homelands and as Expatriates", in Ellen A. Fagenson (ed.), *Women in Management: Trends, Issues and Challenges in Managerial Diversity*, Vol. (4). Newbury Park, Calif, Sage.

3. Buddhapriya, S., and Khandelwal, P., (1995), "Sex Role Stereotypes and Women Managers: A Reality", *Indian Journal of Industrial Relations*, 31 (1), July, pp. 72-90.

4. Chakravarti, M., (1995), "Towards Gender Equality", *Yojana*, April, 39(6): pp. 29-31.

5. Chow, E.N., (1987), "The Influence of Sex-role Identity and Occupational Attainment on the Psychological Well-being of Asian American Women", *Psychology of Women Quarterly*, March, pp. 2, 69-82.

6. Horner, M.S., (1972), "Toward an Understanding of Achievement Related Conflicts in Women", *Journal of Social Issues*, 28(2), pp. 157-75.

7. Horner, M.S., (1968), "Sex Differences in Achievement Motivation and Performance in Competitive and Non-Competitive Situations", *Unpublished Doctoral Dissertation*, University of Michigan.

8. Horner, M.S., (1970), "Feminity and Successful Achievement: Basic Inconsistency", in *Feminine Personality and Conflict*, California, Brooks/Cole.

9. Horner, M.S., (1972), "Toward an Understanding of Achievement Related Conflicts in Women", *Journal of Social Issues*, 28(2), pp. 157-75.

10. Jurma, W.E. and Powell, M.L., (1994), "Perceived Gender Roles of Managers and Effective Conflict Management", *Psychological Reports*, 74(1), pp. 104-06.

11. Kleinplatz, P., Mc Carrey, M. and Kateb, C., (1992), "The Impact of Gender Role Identity on Women's Self-Esteem, Life-Style, Satisfaction and Conflict". *Canadian Journal of Behavioural Science*, pp. 24, 333-47.

12. Kruse, L., and Wintermantel, M., (1986), "Leadership Ms-Qualified", in C.F. Graumann, and S. Moscovici, (eds.), *Changing Conceptions of Leadership*, Springer-Verlag, New York Inc.

13. Laine, L. et at., (1984), "Fear of Success: The Influence of Sex, Sex-role Identity and Components of Masculinity", *Sex Role,* 10(5-6), pp. 341-46.

14. Lenny, E., (1979), "Androgyny: Some Audacious Assertions Toward its Coming of Age", *Sex Roles,* pp. 5, 703-19.

15. Horner, (1969).

16. Johnson, 1988.

17. Laine. 1964.

18. Naisbitt, J., and Aburdene, P., (1990), *Magatrend 2000,* USA, Marrow.

19. Pleck, J.H., (1971), "The Psychology of Sex-roles: Traditional and New Views", in A. Carter, A.F. Scoot and W. Martyna (eds.), *Women and Men in Changing Roles, Relationships and Perceptions,* New York, Prager Publishers.

20. Savage, J.E. Stearns, A.D. and Friedman, P., (1979), "Relationship of Internal External Locus of Control, Self-Concept and Masculinity Feminine to Fear of Success in Black Freshmen and Senior College Women", *Management Review,* 5(3), pp. 373-83.

21. Shifren, K., Bauserman, R. and Carter, D.B., (1993), "Gender Role Orientation and Physical Health: A Study Among Young Adults", *Sex Role,* Vol. 29(5-6), pp. 421-32.

22. Surti, K., (1982), "Some Psychological Correlates of Role Stress and Coping Styles in Working Women", *Ph.D. Thesis in Psychology,* Gujarat University, Ahmedabad.

23. Surti, K. and Sarupria, D., (1981), "Psychological Factors Affecting Women Entrepreneurs: Some Findings", *Paper Presented at the Second International Conference of Women Entrepreneurs,* New Delhi, November.

24. Towards Equality, (1974), "Committee on Status of Women", *Government of India,* p. 150.

25. Towards Equality., (1974), p. 215.

26. Vidya Rani, G., (1990), *Women in Public Employment,* Mittal, Delhi.

27. Webb, J., (1991), "The Gender Relations of Assessment", in J.F. Cozens and M.A. West (eds.), *Women and Work,* Philadelphia, Open University Press, pp. 13-25.

4

POLITICAL PARTICIPATION AND DALIT WOMEN

Pradeep K. Sharma

The very first question that comes to our minds is that of a definitional perspective regarding who is a Dalit? The confusion centres around the connotation of the word 'Dalit' which was originally used as a Marathi and Hindi translation of the British term 'Depressed Classes.' There are varieties of nomenclatures such as Untouchables, Harijans, Depressed Classes, Dalits, servile classes, weaker sections, Panchamas, Atishudras, Avarnas and the Scheduled Castes. The term 'Depressed Classes' refers to those castes who belong to the lowest rung of the Hindu caste hierarchy and whose touch and proximity is considered polluting by the caste Hindu. This is a British innovation from the article written by Dr Annie Besant in the *Indian Review*, February 1909 captioned "The Uplift of the Depressed Classes." Further, the term 'Depressed Classes' was mentioned in the Census Report, 1921, but the castes constituting the 'Depressed Classes' were not defined and it was used before 1930, but since the enactment of the Government of India Act, 1935, they are consistently referred to as the 'Scheduled Castes' (SCs).

This term was coined by the Simon Commission, 1928 and subsequently the British Government issued the Government of India (Scheduled Castes) Order, 1936, specifying certain castes and tribes. This category of the Scheduled Castes was known as the Harijans, that is, the children of God—a term coined by Mahatma

Gandhi in 1933. Some leaders of the aforementioned castes consider the Harijan nomenclature pejorative and they prefer to be called 'Dalit', that is, oppressed. Since then the term has undergone a drastic change and this oppressed section of the Indian society has chosen for themselves 'a new identity', 'a revised self-image' to indicate their lack of belief in being polluting and their inclusion in the Ambedkar movement, their sense of denial that their condition is the fault of the caste system and to assert their rights and denial of being subordinated by the religious, social or economic status.[1] The Dalit Panthers, once a militant organisation had used this term and has widened its scope as it defines "members of Scheduled Castes and Scheduled Tribes, neo-Buddists, the working people, the landless poor peasants, women and those who are being exploited politically, economically and in the name of religion, are called Dalits."[2] Through this asserted identity, the Dalit Movement directed itself "towards status improvement vis-a-vis social mobility among Dalits and shaping their agitational sensitivity and assertion for achieving the rights of equality and equal opportunity, self-respect and respectful identity."[3] Thus the Marathi word 'Dalit' was chosen by this section of the society itself and is used proudly. Even in the English Press this word has to be used without translation. "None of the normal words as Untouchables, Scheduled Castes, Depressed Classes, etc. had the same connotation. *Dalit* implies those who have been broken, ground down by those above them in a deliberate and active way. There is in the word itself an inherent denial of pollution, Karma and justified caste hierarchy."[4] Professor Gangadhar Pantawane, founder-editor of *Asmitadarsh* (Mirror of Identity), the chief organ of Dalit literature, defines the word as follows:

> "To me Dalit is not a caste. He is a man exploited by the social and economic traditions of this country. He does not believe in God, rebirth, the soul, holy books teaching separatism, fate and heaven because they have made him a slave. He does believe in humanism. Dalit is a symbol of change and revolution."[5]

Thus the definitional perspective of the word 'Dalit' is wide enough to address the oppressed sections of the society and it includes in its paradigm not only those castes who are oppressed for centuries but all those who are subject to multiple exploitation thereby including women as a 'category' cutting across the caste, creed or community lines because it is a proven fact that almost half of the humanity in this country has been subject to subordination at various levels.

The second definitional perspective that needs equal attention is that of political participation. As a matter of fact, in the developing societies like India, political participation is not confined to a relatively limited set of acts such as exercise of franchise campaigning or participation through very formal institutions but it certainly has a wider context which refers to "any voluntary action, successful or unsuccessful, organised or unorganised, episodic or continuous, employing legitimate or illegitimate methods, intended in influencing the choice of public policies, or the administration of public affairs or the choice of the political leaders."[6]

What is of crucial importance in terms of political participation is the vision to associate oneself with the larger social movement for equality and justice. This kind of political participation requires a large level of mass mobilisation with very clear and coherent understanding of one's socio-political context, a vocal and committed leadership and mutually confident and transparent organisational structure which can associate people in different ways: formal and informal as well.

Having such a kind of understanding of political participation one wonders whether women as a category have the required level of political participation in their movements which are variously termed as fragmented, sparse or even fizzled out. Whereas the role of women in the changed domestic and global perspective has been considered most important to the political life of our society, it is the area of socio-economic equality, liberty and decision making where they have to crave out a meaningful space for themselves. Though constitutional safeguards and progressive legal enactment have endowed juridical equality but the right to equal status and opportunities in education, law and political participation influencing the key decisions having serious imprints on socio-economic structures have still been a distant dream that needs urgent attention. We find that the majority of the womenfolk, particularly in rural India, are operating in a closed social system where they are subordinate to their male counterparts in almost every sphere of their lives and are left with no option other than the 'kitchen affairs' to display their skills. The situation of Dalit women is more precarious and what is worse is that they have to face two-way simultaneous oppression; one, from their male counterparts in their own family and kinship as well as from the upper castes males, and second, due to their so-called low status in the caste hierarchy. There are numerous examples in our country where women of the lower castes are being exploited in various ways including physical but the level and degree is minimum or sometimes absent and people don't have the will to protest against the shameful and heinous acts of physical violence. Though with the spread of the communication technology cases of exploitation are coming to light but the punishment and deterrents are not working somehow and many a time the culprits go scot-free. It is now widely accepted that assertion by women for their rights and admissions in civil society is of utmost importance for the overall development of the democratic fabric of our society. But its proper execution is sometimes interpreted in a diffused manner by the government and other institutions. The concerned agencies shirk their responsibility towards them and only a wish well which does not augur well for the vision of a mass-based women's movement. They tend to ignore that the specific socio-economic structure of our society where the nature of women's subordination adversely affects the forms, character and effectiveness of their participation. In fact "political equality is meaningless where the mass of the population suffers from poverty, continuous threats of starvation, lack of health and inequality of class, status and power. It is more so in the case of women who suffer from another dimension of inequality, namely, the weight of traditional attitudes that regard them as physically and socially inferior to men."[7] Women's participation in the political process is central to their struggle against oppression. All the different aspects of women liberation depend on their articulation to express their demands and aspirations politically associating themselves with the larger movements of liberation, equality, liberty and justice. Issues relating to women emancipation have to be addressed in almost all fields and only through consistent organised political behaviour and action can they achieve their objectives in the social, cultural, religious and economic fields; whether it is health, employment, education and training or demands for their basic rights, it is through collective endeavour that they can achieve their particular objectives. Political participation in India, particularly by women, has been considered in the narrow sense of participating in the elections and casting their votes. Party politics is not the only expression of political participation. People's organisations and movements both at the grassroots and macro levels for transformation of society and women's liberation are to be amply recognised. As was pointed out earlier there are various levels of political participation, institutional and non- institutional as well as formal and informal. Hence all these issues have to be seriously considered and only then can a comprehensive approach to the women's development emphasising on the issues of education, employment, health, nutrition and empowerment be chalked out leading towards women's empowerment thereby making an empowered society at large.

Amidst this background I shall now focus on the crucial issues or concerns which definitely need urgent attention.

First of all, the chief task of the women movements, particularly of the Dalit women's movement, is to fight for economic and social equality, not only formal equality as we know that equality before law is not necessarily equality in fact. Women's movement which are essentially an important component of the larger mass movement must address the issue of equality along with justice. For achieving this goal they must be aware themselves and of society and its context.

Dalit women have to struggle at two basic levels: one, they to fight for their social recognition as an equal human being in the Indian social system dominated by the caste hierarchy and, two, for the recognition of their rights along with the larger movements for women emancipation. Their struggle has to be two-fold making their movement more complex and requires a holistic approach. What is more important here is that women's right to organise and struggle against their oppression must be linked to the question of the democratic rights of the people and strategy should be evolved to delineate their participation in the struggle in a more active manner.

Another issue concerning women's political participation is their household and child-rearing responsibilities and tasks. Lack of maternity and child-care facilities not only prevent women from participating in productive labour but are a barrier to their participation in public life. The State policies have been ineffective in addressing this problem and are hampering their development. Along with this they need to take part in the administration of the private and public affairs. Here we must concentrate on the life-skill development where both the genders should equally participate on mutual basis. One of the major causes of gender discrimination is the negative attitude created among both boys and girls at an early age. Gender discrimination at the societal level begins at birth and is powerfully reinforced at various stages. Even children starting school at the age of five already have a gender identity and hold stereotypical assumptions about different gender roles of adults as well as themselves. Gender relationship in our society have been stereotyped in a characteristic way, in which men dominate and women are subordinated. The woman is supposed to perform all domestic tasks and is often not assigned a decision-making or important role in day-to-day life. There is a tacit gender based division of labour which determines who does what, when and where. Gender identity is one of the first and far-reaching identities that a human being acquires, and this is overshadowed by traditional gender roles. The application of traditional gender roles leads to many forms of differentiation and discrimination between men and women. In order to achieve gender equality, a vital component of the overall strategy of securing equity and social justice, education needs to be interventionist, empowering and reflective of social reality. The education system, its curriculum and its teacher have a prominent role in developing a future generation inculcating a spirit of equality among children and sharing responsibilities equally. Here the role of the life-skill development becomes more important. Life-skill development broadly includes:

(*a*) empowering financial management where women are given more autonomy and freedom to manage the financial affairs of the family life;

(*b*) family health and child care where the male counterparts have a very important role to play as child rearing is not only the women's responsibility; but the man's as well;

(*c*) nutrition and cooking;

(*d*) general house management and related household tasks which should be performed mutually and should be shared.

Associated with the above issues is the major concern for a dignified human life.[8] Every individual must enjoy a dignified life and not be subjugated or a subordinated nor made to lead a life that is appropriated by the male-dominated social order. We must strive for a society that should work out for the dignity of the individual and everyone should be so nurtured that she/he should have respect for the human life and should cherish equality, liberty and fraternity in his/her life approach. This can be an ideal but does not unachievable if the whole society works collectively and consciously for its attainment. This objective needs a serious introspection on the part of the each individual and the entire structures of the social system to impart training towards that direction. This also demands certain commitment and more so in shedding down one's own prejudices and inhibitions regarding gender, caste, colour, creed and region, etc.

There are other issues of equally utmost importance which also need thorough analysis but it is the limitation of this book that they are not within the purview of this book. The crucial issues of equality (social, political and economic), household and child-rearing responsibilities, life-skills development and a dignified human life are dealt with touching upon the issues of education, health, nutrition, employment, etc. which certainly need further attention.

Analysing these issues at length one dwells on the double strategy which has been phrased in the concept of empowerment where empowerment means a restructuring of gender relations within both the family and in society at large and it is society's recognition of women's equality vis-a-vis men as independent human beings which will bring the real change. Empowerment is a continuous process encompassing several mutually reinforcing components that are ushered in through an increased level of politicisation and participation in the public affairs.

If politics means power then women must achieve power. They must achieve power themselves and by their own struggle. They must fight for their recognition as an equal partner of social life. Dalit women in particular have to fight against oppression in more active and vocal ways. They have to fight against the caste system and against the male-dominated patriarchal social structure. At the primary level, they have to associate their movement with larger anti-caste Dalit movements[9] while at the secondary level they have to align themselves with the feminist movements. The task is definitely a tough one but hope sustains, though in a fragmented way when in the Marathi literature Dalit women have challenged male supremacy and also the caste system. In other areas of human life politics, training, management, development, etc. women are becoming conscious of their rights and they are in the continuous process of defining and re-defining their self-image and striving for autonomy and freedom. What is needed at this decisive juncture is a gender-sensitive approach towards overall human development and I think one important change or step that can be taken immediately is to question one's own conscience for human equality which will certainly culminate in the continuous process of women's empowerment. If our democratic fabric has to be enriched then a comprehensive approach to equality has to be evolved ensuring democratisation, decentralisation and transparency in the private and public affairs which will lead towards the establishment of an egalitarian society and will have a meaningful transformation of the social structures.

REFERENCES

1. Zelliot, Eleanor. From Untouchable to Dalit: Essays on the Ambedkar Movement, Delhi : Manohar Publishers, 1992.
2. Manifesto of Dalit Panthers.
3. Ram, Nandu. Beyond Ambedkar, Delhi: Har-Anand Publications, 1995, p. 87.
4. Zelliot, Eleanor, *ibid.*, p. 267.

5. Zelliot, Eleanor, *ibid.*, p. 268.
6. Weiner, Myron. "Political Participation: Crisis of the Political Process" in L. Binder et al., Eds. *Crisis and Sequence in Political Development*, Princeton: Princeton University Press, 1979, p. 164.
7. Committee on the Status of Women in India, 1974.
8. For more detail please see a very powerful empression in Dalit Literature all over India which, inherently, is a protestant literature and on visions a society where each individual enjoys a dignified human life.
9. Omvedt, Gail. Dalits and the Democratic Revolution: Dr. Ambedkar and the Dalit Movement in Colonial India. Delhi: Sage Publications, 1994.

5

POLITICAL CONSCIENTIZATION PARTICIPATION OF WOMEN IN A SQUATTER SETTLEMENT[1]

Saraswati Haider

Western philosophers and political theorists, with their penchant for thinking in terms of non-interacting, impermeable dualisms and binaries for Women and Dualism: A Sociology of Knowledge Analysis (see Glennon 1979), saw society as divided into what came to be viewed as distinct, separate private and public sphere (see Elshtain 1981). Women and their patriarchally constricted, ordained activities revolving around reproduction[2] were decisively confined to the private domain, while men were the sole, supreme role players in the public domain of politics, civil society and what was, in an unabashedly male-biased, male supremacist stance, perceived as 'productive'[3] work—culture—while child bearing and child rearing and the housework done by women in the home was seen as non-productive. Women's reproductive work was not viewed as productive, but 'natural' (see Ortner 1974)[4]. Neither was the unpaid extensive production work women did in the home and outside in subsistence and semi-capitalist economies (semi-capitalist economies incorporating pre-capitalist primitive modes of accumulation of capital) (see Mies 1986, Werlhof 1988b) seen as of productive value. The private sphere, however, was also not a space of complete autonomy and supremacy for women. Men were the lords and masters—the watchful eyes and the restraining hands—in the private realm as well as, resulting in strict control by males of women's bodies, sexuality, movements, much of women's space, women's doings and even, women's thinking. The distinction between the private and public spheres still persists to a large extent in spite of feminism and women's movements critiquing it (Pateman 1987; Elshtain 1974; Helly and Reverby 1992) and persistently trying to break the false, socially constructed (for amplification of the social construction of reality see Berger and Luckmann 1976) patriarchally-premised barrier, but with only limited success. The significant and the top, most valued, controlling positions and activities in the public sphere, including politics, still remain by and large male-dominated bastions.

In India too the division between the private and the public sphere prevailed more or less on the same pattern as in the West—the *ghar* (home) and the *baher* (outside—for an account of the construction of *ghar* and *baher* in the nationalist discourse in India see Chatterjee 1997a, 1997b. See also Rajan 1999a, for explication of the sexual abuse perpetrated on women, who venture into, or find themselves, in the public space in India in the same way as Draupadi in the *Mahabharat*). The distinction of the private/public was in fact, far more stringently upheld in India than in the West with the private physical space also demarcated between that reserved for males and that for females restricting further the movement and contact with men of women—the *zenana* (women's quarters, the space for women's patriarchally prescribed activities, which quarters men occasionally visited) and the *mardana* (men's quarters, where women were not allowed to enter).

In India also women were firmly kept out of politics, but for a few exceptions. Even women, usually of the lower castes, who participated actively and substantially in the so-called 'productive' work (which women's work, more often than not, remained unpaid, unrecognized and unregistered) were denied access to political space. This one presumes was so in all the 'multiple patriarchies' in India (for information on the 'multiple patriarchies' in India see Sangari 1995 and for an affirmation of different caste patriarchies see Rao 1999). Politics in the public domain in India was exclusively a male preserve and is still so to a very large extent.

The Indian Constitution drafted after India's independence, however, gives Indian women the right to vote and hence, participate in the democratic political process of the country. It also guarantees to women, with men, equal rights in all spheres, including ostensibly politics, though there exists a considerable hiatus between the *de jure* and *de facto* situation where participation of women in the political affairs and political decision making in the country is concerned[5] even, though so far as voting goes the gap between male voters and female voters is not much.[6] Thus, women seem to have made some excursion in the public domain in India though in all likelihood guided there by males and influenced by the latter also, to serve male interests.

One must make clear here that politics today has come to acquire a very wide, expansive and multi-nuanced meaning, which not only embraces formal politics concerning state and citizenship, but has been extended to include the various, diverse strategies and manouvres, covert and overt, adopted in any relationship either between individuals or groups including the relationship between the two genders (see Millet 1972—for women the personal also declared as political) or in any sphere to gain power, authority and social, political, economic, cultural, symbolic capital (for information on the different kinds of capital see Bourdieu 1979, 1986, 1987, 1989) and as a consequence dominance and control over human beings, things, processes and events. In this paper, however, politics implies only formal politics of state and citizenship including women's politics of the Indian Women's Movement (IWM).

No significant studies, as far as one's knowledge goes,seem to exist in India on the political conscientization (on 'Conscientization' see Freire 1973, 1974)[8] and political participation of the different sub-groups of women with gender identity criss-crossed and intricately enmeshed in caste, class, community, religious, ethnic, urban-rural and regional differences creating divides and sub-groups among the phalanx of Indian women and influencing Indian women's differential conscientization, experiences and behaviour patterns including, no doubt, their political behaviour, experiences and conscientization.

It is interesting to note that at least two important books—one on *State and Politics in India* (Chatterjee 1997 c) and the other *Wages of Freedom: Fifty Years of the Indian State* (Chatterjee 1998)—though they contain the usual, now almost ritualistic, tokenist papers on gender, however, in the first publication the paper on gender is entitled Protecting Women Against Violence? *Review of a Decade of Legislation 1980-1989* (Agnes 1997) and in the second, *Women and Citizenship* (Menon 1998), with citizenship here constricted to mean the discourse and campaign on the Uniform Civil Code (UCC) of the IWM. There is nothing in the above two books on women's 'conscientization' of India's larger political system, ethos, issues and processes and Indian women's participation in them or for that matter, the conscientization, of Indian Women of issues and their (the women's) experiences in participation in the IWM's campaigns. Women's political activities in the above two tokenist papers on gender are minimized and confined to a description of the major issues taken up by the IWM since, the latter's resurgence in the mid-1970s, after a 'silent period' (see John 1999 a), from the year of Independence to the 1970s.

The IWM, or the 'Autonomous Women's Movement', as it has come to be called (see Sen 1998; Patel 1998), no doubt, focused mainly on violence perpetrated on women and sought to bring about changes in this sphere through pressurizing the state *vide* wide scale, though not really mass campaigns, despite the IWM claiming them to be so (see Gandhi and Shah 1991; Kumar 1993; Calman 1992; Agnes 1997; Palriwale and Agnihotri 1998; Kapur and Cossman 1996). The campaigns apparently did not meet with much success. In fact, the situation worsened after some minor amendments were made in the law (see Agnes 1997). One of the IWM's major campaigns was also, no doubt, on the UCC (see Menon 1996; Parashar 1992), on which today the IWM finds itself in a quandry with the Hindu nationalist Bharatiya Janata Party (BJP), having incorporated the UCC in its political agenda mainly to beat the Muslims with this stick (see Sangari 1995). However, Indian women have been also implicated in a few mass movements (Sen 1990), in the country and as Indian citizens take part in general elections and thus, also participate to some extent in India's liberal parliamentary democratic political system making forays in the public sphere of politics though, as said before, perhaps driven and influenced by males for the benefits of the latter. Indian women's political activity thus, has not been confined only to agitating against increasing violence on women and the UCC. Besides, as pointed out above, the two studies cited, concentrate on the historical progression of the IWM's agenda and not 'conscientization' of the agenda or campaign experiences of the critical mass of India's women.

Some literature, however, has been produced in the ghettoised 'women's studies' (see John 1999 b), on Women and Politics (see Ray and Basu 1999; Kumari and Dubey 1994; Fredrich Ebert Stiftung 1993; Kaushik 1993; Kumari and Kidwai 1998), in the wake of the 73rd and 74th Amendments to the Indian Constitution in 1993 giving women 33 per cent reservations in all rural and urban local governing bodies (for literature on the Amendments see d' Lima 1993; Gawankar 1993, Kaushik 1993 b; Datta 1998, Narayanan 1996); the controversial, aborted 81st Amendment Bill reserving 33 per cent seats for women in the central and state legislatures (for writings on the 81st Amendment Bill see Seminar 1997), on which the IWM stands divided (see Kishwar 1998); the upsurge of religious fundamentalism and casteism (see Patel 1993; Tanwar 1998; Jayawardena and de Alwis 1996; Sarkar and Butalia 1995; Jeffery and Basu 1999; Bhasin et al 1996), which has led to fissions among Indian women of different religions and castes; stock-taking of the past and plans for the future of the IWM (Agnes 1995; Jain 1996; Agnihotri and Mazumdar 1995; Tharu and Niranjana 1994) and contemporary gender issues in a drastically changed socio-economic and cultural scenarios in India in the 1990s, (see Rajan 1999 b). But, again, in all this body of literature also studies on the political 'conscientization' of the critical mass of Indian women and their participation in the larger Indian political milieu, or for that matter in women's politics of the IWM are low and far between.

In this chapter I document the political conscientization of rural migrant women (henceforth, referred to as migrant women) residing in the squatter settlement (or *Jhuggi-Jhompri* (hutment) colonies, as squatter settlements are called in Delhi), Rajpur[9], i.e., the rural migrant women's 'conscientization' of the liberal Parliamentary democratic system of India; its processes, issues, its institutions, the role the migrant women are expected to play in the system, their rights and duties within the liberal Parliamentary democratic grid as well as the migrant women's 'conscientization' of women's politics as charted out by the IWM, which has been able to make some of Indian women's 'personal troubles of milieu' into 'the public issues of social structure' (for explanation of 'personal troubles of milieu' and 'public issues of social structure' see Mills 1973), politicizing them.

The study also includes presentation of findings on the participation of the migrant women in the political process and institutions in India as well as in the IWM.

The Setting

Squatter settlements, as pointed out above, are known as *Jhuggi-Jhompri* colonies like, JJ colonies in Delhi. Most of the inhabitants of these JJ colonies are rural migrants from all over India. JJ colonies in Delhi are increasing at a very rapid rate. From 929 JJ colonies in 1990, with about 0.26 million *Jhuggis* (see Sridharan 1995:338) and a population of about 1.5 million (Voluntary Health Association of India 1993; 16) the number of JJ colonies in Delhi increased to 1080 in 1994, with a population of about 2.7 million and in '1997, JJ colonies in Delhi numbered 1080 (*The Times of India*, New Delhi, Thursday, 15 May 1997), with an expected population of more than 3 million, i.e., almost one-third of population of Delhi. The JJ colony population in Delhi thus, forms a large vote bank and the votes of the *Jhuggi* dwellers can make or mar the career of a candidate contesting for elections either for the Lok Sabha, Delhi Assembly or the Municipal Corporation of Delhi (MCD). The JJ colonies are, therefore, hotbeds of politics in Delhi (see de Wit 1996, for the same in Madras slums).

Rajpur is a large, unauthorized illegal JJ colony in Delhi, in an industrial area situated on a hillock on land allotted to a government agency. It is surrounded by residential buildings functioning as small-scale manufacturing units. According to a survey by the Slum and JJ Wing of the Delhi Development Authority (DDA), in 1990, the colony had a total of 2708 *Jhuggis* with a population estimated at approximately 12000. In a recent conversation with one of the active Pradhans [10] of Rajpur I was told that the number of *Jhuggis* had increased and was at present 3500 and the population approximately 16000.

Rajpur has a considerable population of the Scheduled Castes, about 75 per cent I was told. The majority of the inhabitants have come from the rural hinterlands of the state of Uttar Pradesh (62.3 per cent) followed by much smaller numbers from the states of

Bihar, Rajasthan and Haryana. There were about 150-200 Muslim households in Rajpur and 1 Sikh household. The average household size comprised approximately 5 members.

Males in Rajpur outnumbered females with their population being 58 per cent and the female 42 per cent. Illiteracy was high at 52 per cent and of the so-called literates 36.2 per cent had only primary level education. Data was not collected on women's literacy, but it is bound to be very low as most of the inhabitants belong to the Scheduled Castes and the literacy of Scheduled Caste women was only 10.93 per cent in 1981, (see Anthropological Survey of India 1993:12). About 83 per cent households had a monthly income of Rs. 1000 or below, i.e., the majority of the families were living below the poverty line.

The Rajpur population is a young population with most of the inhabitants being in the age group 18 to 45 years. In 1990, Rajpur, there were 13 per cent unskilled workers, 13.2 per cent had their own businesses and were self-employed owning small shops or doing *kabadi ka kaam* (buying and selling junk—in Rajpur a business of selling cloth cuttings purchased from readymade garment making units), 30.2 per cent were in service jobs mostly of lower levels and as many as 37 per cent were unemployed.

Data on employment of women was not collected. Most of the women in Rajpur, however, surprisingly, are unemployed and are housewives.

The maximum number of population settled down in Rajpur unauthorizedly during the period of 1977-1985 was 94.2 per cent and the majority of them were first generation migrants.

The situation in Rajpur has worsened on all fronts since 1990, though some upwardly mobile households have amassed considerable wealth vide *kabadi ka kaam* or running shops and have become the haves of Rajpur envied by the other poor dwellers.

Political Conscientization of Migrant Women

Gendering politics does not only imply the participation of women in campaigns on women's issues organized by the IWM, but something more. It also means an awareness and 'conscientization' of the larger Parliamentary democratic political system of the country; its processes; its institutions, issues involved; what role women should be playing in the larger political system; what are the rights and duties of Indian women in the political system and together with this an awareness and 'conscientization' of the agenda of the IWM and participation in the political process, institutions and IWM campaigns.

Conscientization of the liberal Parliamentary Democracy of India

More than a half century after independence the crises of governance which have occurred since the mid-1970s, in India have on the one hand led to the conclusion that the liberal democratic system of India has been eroded by rising corruption, criminalization of politics, debasement of democratic institutions (see Kothari 1995, for a trajectory of the erosion of democracy in India; on the crisis of governability in India see Mitra 1995); democracy in India has been reduced to an electoral democracy only (Khilnani 1998), a mere game of numbers marred by communalism, casteism and cessationism. On the other hand it is also believed that India's democracy has struck strong roots in the country and it is because of the deep roots that democracy has struck in India that today's marginalized and peripheral sections of the population have been brought into mainstream politics, where they can represent their interests and musterup support for them (see again Kothari 1995; Mitra 1995). In this rather ambiguous 'conceptualization' it is interesting to investigate how much awareness and 'conscientization' of the liberal parliamentary democratic system is present among the migrant women of Rajpur, who are at the grassroots level and are part of the critical mass of Indian women.

The migrant women of Rajpur of all types were unaware of the word *Loktantra* (democracy). Even, the handful of women who were active in politics including one who styled herself as a *Pradhan* and worked vigorously during elections having dreams of contesting for an election herself—Asha Devi—could not explain clearly, coherently what *Loktantra* implied.

The migrant women were also unfamiliar with word *Rajniti* (politics) except the few politically active ones who, however, thought it to be the work of the *netas* (political leaders).

When asked as to who makes public arrangements of basic amenities, such as authorization of the shelter of the migrant women, and make facilities of water, sanitation, health care, schools, etc., the answer of practically all the migrant women was *sarkar* (government).

Sarkar is a word which is often used to refer to big landlords in many parts of rural North India. Rural big landlords on whose paternal patronage small and tenant farmers' and agricultural labourers' livelihood and peace depends. Thus, government apparently is perceived by the migrant women, as it is by most other Indians, as *sarkar*—an entity that is hierarchically above them and on whose benevolence the lives of the citizens depends and not as an institution of which they are the masters and forgerers and that it is incumbent up on the *sarkar* to make available basic amenities for its citizens not as largesse, but as their (the citizens') right. This concept of *sarkar* as a dominant superior power on whose benevolence one depends was the understanding of the migrant women also. Thus, a patron-client sort of relationship (see on *Jajmani* system Wiser 1958; Caldwell 1991), which was one of the hallmarks of India's hierarchical society divided into hierarchical castes (see Dumont 1980), was superimposed on a modern structure of governance. Democracy, an alien concept, not an Indian one, understood as *sarkar*, has thus, been Indianized to conform to an Indian feudal hierarchical way of thinking. When the migrant women were asked why did they not think that they were the *sarkar*, most of them exclaimed how could they be the *sarkar* as only the well off and well-educated people can be the *sarkar* not poor and illiterate women like them.

When they (migrant women) were questioned whether it was not the duty of the *sarkar* to provide them with basic amenities as their *adhikar* (right), the women had no idea about what *adhikar* meant. They were only familiar with *maang* (demand), but *maang* here included more connotations of asking for rights not demanding them. Asking being a more supplicant kind of request not a forceful claim.

Thus, as far as government was concerned the migrant women saw it as a dominating power to whom only requests could be made and which had the power to make 'whatever' decisions it liked uninfluenced by the migrant women.

When inquired why the *sarkar* should not let them to make their own decisions about their own lives, my protagonists asked me instead how can they make decisions? As they are illiterate and have no idea about the world outside their homes. Thus, they did not have much of a clue about participatory democracy in which decision-making would be in their hands. They did not have even, think themselves as fit for taking any decision. The *sarkar* was viewed as some kind of superpower that had the cleverness and right to direct their lives as it decided.

In the above context it is interesting to reproduce here two answers, which I received when I asked the migrant women about *sarkar*. One migrant woman replied the *sarkar* was like one's man[11] (in some parts of North India especially among the princely households a husband is also referred to as *sarkar*). Who is more powerful, strong, more clever and worldly wise and whose duty is to look after his wife and children in what he thinks is the right way for he knows best. Another woman compared the *sarkar* to a *raja* (king) and the citizens of the country including herself as the *parja*, (subjects) and that it was the *raja* who is supposed to make all decisions. However, it was the duty of the *raja* to make such decisions as would these be beneficial for the well-being of the *parja*.

Another belief that was prevalent among the migrant women was that they could not be in direct touch with the *sarkar* and the *sarkar* was also too far from them. They had to have mediators to convey their requests to the *sarkar* and these mediators were the *netas*. But sometime they added that they could not be in direct touch with the *netas* also, who too were far reached from them. To be in touch with the *netas* once again one needed mediators and these were the *Pradhans* of Rajpur. The migrant women, however, said that to be in touch with the *netas* and the *sarkar* and all the mediators were totally of men's area of concern. The women remained away from it. They revealed that they did not also have any links with the *netas* or the *Pradhans*.

Thus, at the grassroots level at least middlemen had an important role to play in a link of the people with the *netas* or the *sarkar*. Middlemen in fact are important personnel in a non-contractual, unequal society. In India thus, middlemen have a significant role to play in all spheres, even, that of religion where the Brahmin *pandit* (priest) acts as a mediator—a middleman—in the relationship between God and His (god's) devotees (for information on connection between middlemen and corruption in India see Oldenburg 1987).

It is necessary to elaborate here that the *Pradhans* in Rajpur and in other JJ colonies act as vote-brokers for political leaders contesting for elections[12]. It is through the *Pradhan* that political leaders procure votes for themselves (in the five elections that I have witnessed in Rajpur the candidates have always been men never a woman). The *Pradhans* are able to solicit the votes of the *Jhuggi*-dwellers by establishing a reciprocal, but vertical, hierarchical patron-client relationship. The *Pradhan* becomes a patron by doing several favours for the *Jhuggi*-dwellers, because the *Pradhan* is better-off, educated, more resourceful and has connections with the police as well as, of course, political leaders. The *Jhuggi*-dweller becomes obligated to the *Pradhan* and his (the *jhuggi*-dweller's) reciprocal repayment is made in the form of his and his families votes for the candidate whom the *Pradhan* is supporting in the elections. The *Pradhan* himself is in a similar kind of patron-client relationship as he has with the *Jhuggi*-dweller and with the political leader, though this relationship is often not a direct one, but is mediated by the minions of the political leader (for a detailed amplification of the patron-client relationship in politics in South East Asia see Scott 1972; also see Haider 1993).

The *Pradhans* are mostly men. There are a few women *Pradhans* also, but they are the exceptions rather than the rule. There is an upwardly mobile woman in Rajpur who styles herself as an important *Pradhan*—Asha Devi—and there are a few women who are small-scale women *Pradhans* with women as their following, but none of the male *Pradhans* take them seriously and only use them to get the votes of women. Apart from this, the women *Pradhans* are mostly ignored and not allowed to be over active politically.

Conscientization of Democratic Institutions

The migrant women had no idea about what the Lok Sabha and the Vidhan Sabha were. Neither were they familiar with the Delhi Assembly nor the Municipal Corporation of Delhi. They could not, 'even' distinguish between the four institutions, and these institutions were all *sarkar* for them. Those women who were politically active were familiar with the names of the four institutions because of the separate elections that are held for them.

The awareness of the politically active women of these institutions was based on their involvement with the elections of these institutions, but they too could not make any distinctions between these institutions and these institutions in governance and what was the work each institution did. Both the common migrant women in Rajpur and those politically active were not sure, how the Lok Sabha, Rajya Sabha, the MCD and the Delhi Assembly were connected with Rajpur and themselves, even, though one woman in Rajpur, Asha Devi, as pointed out earlier, who styled herself as a *Pradhan*, wanted to contest for elections, but, which election she had no idea. She would not mind standing for any election she said.

It is not only the migrant women who are not familiar with the above democratic institutions of the country, but, even, many men in Rajpur could not tell the differences between the institutions referred to above.

Surprisingly, the migrant women neither did know what was a President nor could name.

The migrant women were familiar with the name of Indira Gandhi, but were not aware that she was the *Pradhan Mantri*. They thought she was a *neta* and all were of the opinion that Indira Gandhi was good to the poor and wondered why she had been killed. They said that, if she had been alive she would certainly have done something to alleviate their (the migrant women's) poverty. Some migrant women were also familiar with the name of Rajiv Gandhi, but not as a *Pradhan Mantri*, but as Indira Gandhi's *bitwa* (son—*beta* in Hindi). The migrant women were also familiar with the name of Sajjan Kumar an ex-MP of the Congress Party, who has organized many rallies of the JJ-dwellers. Now the migrant women also know the name of Ram Singh the current popular leader in Rajpur, because of the water tankers he sends to Rajpur conducting enough publicity about them *vide* his vote-broker *Pradhans*.

The migrant women were only familiar with the party with *panja* (hand—the symbol of the Congress (I)) and the party with *kamal* (lotus—the symbol of the BJP) as its *nishan*. They were, however, not familiar with the names of the party. Some women also were aware of the party with *haathi* (elephant—symbol of the Bahujan Samaj Party). However, politically active women were familiar with the names of the important parties and their respective symbols.

Conscientization of the Democratic Process

All the migrant women were familiar with what elections were and that elections were held to choose *netas*. However, when asked why the *netas* were chosen they replied that *netas* were chosen so that they (the *netas*) could ask the *sarkar* to fulfil the needs of the *Jhuggi*-dwellers like not demolishing *Jhuggi*, making provision for adequate water, schools, health care, latrines, etc.

It was not surprising that the migrant women knew what elections were, because elections in Rajpur are held with great fan fare except for a short period, when T.N. Sheshan's[13] strictures curtailed expenditure on elections considerably. During that period one could not, even, make out that elections were being held in Rajpur, things became so quiet. Otherwise, elections in Rajpur are like a festival and perceived as such by the migrant women. On the dirt road opposite the colony, offices of all prominent parties are opened. Leaflets of various parties are strung right across the width of the dirt road. Loudspeakers blare slogans; songs specially composed for the elections; play casettes of speeches of important leaders. Three wheelers ply up and down also blaring slogans. Meetings of political leaders are held. A lot of tea is drunk for which the *Pradhan* gives a contract to a tea-shop taking of course his commission from the payment made from the election fund of the electoral candidate for whom the *Pradhan* is working.

Tea-shops become gossip joints where heated political arguments take place and often ending in fisticuffs. There is a lot of haggling on the payment to the workers, the latter working more for the money paid to them than for the love of the candidate for whom they are labouring. The workers argue to get the maximum payment whereas, the endeavor of the *Pradhan* is to underpay the workers and keep the money, thus, saved for himself. Elections in the JJ colonies including Rajpur are a money-making time for many. It is indeed difficult not to be aware of election in Rajpur and the migrant women are thus, knowledgeable of them though not of their significance. But, the migrant women watch all the activities from the periphery—from afar, never venturing anywhere near the offices of the political parties or the tea-shops going about their work as usual in spite of the din and noise. Only the handful of women workers who are active at election time can be seen in the offices of the political parties and at the tea-shops but their role is kept low-key by the male *Pradhans*.

Conscientization of Political Issues

The migrant women, including the politically active ones, were not aware of the many abstract issues on which elections are usually fought at the national level such as defence of secularism (the migrant women had no idea what secularism stood for), anti-communalism, need for a stable government, saving the integrity of the nation, etc. The migrant women were of the opinion that elections take place so that a *neta* could be chosen who would see to it that the *Jhuggis* of Rajpur are not demolished and provision make for sufficient supply of water. The above are two major local issues in Rajpur. The migrant women also expected the *netas* to see it that there are proper latrines constructed, schools and medical care is easily available to the *Jhuggi*-dwellers. The migrant women said that they had come to know that these are the issues on which elections are fought from their menfolk, who were in the knowledge of all such things. It is important to note here that most of the migrant women live their lives, including their political experiences, vicariously in the urban milieu in which they are placed with their voiced beliefs and knowledge, repetitions of what their husbands have told them and not an expression of something that they have thought of or experienced themselves (see Haider forthcoming.)

It is not surprising that the migrant women are not aware of the abstract issues on which elections are fought at the national level for at the level of the JJ colonies politics is the politics of basic amenities (see Haider 1993). Election are fought in JJ colonies on more localized, basic, practical issues like the guarantee that the

Jhuggis of the JJ colony dwellers, which are to be demolished, sufficient notice would be given and adequate land provided to the *Jhuggi* dwellers as compensation; alleviation of the acute scarcity of water, which is the most vexing problem that JJ colony dwellers are facing and is especially grim in Rajpur; schools and medical care to be made available easily to the *Jhuggi*-dwellers; provision of suitable latrines, etc. The JJ colony politics is, therefore, an insular politics. Votes are given to the candidate who has been successful in fulfilling the demands of the JJ dwellers in the years gone by or make promises to fulfil the demands, if elected, which promises are so convincingly made that the JJ-dwellers repose their confidence in the candidate and elect him or her (the latter so far never being the case).

Most often, however, as the migrant women complained (again echoing their husbands' opinions and knowledge), that the candidates once elected often easily forget their promises. The migrant women were very delusioned with *netas* and uttered that their men say that all *netas* are *chors* (thieves) and *badmash* (scoundrels). However, though this is the prevalent belief once the elections come around the JJ dwellers, including the migrant women of Rajpur, venture out again to choose a *neta,* no doubt, thinking that this time they would make the right choice.

Conscientization of the Role the Migrant Women Should be Playing in the Political System

When inquired what role the migrant women should be playing in forming the *sarkar* they revealed that they thought their only role was to vote and choose a *neta* who would work for their good. The same opinion was also voiced by politically active women. None of the women saw themselves as active agents in forming the *sarkar* or being a part of it. They did not seem to be conscious of the fact that through elections they can be instrumental in making or breaking a *sarkar*. Their motive for participating in the elections was, as they said, only to choose a helpful *neta*.

The politics of the JJ colony level is a very individual and charismatic personality-oriented politics where political leaders are concerned. A *neta* who has the gift of the gab and is adroit in bluffing can easily sway the support of the gullible JJ-dwellers in his favour and more so if he has an influential *Pradhan* working for him. Political parties or their manifestos have no role to play in the JJ colony elections. It is the candidate who draws support or repels it.

An influential *Pradhan* can through persuasion, but more often by outright, or, subtle coercion, amass votes for his patron political leader and thus, gain favours from the latter in cash and kind. If a *neta* has worked for the JJ-dwellers, which is rare, such a *neta* has substantial support from the latter. What is more important is that the *neta* should put up a show that gives the impression that he is sincere and hard working to improve the condition of the JJ-dwellers, which is enough to fool the JJ-dwellers into believing that this is really so.

From observing the elections in Rajpur one cannot, but come to the conclusion that the *netas,* the JJ-dwellers elect are perhaps not really interested in improving the living conditions of the JJ-dwellers. They, it is felt, want to keep all the local issues of provision of basic amenities ever alive for it is on promises made to make the basic amenities available that the *netas* can register a victory. Hence, if the basic amenities are made available to the JJ-dwellers the *netas* main lever propelling factor to victory would be lost. The politicians, thus, it is one's impression, have a vested interest in keeping the JJ-dwellers deprived of basic amenities.

Conscientization of migrant women's rights and obligations in the democratic political system

As noted earlier the migrant women were not familiar with the word *adhikar* (right). When asked what they thought about their rights in the political system in India their reply was that they had the *adhikar* to vote. When again questioned what they thought *adhikar* to vote meant they had no answer. In saying that they had the *adhikar* to vote the migrant women, in all probability, were repeating what has so often been said by political leaders to persuade the masses to vote. When asked if they were familiar with India's *Samvidhan* (Constitution) they sheepishly admitted that they have no idea about what *Samvidhan* was. Even, politically active women believed that their main *adhikar* in the political system was to cast their vote and elect a *neta*. Though, politically active women were, however, aware of the *Samvidhan*, but they had hardly any idea about its role in their lives and for the country.

When the migrant women were queried as to what other rights were their's in the particular political system of India they kept quiet. *Adhikars* seemed to be something that were not part of their thinking. This was so most probably because in India girls are brought up not to claim *adhikars*, but to do their duties. Their socialization inhibits them in making demands. Theirs is not to claim, but to give. The politically active women, however, thought that they also had the *adhikar* to stand for elections and become *netas*, but beyond that they were as much at sea about their *adhikars* as the other migrant women.

The migrant women were also not clear what their duties in the Indian political system were. What it meant to be a good citizen. They had never thought in terms of citizenship. The politically active women on the other hand glibly proclaimed that their duty in India's political system was to serve the poor and downtrodden the sentiment, which they have, no doubt, picked up from the *netas* who repeat this duty of their's to the country *ad nauseam*. The politically active women had nothing to say on their duty to get rid of rampant corruption in the political system, which corruption is so visible at the JJ colony level where both the *netas* and the *pradhans* are concerned. This was, no doubt, so because the politically active women, especially the self-proclaimed women *Pradhan*, who dreams of fighting an election, Asha Devi, expected to climb up in the political system *vide* the same ladder of corruption as the *netas* and *pradhans* have done with the sole purpose of amassing wealth. Asha Devi, in fact, admitted it to be so quite candidly.

The migrant women when asked about what their duties were towards their country, said that their duty was only to lookafter their husbands and children and their homes. This is what is meant to be done by all women in their *biradari*[14]. For the migrant woman what their *biradari* ordained was more the letter of law than what the Constitution instituted. The *biradari* dos and don'ts had a strong hold on not only the migrant women, but also the migrant men in

Rajpur, even, though they are living so many kilometres away from the area of the jurisdiction of their *biradari*. The *biradari* acts as the 'collective conscience' of the migrants in Rajpur (for information on 'collective conscience' see Durkheim 1947) and brooks no breaking of its tenets, it governs through the panchayat and for the migrant women it is the panchayat of their *biradari*, which has the right to settle feuds and disputes of all kinds rather than the law of the nation (see Haider 1997).

Conscientization of the Agenda of the Indian Women's Movement

The migrant women of Rajpur who had not, even, heard of the IWM leave alone taking part in its campaigns. When asked that should not they demand that the *sarkar* take some measures to stop their husbands beating them (wife battering being quite common in Rajpur) they replied that their husbands should not beat them, but what the *sarkar* got to do with it? Why should the *sarkar* do anything? The migrant women, in fact, gave all sorts of excuses, to justify the violent behaviour of their husbands (see Sangari 1998, for consent of women in patriarchy for compensations like, protection from outside males and different kinds of power they are allowed to exercise often over other women; also see Haider 1998).

The migrant women were reluctant to give any information of rapes and were quite unfamiliar with two other major issues of the IWM—the UCC and sati. Sati as alien to the migrant women most probably because they were mostly of the Scheduled Caste where widow remarriage was permitted, hence, there was no question of the immolation of the wife on her husband's funeral pyre. However, in a bid to Sanskritise (for explanation of Sanskritization see Srinivas 1989 a, 1989 b, 1989 c, 1951, 1984, 1988, 1994 and 1994 b) the Scheduled Caste men are forbidding their widows to remarry, but have not reached the stage where they would ask their wives to commit sati.

Where dowry deaths were concerned the migrant women said that there had been no dowry deaths within their *biradari* as far as they were aware, but that dowry has to be given and is given if one wants a good boy for one's daughter to marry. They were unaware of any law forbidding dowry-giving and said dowry was being given by everyone who had daughters and claimed by all those who had sons quite openly without any one getting arrested. The politically active women also agreed to them. As already mentioned that most of the migrant women belonged to Scheduled Castes among whom earlier bride price was given, but now dowry has come to replace it.

The migrant women, including the politically active ones, have get their daughters married at the early age of about 12 years. Yet, they were again unaware of any law against child marriages (even, there has been no campaign by the IWM on stopping of child marriages) and said that though now some families give their daughters in marriage at a fairly late age marrying daughters at an early age, if one can get a good boy, is still common. According to them, the daughter, is a *bhoj* (burden) on one's head and the sooner one got one's daughter married the better.

The migrant women said that they guard their daughters as closely as possible and hence, there was no possibility for them to be sexually harassed. The migrant women, however, said that they had to be extra strict with their daughters in Rajpur where the young boys are adopting urban ways and have no respect for their elders and hence, chances of them sexually harassing girls are very much there. Again the migrant women were ignorant that there was a law against sexual harassment.

The migrant women, including the politically active ones, also informed me that they were not aware of any law, which says that daughters could inherit their father's property. As far as they knew in their *biradari* the girls only got ornaments and clothes at marriage and dowry was given and that gift-giving to the daughter, her husband and her in-laws continued for a long time if not by the father then the brothers, but there was no question of a girl getting a share of her father's land or money. North Indian society is primarily patriarchal, patrifocal and patrlineal.

Where divorce was concerned the migrant women said they never thought about divorce, for where would they go if they left their husbands? Who would bring up their children? How will they fend themselves alone in a male world?

Political Participation of Migrant Women

One would assume that it is when one has been 'conscientized' of some reality and has gained 'critical consciousness' (see Freire 1973, 1974)[15], of it then only one can act to transform that reality. Of course it is only when one has been 'conscientized' of a reality and developed 'critical consciousness' about it, then only can one take active action to transform the reality. Not being conscientized of and not developing 'critical consciousness' of an oppressive reality would leave one in what Paulo Freire calls 'semi-intransitive consciousness' (see Freire, 1974, 1973)[16], which is a passive state. Such is the case as far as the migrant women are concerned about their political consciousness in the political system of India, which *de jure* gives them rights, but *de facto* does not see to it that these rights are actually conferred on them and an environment created wherein women can exercise their rights.

Participation in the Political Process

The Constitution of India gives all women citizens of the country the right to vote and thus, take part in the democratic political process of the country to form a democratic government. All the migrant women living in Rajpur exercise their vote. Election time, as said before, is like a festival for them. They lookforward to the elections perhaps as a welcome break from the monotonous, uneventful tenor of their lives. The migrant women dressup in their finery to go for vote. They are accompanied by their husbands or form a women's group and go for casting their votes.

The migrant women have by now come to believe that they should not let anybody know who they have voted for and kept their vote has to be a secret. They have in all probability been instructed in this by their husbands. However, when asked who they voted for they said that they voted for whoever their husbands told them to vote. The politically active women of course voted for the candidate for whom they were working. They tried also to make the women whom they could influence to vote for the candidate supported by them, but most of the women who came with them to vote were wives of men who were working for the same candidate that the politically active women were working for.

The migrant women, therefore, were very much influenced by their husbands' wishes where voting was concerned. However, the very act of voting and that too on one's own, secretly, must surely be giving the migrant women a certain sense of self-importance and thrill. Voting is an independent act and even, this iota of independence must surely be an exhilarating experience for the women. May be some of them go against their husbands' wishes and vote for, whoever, they like just to enjoy a sense of freedom.

Quite a few women had participated in the huge rallies of JJ colony dwellers organized off and on by political leaders in outer Delhi within, which constituency Rajpur is situated especially by Sajjan Kumar the erstwhile Congress MP. The women, however, went to these rallies for get the fun of it. To get out of Rajpur for a change and for the food that they would be given to eat rather than due to a commitment to the demands of the JJ-dwellers for which the rallies were organized. Special buses were arranged to take them to these rallies, which rallies the migrant women gigglingly told me were more like a good *sair* (outing) for them.

For a few years the Bahujan Samaj Party (BSP)[17] has gained a foothold in Rajpur. It has some very active and very angry young men as its supporters. The BSP put up Shiv Shankar, an important *kabadi ke kaamwala* (cloth cuttings buyer and seller), who is of the Scheduled Caste and is a leader of the BSP in Rajpur, as the candidate for the MCD's elections held in 1998, for the post of a Corporator. A whole lot of the wives of the BSP supporters came out to work for Shiv Shankar not because they were politically 'conscientized' or were familiar with the party's beliefs and aims, but because their husbands wanted them to work for Shiv Shankar. A rally was organized in which the wives of the BSP workers dressed in their best and were very much excited in the forefront shouting slogans. Many of the women, however, did not know what the BSP stood for and what post Shiv Shankar was standing for. Shiv Shankar's wife in fact, disapproved of his party activities and his progressive for their daughter (see Haider 1995).

The politically active women were very visible during the elections with each of them trying to prove that they were working very hard and had brought in a whole lot of women to vote for the candidate they were supporting. The most visible of these was Asha Devi, who at one election was working for two candidates at the same time supposedly in a grand intrigue. However, her two-timing was not hidden from anyone. Asha Devi is one woman who tries very hard to be in the select coterie of political leaders and does her level best to push herself forward, but does not succeed very much. The male *pradhans* tolerate Asha Devi's shenanigans, but give her no importance and to it that she does not progress very far.

Participation of the Political Institutions

The migrant women, as noted above, are not aware of any of the institutions that are a part of a liberal Parliamentary democracy and have never thought they could be in a position of decision-making in any such institutions. As observed earlier, the women feel that they are unfit for such positions because they are illiterate and not worldly-wise. This feeling of inferiority is compounded by the fact that their husbands also treat them as illterate and inexperienced in worldly matters and are only fit for bearing and rearing children and doing housework.

The politically active women, like Asha Devi, dream of fighting elections—any election—themselves, and becoming a *neta*. Asha Devi in fact did fight a mini election of the *pradhan* of JJ colony of Rajpur as a candidate. A couple of years back the Rajpur *pradhans* decided that they would hold a democratic election to choose a *pradhan* for the whole colony and conducted all the proceedings in the same way as are conducted in a national election or the state and city election. They had a most wish-fulfilling time pretending to be and aping, the *netas*. Asha Devi filled her papers as a candidate, spent considerable money on her election, but got only very few votes. Even, the women of Rajpur did not vote for her. They apparently voted for the *Pradhan* candidate whom their husbands wished them to vote for. Asha Devi was sorely disappointed. She then tried to be a candidate for the MCD election, but did not succeed in getting a ticket, even, when two male *Pradhans* from Rajpur were chosen as candidates.

Political Participation in the Indian Women's Movement

As has been documented above, neither the migrant women were aware that there was such an activity as the IWM, nor were they in line with the thinking of the IWM on several issues. This was, no doubt due to the fact that the IWM did not have the outreach to touch the lives of the migrant women of Rajpur. The

IWM whose 'second wave' upsurged in the mid-1970s, is perceived by many as primarily an urban movement (see Sen 1998) and a Brahaminical one at that (see Rao 1999). However, in spite of it being an urban movement though with many autonomous groups working in rural areas now, the women's groups seem to be functioning in small pockets only and they have not been able to make the movement a mass movement. Thus, many women remain out of the stretch of the IWM. The migrant women of Rajpur too do not form part of the IWM and have participated in none of the IWM's activities.

Conclusion

It is very obvious from the above account that the migrant women of Rajpur, even the handful of those who are politically active. have no 'conscientization' of what the Indian democratic system of goverance is and what it means for them. This is not because the women are incapable of understanding the democratic way of thinking and operation, but more because the Indian state having adopted an alien concept of democracy and its institutions superimposed in on what was traditionally a hierarchical society. The state did not take up the task of educating the Indian masses to become knowledgeable about the new democratic ethos and imbibe new democratic norms and values. To do this was very necessary especially because Indian thinking was suffused with hierarchical concepts and the behaviour of the Indian masses also conformed to a hierarchical way of functioning. What has been the result, for instance, in the case of migrant women of Rajpur, (no doubt under the influence of their menfolk) is that the women too have superimposed their hierarchical way of thinking on to a democratic setup and institutions. They see the democratic government not as one, which they have forged and of which they are the main role players, but as a paternalistic patron comprising of the educated and the better-off. The migrant women, thus, are well entrenched in a dependency syndrome, in which they expect the government to take decisions for them and to provide for their well-being like a benefactor not comprehending that the government is they themselves and as such it is they who should lay down the rules and make it incumbent on the government to provide needful for their well-being and ensure their democratic rights as rights not as doles.

The migrant women have no conception of their rights in a democratic system. This is because Indian women on the whole are brought up not to demand anything but to give, to abnegate, to sacrifice and not assert. Indian women, thus, are supposed to have only duties not rights. Hence, a thinking in terms of rights and a readiness to demand them also needs to be inculcated among Indian women by political parties and the government, if they want to mete out justice to the latter. The Indian women are in great need of 'conscientization' of their rights, which 'conscientization' should also be effected by the IWM. Apparently neither the state nor the IWM have thought it necessary to take up this incumbency in earnest for the migrant women of Rajpur at least do not feel they can claim any service for themselves from the state as a right.

The migrant women also do not feel that they have any role to play in the democratic set-up of the country. First of all they have always been told that their work is to bear and rear children and lookafter the house and secondly the women feel that the democratic set-up of the country is too far removed from them. Here again we see a failure on the part of the state. The Indian state has made itself an aloof entity with, which at least the migrant women of Rajpur cannot connect, or identify, and in which they feel they cannot participate and to which they feel they have no access except through mediators who corrupt the system. This is not a very happy state of affairs and is an indication of democratic centralization not decentralization. Thus, the Indian democracy remains a tightly controlled system by a centralized group of individuals not a decentralized truly participatory democracy that it should be whose main ingredient is dialogue and consensus and in which power is not allowed to congeal at one point, but is fluid moving from the people to its representative and then back again to the people. Power in democracy needs to be widely and thinly spread out not aggrandized by a few individuals or groups of people for their own advancement. It is in such a participatory democracy that women have to be given and will find precedence and space with special efforts made to accomplish this in view of the deprived state of the majority of Indian women and their subordination to males.

One effort, which will go far in helping women to become more knowledgeable of what democracy entails for them and what their rights and duties in, it are, is the launching of a massive literacy campaign for making women literate. This one presumes would make them more independent too. The migrant women also felt that they have lack knowledge of many aspects of the country's political ethos and do not see themselves as important participants in it, because they are not literate and worldly-wise. Education may not be a significant factor, but is a necessary condition to help women come into their own.

Meanwhile, just as the Indian state has taken the commendable step of undertaking the 73rd and 74th Amendment to the Indian Constitution, which guarantees 33 per cent reservation for women in all rural and urban local governing bodies, there is a need to pass the 81st Amendment Bill as soon as possible. The IWM should launch a wide scale campaign to see to it that the Bill is passed, which would guarantee 33 per cent reservation for women in all the legislatures at the centre and the states. It has, however, to be ensured by whatever means considered suitable and ethical as per the Indian Constitution that the reservation does not lead to *beti-biwi raj* (daughter-wife governance) with the better endowed and better-off women usurping the reserved seats and serving the interests of their male relatives. Arrangements have to be made to ensure that in both the rural and urban local bodies and the legislatures women from all sections of Indian society get a chance to become decision-makers and that they are allowed to function independently and not serve as proxies for the males of their families. The placement of women in decision-making will create its own momentum and would 'conscientize' women to the political ethos of the country and compel them to find out more about how politics in India functions so that they can utilize it to better the condition of women.

Hand in hand with the passing of the 81st Amendment it is very necessary that all political parties in India reserve places for women in their organization and assign at least 33 per cent of seats to women candidates in elections. The political parties, including the Left parties are all guilty of ignoring women so far (see Kumar and Kidwai 1996; Seminar 1997:51).

It is very obvious that the IWM does not have a widespread. It has in any case been and is so, even, now, active on some issues only, the campaigns of which peaked a high and then have petered out. This is because of non-achievement of the IWM of the 'conscientization' of the critical mass of Indian women of its issues and agenda and a sustained continuous struggle. The IWM at present stands paralysed by the divide in whatever solidarity among women that it had achieved because of religious, caste, ethnic, community plus regional differences. The IWM needs to galvanize itself and change this situation. It needs to upsurge again this time with more coordinated campaigns and a clearly thought out comprehensive plan, which stretches wide enough to embrace women like the migrant women of Rajpur also. The IWM has to be transformed into a movement that works in isolated pockets and carries all the women of India together. A way has to be found by the IWM to become far-reaching not only to fight for women's rights, but also the rights of all the downtrodden and deprived sections of the country on all fronts for women suffer oppression not only as women, but also as members of oppressed castes, classes, deprived ethnic groups, religious minorities and backward regions. This 'multiple jeopardy' of women needs to be confronted. The IWM has before it a mighty challenge to reform the Indian society by subverting the very structures of all kinds of domination in every sphere and usher in an absolutely new kind of just, liberated and humane society. One expects that in the future with the soul-searching that the IWM is at present involved in it will surface as a more resolute and strong movement and will meet the above challenges cohesively and decisively.

NOTES

1. I would here like to convey my gratitude to Prof. Kiran Saxena for giving me a chance to write this chapter. I am also grateful to my friend Sandhya Gupta for introducing me to Prof. Kiran Saxena. My thanks also goes to Taqui Haider who has always been a very supportive friend boosting my morale, when I have been plagued with self doubts.
2. Reproduction role of women does not only mean the bearing and rearing of children to continue the existence of the human species, but also includes housework—the reproduction of the energy of the existing male labour force. Moser (1993), demarcates three roles of women: (1) the reproductive role as outlined above, (2) the productive role in which women work and labour for

remuneration and (3) organizing the provision of utilities of collective consumption. Men do not have a reproductive role. They have a major so-called productive role and their role is involvement in politics for making utilities of collective consumption available.

3. 'Productive' work is supposed to be work that has remunerative value and is paid for in cash or in kind. It is a paradox that Karl Marx, the greatest critic and theoretician of oppression made the distinction between reproductive and productive work and then completely ignored the former, which is the work of women. It was left to Engels to explain the origins of male domination of women (see Jaggar 1983; Barett 1987; Engels 1942).

4. The duality of 'nature' and 'culture' are used by Ortner in an attempt to account for the apparent universality of male domination across cultures. Ortner declares that the pan-cultural second class status of women could be accounted for quite simply by postulating that women are being identified, or are symbolically associated with nature as opposed to men, who are identified with culture. Since, it is always culture's project to subsume and transcend nature, if women are considered, as part of nature, culture finds it 'natural' to subordinate them. It all begins with the body and the natural procreative functions specific to women alone. There are three levels at which physiological facts have significance: (1) Women's body and its functions are more involved most of the time with 'species life' thus, placing her closer to nature in contrast to man's physiology, which allows him more completely to take up the project of culture; (2) Women's body and its functions place her in social roles that in turn are considered to be at a lower level of the cultural process than that of men's and (3) Women's traditional social roles are being imposed on her because of her body and functions in turn give her a different psychic structure, which like her physiology and her social roles is seemed as being closer to nature (see Ortner 1974). For a criticism of Ortner's thesis see Pateman 1980,1987; Rosaldo 1980; Haraway 1979; MacCormack 1980. Jordanova demonstrates how by the mid-eighteenth century a well established bio-medical tradition observed and defined humans, hardening the conceptual division between unique feminine and unique masculine attributes. A biological determinism 'explained' women, but men were defined by their social acts, an attitude of enquiry, which finds expression in Ortner's thesis—see Jordanova 1980. The most thorough attempt to find a universal answer to the question of why it is that women are in subjection to men, and the most stark opposition

between 'nature' and 'culture' can be found in the writings of the Western radical feminists, who argue that nature is the single cause of women's domination by men. For the best known version of this argument see Firestone 1970. For a criticism of Firestone thesis see Elshtain 1978. Von Werlhof offers a rather original interpretation of the concept of 'nature' within capitalism, which encompasses within 'nature' women. Von Werlhof argues that the concept of 'nature' in capitalism is not determined by biology, but by economics. It does not distinguish between people and animals, but between people and people. At any given historic instant 'nature' is what the economic process consumes as 'inputs'; this embraces the land and the soil, the products of the soil, mineral resources, the products of industry and handicrafts, services and first and foremost—the people, who work and produce services; without human labour-power none of the other products would be available, i.e., convertible into 'nature'. The what of nature, therefore, ultimately is why labour-power above all is indispensable in the workplace and the family, hence, including women. According to Von Werlhof these products and resources and especially workers, be available, but they should be as cheap as possible. That is, their own production and reproduction, their genesis and maintenance before, during and after their use should incur either only minimum or no costs to whoever needs and uses them. Seen from this standpoint of dominant logic (the logic of dominance) there is, then, a tendency to maximize the range of resources and people including women (as bearers or possessors of labour-power) to be treated as if they were nature available gratis, like air. The labour of these people, including women, is therefore, pronounced to be non-labour, to be biology; their labour-power, i.e., their ability to work appears as 'natural' resource and their products akin to a natural deposit. Von Werlhof professes that we are witnessing a progressive extension of the concept of nature to cover all people, their work and what they produce. This concerns not only women, blacks and wageless, but in the final analysis white, male wage workers also. Von Werlhof writes that in contrast to the usual assumptions about advancing 'humanization' or 'socialization' with its implied limitation of what belongs to nature, the real process is leading to the opposite direction. An ideological and material process of 'naturalization' or 'feminisation' is taking place. Based on the ideal type of 'women's nature', domestic labour and the housewife the process may be termed 'domestication, or 'housewifisation' (see Von Werlhof 1988 a).

5. The representation of women in the Lok Sabha has been an average of 6 per cent from 1952 to 1998, (see Seminar 1997:51, Table 1; Kumari and Kidwai 1996:2; Rana 1998:62) and in the Rajya Sabha from 1952 to 1996, just 10.3 per cent. In State Assemblies women's representation on an average since, 1952 to 1997, has been just 4 per cent (Seminar 1997:51, Table 2).

6. The voting pattern of males to females has been the following in the Lok Sabha elections from 1952 to 1991:—

WOMEN VOTERS

General Elections	*Percentage of Voters Participating in Elections*			*Gap Between Male and Female voters* (per cent)*
	Female	*Male*	*Total*	
1952	—	—	61.2**	—
1957	—	—	62.2**	
1962	46.6	62.0	55.0	15.4
1967	55.5	66.7	61.3	11.2
1971	—	—	55.3**	—
1977	54.9	65.6	60.5	5.7
1980	51.2	62.2	56.9	11.0
1984	59.2	68.4	64.0	9.2
1989	57.3	66.1	61.0	8.8
1991	49.5	61.6	55.7	12.2

*Calculated by author

**Calculated on the basis of valid votes polled. Sex wise breakup is not available for 1952,1957 and 1971. Dates relate to Lok Sabha elections (Government of India 1995:68).

7. It was the Western feminist group known as radical feminists, who recognized politics as an important issue for feminism and articulated new thinking on it within the wider women's liberation movement. Firstly, the radical feminists rejected the definition of politics as a particular kind of activity. The foundation for this was laid by Kate Millet in her path breaking book *Sexual Politics* (1972), in which she redefined politics as 'power structures, relationships and arrangements, whereby one group of persons is controlled by another' (Millet 1972:27). Kate Millet's book created a storm of discussion and reaction within the Western feminist movement, the everyday world and just about everywhere else. Subsequent

radical feminists implicitly if not explicitly followed Millet's approach to politics because it accorded with their experience of male dominance as *systemic,* reliant on conditioning, and the diffused threat of violence as well as conscious actions. The second feature of this approach of radical feminists to politics, which is more important and in a way it was applied in a much more original way, was the attack on the split notion of the distinct political arena and the public-private split that went with it. This reflected the experience of radical women students in the 1960s, which they applied to their own situation. Many American radical feminists owed their political education in particular to the civil rights campaign. It was here that they learnt that the 'personal is political also', the phrase being coined to apply to the thinking of the radical feminists by Carol Hanisch (1971), which became an important slogan of what is called in the West its 'second wave of feminism'.

8. 'Conscientization', refers to the process in which human beings, not as recipients, but as knowing subjects, achieve a deepening awareness both of the socio-cultural and political reality, which shapes their lives and of their capacity to transform that reality (see Freire 1974:49-84; 1973).

9. Since some sensitive political and personal data is being collected in the JJ colony, that I am studying the name of the latter and the characters that appear in this study have been changed.

10. The *Pradhan* is the headman of a community or group as well as a panchayat. There are about 35 *Pradhans* in Rajpur who can be said to be influential.

11. Among orthodox Hindus, now also among the 'untouchable' castes, it is considered disrespectful to take one's husband's name. The women of orthodox upper castes among the Hindus refer to their husbands as 'he' or 'him' and the lower-castes as 'my man' or as the father of their child, e.g., 'Bhim's father'.

12. The *Pradhan* as middleman is not a peculiar feature of the Indian squatter settlements. Manuel Castells talks about caciquism in Latin America. Castells informs that in the traditional, long standing squatter settlements on the periphery of big cities, the key elements in a very strong community organization is the tight control of leaders who are the intermediaries between the squatters and the administrative officials in the early stages of this form of community organization can be considered to be dominated by the caciquis namely by the personal and authoritarian control of a leader, himself backed and recognized by the local authority

(Castells 1990). Lomitz (1977), also talks about 'cacicazzo'. She writes that 'cacicazzo' is the emergence of a patron as broker—caciquis who are intermediaries between the squatter settlers and the urban industrial society.

13. T.N. Seshan was the erstwhile Election Commissioner of India.

14. The *biradari* is a community comprising a number of families of the same caste spread over a certain number of villages. The *biradari* has it own panchayat.

15. 'Critical consciousness' is the apprehension and perception of a reality objectively as a subject. Critical consciousness forms part of the process of praxis, i.e., reflection and action and then once again reflection on the previous action and further action *vide*, which human beings transform and retransform, create and recreate social reality (see Freire 1973, 1974).

16. There is a mode of consciousness, which corresponds to the concrete reality of dependent societies and dependent human beings. It is a consciousness conditioned by the social structures. The principal characteristic of this consciousness as a dependent consciousness is its 'quasi-adherence' to objective reality, or 'quasi-immersion' in reality. The dominated consciousness thus, does not have sufficient distance from reality to objectify it in order to know it in a critical way. This mode of consciousness Paulo Freire calls 'semi-intransitive' (see Freire 1974, 1973).

17. The Bahujan Samaj Party (BSP) is a party of the Scheduled Castes with its leader Kanshi Ram. The BSP, however, now claims a wider base including the other backward castes and the minority groups.

REFERENCES

Agnes, Flavia, 1995, ' Redefining the Agenda for the Women's Movement Within a Secular Framework' in Tanika Sarkar and Urvashi Butalia (ed.) *Women and the Hindu Right*. New Delhi, Kali for Women, pp. 137-57.

____________ 1997, 'Protecting Women Against Violence: Review of a Decade of Legislation, 1980-1989.', in Partha Chatterjee (ed.), *State and Politics in India*, Delhi, Oxford University Press, pp. 521-65.

Agnihotri, Indu and Mazumdar, Veena, 1995, 'Changing Terms of Political Discourse: Women's Movement in India, 1970s-1980s', *Economic and Political Weekly*, Vol. 30, No. 25, July 26, pp. 2308-19.

Anthropological Survey of India, 1993, The Scheduled Castes: People of India, National Series, Vol. II. Delhi, Oxford University Press.

Barett, Michele, 1987, 'Marxist Feminism and the Work of Karl Marx', in Anne Phillips (ed.), *Feminism and Equality*, Oxford, Basil Blackwell, pp. 44-61.

Berger, Peter L. and Luckmann, Thomas,1976, *Social Construction of Reality : A Treatise in the Sociology of Knowledge*. Harmondsworth, Penguin.

Bhasin, Kamla, Menon, Ritu and Khan, Nighat Said, 1996, *Against All Odds: Essays on Women, Religion and Development from India and Pakistan*. New Delhi, Kali for Women in collaboration with Isis International and South Asian Women's Forum (SAWF).

Bourdieu, F., 1979, 'Symbolic Power', *Critique of Anthropology* 4, pp. 77-85.

____________ 1986, *Distinction: A Social Critique of the Judgement of Taste*, London, Routledge.

____________ 1987, 'What Makes a Social Class? On the Theoretical and Practical Existence of Group', *Berkeley Journal of Sociologis*, pp. 1-17.

____________1989, 'Social Space and Symbolic Power', *Sociological Theory*, 7, pp. 14-26.

Caldwell, Bruce, 1991, *The Jajmani System: An Investigation*, Delhi Hindustan Publishing Corporation.

Calman, Leslie.J., 1992, *Toward Empowerment: Women and Movement Politics in India*, Boulder, San Francisco, Oxford, Westview Press.

Castells, Manuel, 1990, 'Squatters and Politics in Chile, Peru and Mexico' in A.R. Desai and D. Pillai (ed.), *Slums and Urbanization*, Bombay, Popular Prakashan.

Chatterjee, Partha, 1997 a. ' The Nation and its Women' in Partha Chatterjee, *The Nation and its Fragments: Colonial and Post colonial Histories*, Delhi, Oxford University Press, pp. 116-34.

____________, 1997 b, 'Women and the Nation' in Partha Chatterjee, *The Nation and its Fragments: Colonial and Post colonial Histories*, Delhi, Oxford University Press, pp. 135-57.

____________ (ed.) 1997 c, *State and Politics in India*, Delhi, Oxford University Press.

____________ (ed.) 1998, *Wages of Freedom: Fifty Years of the Indian Nation-State*, Delhi, Oxford University Press.

Datta, Bishakha (ed.), 1998, *'And Who Will Make the Chapatis?', Study of All Women Panchayats in Maharashtra*, Calcutta, Stree.

Dede Wit, Joop, 1996, *Poverty, Policy and Politics in Madras Slums: Dynamics of Survival, Gender and Leadership*, New Delhi, Sage Publications.

d'. Lima, Hazel, 1993, 'Participation of Women in Local Self Government' in Susheela Kaushik (ed.), *Women's Participation in Politics*, under the auspices of the Indian Association of Women's Studies, New Delhi, Vikas Publishing House Pvt. Ltd., pp. 21-30.

Dumont, Louis, 1980, *Homo Hierarchicus*, Chicago, University of Chicago Press.

Durkheim, Emile, 1947, *The Division of Labour*, translated and with the Introduction by G. Simpson, New York, Macmillan.

Elshtain, Jean Bethke, 1974, 'Moral Woman and Immoral Man: A Consideration of the Public-Private Split and its Political Ramifications', *Politics and Society*, Vol. 4, No. 4, pp. 443-61.

____________ 1978, 'Liberal Heresies: Existentialism and Repressive Feminism, in M. McGarth (ed.), *Liberation and the Modern Polity*, New York, Marcel Dekker, pp. 49-72.

____________ 1981, *Public Men, Private Women: Women in Social and Political Thought*, Princeton, Princeton University Press.

Eltain Engels, Fredrich,1942, *The Origin of the Family, Private Property and the State*, New York, International.

Firestone, Shulamith, 1970, *The Dialectis of Sex*, New York, William Harrow.

Fredrich Ebert Stiftung (ed.), 1993, *Women in Politics: Forms and Processes*, New Delhi, Har-Anand Publications.

Freire, Paulo, 1973, *Pedagogy of the Oppressed*, Harmondsworth, Penguin Education.

____________, 1974, *Cultural Action for Freedom*, Harmondsworth, Penguin Education.

Gandhi, Nandita and Shah, Nandita, 1991, *The Issues at Stake: Theory and Practice in the Contemporary Women's Movement in India*, New Delhi, Kali for Women.

Gawankar, Rohini, 1993, 'Role of Women in Panchayati Raj' in Susheela Kaushik (ed.), *Women's Participation in Politics*, under the auspices of Indian Association for Women's Studies, New Delhi Vikas Publishing House Pvt. Ltd., pp. 88-100.

Glennon, Lynda, M. 1979, *Women and Dualism: A Sociology of Knowledge Analysis*, New York and London, Longman.

Government of India, 1995, *Fourth World Conference on Women, Beijing 1995—Country Report*, Department of Women and Child Development, Ministry of Humán Resource Development.

Haider, Saraswati, 1993, 'The Politics of Providing Basic Amenities to the Urban Poor' in Bidyut Mohanty (ed.), *Urbanization in Developing Countries: Basic Services and Community Participation*, Delhi, Institute of Social Sciences and Concept Publishing Company, pp. 389-411.

____________, 1995, 'Lifting the Veil of Silence: Jamuna's Narrative of Pain', *Sociological Bulletin*, Vol. 44, No. 2, September 1995, pp. 241-54.

____________, 1997, 'An Ethnographic Profile of Family and Kinship among Eastern Uttar Pradesh Chamar Migrants in a Delhi Squatter Settlement', *Guru Nanak Journal of Sociology*, Vol. 18, No. 2, pp. 1-32.

____________, 1998, 'Dialogue as Method and Text' in Meenakshi Thapan (ed.), *Anthropological Journeys*, Delhi, Orient Longman, pp. 237-66.

____________, 1999, 'Migrant Women and Urban Experience in a Squatter Settlement' in Veronique Dupont, Denis Vidal and Emma Tarlo (ed.), *Delhi Games*, forthcoming.

Hanisch, Carol, 1971, 'The Personal is Political' in J. Agel (ed.) *The Radical Therapist*, New York, Ballentine Books, pp. 106-16.

Haraway, D., 1979 'Animal Sociology and Natural Economy of the Body Politic: Part 1: A Political Physiology of Dominance, *Signs*, Vol. 4, No. 1, pp. 42-79.

Helly, Dorothy, O. and Reverby, P. 1992, *Gendered Domains: Beyond the Public /Private Dichotomy*, Ithaca, Cornell University Press.

Jaggar, Alison, 1983, *Feminist Politics and Human Nature*, Totowa NY, Rowman and Allenheld.

Jain, Devaki, 1996, 'Future Directions for the Women's Movement: Some Post-Beijing Thoughts, in Nitya Rao, Louis Rurup and R. Sudershan (ed.), *Sites of Change: The Structural Context for Empowering Women in India* , Fredrich Ebert Stiftung and UNDP, New Delhi, Tulika Press, pp. 1-16.

Jayawardena, Kumari and de Alwis, Malathi (ed.), 1996, *Embodied Violence:; Communalising Women's Sexuality in South Asia*, New Delhi, Kali for Women.

Jeffery, Patricia and Basu, Amrita (ed.), 1999, *Resisting the Sacred and the Secular: Women's Activism and Politicized Religion in South Asia*, New Delhi, Kali for Women .

John Mary. E., 1999 a, 'Gender Development and the Women's Movement' in Rajeswari Sunder Rajan (ed.), *Signposts: Gender Issues in Post-Independence India* , New Delhi, Kali for Women.

____________, 1999 b, 'Beyond the Ghetto: Studying Women and Gender in the Nineties', *The Book Review*, Gender Special, Vol. 23, Nos. 1 and 2, January-February 1999, pp. 6-7.

Jordanova. L.J., 1980, Natural Facts: A Historical Perspective of Science and Sexuality in Carol MacCormack and Marylin Strathem (ed.), *Nature, Culture and Gender*, Cambridge, Cambridge University Press, pp. 42-69.

Kapur, Ratna and Cossman, Brenda, 1996, *Subversive Sites: Feminist Engagements with Law in India*, New Delhi, Sage Publications.

Kaushik, Susheela (ed.), 1993 a, *Women's Participation in Politics*, under the auspices of Indian Association for Women's Studies, New Delhi, Vikas Publishing House Pvt. Ltd.

____________, 1993 b, *Women and Panchayati Raj*, Fredrich Ebert Stiftung, New Delhi, Har-Anand Publications.

Khilani, Sunil, 1998, *The Idea of India*, Harmondsworth, Penguine Books.

Kishwar, Madhu, 1998, 'The Logic of Quotas: Women's Movement Splits on the Reservation Bill', *Manushi*, No. 107, July-August 1998, pp. 31-39.

Kothari, Rajni, 1995, 'Interpreting Indian Politics: a Personal Statement', in Upendra Baxi and Bhiku Parekh (ed.,), *Crisis and Change in Contemporary India*, New Delhi, Sage Publications, pp. 150-68.

Kumar, Radha, 1993, *History of Doing : An Illustrated Account of Movements for Women's Rights and Feminism in India 1800- 1990*, New Delhi, Kali for Women.

Kumari, Abhilasha and Kidwai, Sabina, 1996, *Crossing the Sacred Line: Women's Search for Political Power*, Delhi, Fredrich Ebert Stiftung and New Concept Information Systems Ltd.

Kumari, Ranjana and Dubey, Anju, 1994, *Women Parliamentarians: A Study in the Indian Context*, Fredrich Ebert Stiftung under the auspices of Centre for Social Research, New Delhi, Har-Anand Publications.

Lomitiz, I. A., 1977, *Networks and Marginality: Life in a Mexican Shantytown*, New York, Academic Press.

MacCormack, C. P., 1980, 'Nature, Culture and Gender: A Critique', in Carol MacCormack and Marilyn Stratham (ed.), *Nature, Culture and Gender*, Cambridge, Cambridge University Press, pp. 1-24.

Menon, Nivedita, 1996, *Uniform Civil Code: Debates in Feminism Today*, in Nitya Rao, Luise Rurup and R. Sudarshan (ed.), *Sites of Change : The Structural Context for Empowering Women in India*, Fredrich Ebert Stiftung and UNDP, New Delhi, Tulika Press, pp. 445-59.

____________, 1998, 'Women and Citizenship' in Partha Chatterjee (ed.), *Wages of Freedom: Fifty Years of the Indian Nation-State*, Delhi, Oxford University Press.

Mies, Maria, 1986, *Patriarchy and Accumulation on a World Scale: Women in the International Division of Labour*, London, Zed Books.

Millet, Kate, 1972, *Sexual Politics*, London, Abacus.

Mills, C. Wright, 1973, *The Sociological Imagination*, Harmondsworth, Pelican Books.

Mitra, Subrata, K., 1995, 'Crowds and Power: Democracy and the Crisis of "Governability" in India', in Upendra Baxi and Bhiku Parekh (ed.), *Crisis and Change in Contemporary India*, New Delhi, Sage Publications, pp. 211-45.

Moser, Caroline, O.N., 1993, *Gender Planning and Development: Theory, Practice and Training*, London and New York, Routledge.

Narayanan, Revathi, 1996, 'Empowering Women in Panchayati Raj Struggles in the Brave New World of SAP' in Nitya Rao, Luise Rurup, R. Sudershan (ed.), *Sites of Change: The Structural Context for Empowering Women in India*, Fredrich Ebert Stiftung and UNDP, New Delhi, Tulika, pp. 379-400.

Oldenburg, Philip, 1987, 'Middlemen in Third World Corruption: Implications of an Indian Case', *World Politics*, No. 4, July 1987, pp. 508-35.

Ortner, Sherry, B., 1974, 'Is Female to Male as Nature is to Culture?' in Michelle Zimbalist Rosaldo and Louise Lamphere (ed.), *Women, Culture and Society*, Standford, Standford University Press, pp. 67-87.

Palriwale, Rajni and Agnihotri, Indu, 1998, 'Tradition, the Family and the State: Politics of the Contemporary Women's Movement', in T V. Sathyamurthy (ed.), *Region, Religion, Caste, Gender and*

Culture in Contemporary India, Vol. 3 of Social Change and Political Discourse in India: Structures of Power, Movements of Resistance, Delhi, Oxford University Press, pp. 503-32.

Parashar, Archana, 1992, *Women and Family Law Reform in India: Uniform Civil Code and Gender Equality*, New Delhi, Sage Publications.

Patel, Sujata, 1993, 'Women's Participation in the Anti-Reservation Agitation in Ahmedabad, 1985: Some Issues' in Susheela Kaushik (ed.), *Women's Participation in politics* under the auspices of Indian Association for Women's Studies. New Delhi, Vikas Publishing House Pvt. Ltd. pp. 148-55.

Patel, Vibhuti, 1988, 'Emergence and Proliferation of Autonomous Women's Groups in India: 1974-1989' in Rehana Ghadially (ed.), *Women in Indian Society: A Reader*, New Delhi, Sage Publications, pp. 249-56.

Pateman, Carole, 1980, 'The Disorder of Women: Women, Love and the Sense of Justice', *Ethics*, 91, pp. 20-34.

____________, 1987, 'Feminist Critique of the Public and Private Dichotomy' in Anne Phillips (ed.), *Feminism and Equality*, Oxford UK, Basil Blackwell, pp. 45-68.

Rajan, Rajeswari, Sunder, 1999 a, 'The Story of Draupadi's Disrobing: Meanings for our Times', in Rajeswari Sunder Rajan (ed.), *Signposts: Gender Issues in Post-Independence India*, New Delhi, Kali for Women, pp. 331-58.

____________, 1999 b, *Signposts: Gender Issues in Post-Independence India*, New Delhi, Kali for Women.

Rana, M.S., 1998, India Votes: *Lok Sabha and Vidhan Sabha Elections 1998 (Poll Analysis, Election Data and Party Manifestos*, Delhi, B.R. Publication Corporation.

Rao, Anupama, 1999, 'Understanding Sirsagaon: Notes Towards Conceptualizing the Role of Law, Caste and Gender in a Case of Atrocity' in Rajeswari Sunder Rajan (ed.), *Signposts: Gender Issues in Post-Independence India*, New Delhi, Kali for Women, pp. 204-47.

Ray, Bharati and Basu, Aparna, 1999, *From Independence Towards Freedom: Indian Women Since 1947*, Delhi, Oxford University Press.

Rosaldo, M.Z., 1980, 'The Use and Abuse of Anthropology: Reflections on Feminism and Cross Cultural Understanding' *Signs*, Vol. 5, No. 3, pp. 396-401.

Sangari, Kumkum, 1995, 'Politics of Diversity: Religious Communities and Multiple Patriarchies', *Economic and Political Weekly*, Vol. 30, Nos. 51 and 52, 1995, pp. 3287- 3310, pp. 3381-89.

____________, 1998, 'Consent, Agency and Rhetorics of Incitement', in T.V. Sathyamurthy (ed.), *Region, Religion, Caste, Gender and Culture in Contemporary India*, Vol. 3 of Social Change and Political Discourse in India: Structures of Power, Movements of Resistance, Delhi, Oxford University Press.

Sarkar, Tanika and Butalia, Urvashi, 1995, *Women and the Hindu Right: A Collection of Essays*, New Delhi, Kali for Women.

Scott, James C., 1972, 'Patron Client Politics and Political Change in Southeast Asia', *The American Political Science Review*, Vol. LXVI, No. 1, March 1972, pp. 95-113.

Seminar 1997, Empowering Women: A Symposium on Political Reservation for Women, 457, September 1997.

Sen, Ilina, 1990, *A Space Within the Struggle*, New Delhi, Kali for Women.

____________,1998, 'Women's Politics in India', in T.V. Sathyamurthy (ed.), *Region, Religion, Caste, Gender and Culture in Contemporary India*, Vol. 3 of Social Change and Political Discourse in India: Structures of Power, Movements of Resistance, Delhi, Oxford University Press, pp. 444-62.

Sridharan, N., 1995, 'Indian Slums: Problems, Policies and Issues', in Brian C. Aldrich and Ranvinder S. Sandhu (ed.), *Housing the Urban Poor: Policy and Practice in Developing Countries*, New Delhi, Vistaar Publications, pp. 385-400.

Srinivas, M.N., 1951, 'The Social Structure of a Mysore Village' *The Economic Weekly*, October 30, 1951, pp. 1051-56.

____________, 1984, 'Sanskritization' in M.N. Srinivas, *Social Change in Modern India*, New Delhi, Orient Longman, pp. 1-45.

____________, 1988, 'A Note on Sanskritization' in M.N. Srinivas, *Caste in Modern India and Other Essays*, Bombay Media Promoters and Publishers Pvt. Ltd., pp. 42-62.

____________, 1989 a, *Religion and Society Among the Coorgs of South India*, Bombay, Media Promoters and Publishers Pvt. Ltd.

____________, 1989 b, 'The Cohesive Role of Sanskritization', in M.N. Srinivas, *The Cohesive Role of Sanskritization*, Other Essays, Delhi, Oxford University Press, pp. 56-72.

____________, 1989 c, Introduction', in M.N. Srinivas, *The Cohesive Role of Sanskritization and Other Essays*, Delhi, Oxford University Press, pp. 1-25.

_____________, 1994 a, 'The Dominant Caste of Rampura' in M.N. Srinivas, *The Dominant Caste and Other Essays*, Delhi, Oxford University Press, pp. 96-115.

_____________, 1994 b, 'The Social System of Mysore Village' in M.N. Srinivas, *The Dominant Caste and Other Essays*, Delhi, Oxford University Press, pp. 60-95.

Tanwar, Reicha (ed.), 1998. *Women: Human Rights, Religion and Violence*, Kurukshetra, Nirmal Book Agency.

Tharu, Susie and Niranjana, Tejaswani, 1994, 'Problems for Contemporary Theory of Gender', *Social Scientist*, Vol. 22, Nos. 3 and 4, March-April, 1994, pp. 93-117.

Voluntary Health Association of India, 1993, *A Tale of Two Cities*, New Delhi, Voluntary Health Association of India.

von Werlhof, Claudia, 1988 a, 'On the Concept of Nature and Society in Capitalism', in Maria Mies, Veronika Bennholdt, Thomson and Claudia von Werlhof (ed.), *Women: The Last Colony*, New Delhi, Kali for Women, pp. 96-112.

_____________, 1988 b, 'Women's Work: The Blind Spot in the Critique of Political Economy' in Maria Mies, Veronika Bennholdt, Thomson and Claudia von Werlhof (ed.), *Women: The Last Colony* New Delhi, Kali for Women, pp. 13-26.

Wiser, William Henricks, 1958, *The Hindu Jajmani System: A Socio-Economic System Interrelating Members of a Hindu Village Community in Services*, Lucknow, Lucknow Publishing House.

6

Pradhanis in the New Panchayats: A Study from Meerut District*

**Sudha Pai*

At independence our Constitution granted women equal rights of suffrage and participation in the political process. This arose out of the important role played by them in the national movement. In the post-independence period, while women have entered the workforce even, in the professional field, their role in politics has remained marginal. Those who have managed to enter Parliament have had little impact upon the policy-making process. Against this background, the 73rd Constitutional Amendment passed in April 1993, by Parliament and ratified by all the State Governments by April 1994, which gives women 33 per cent of the seats at all levels of the Panchayat System, is a significant measure. It has been widely perceived as a crucial step for empowering women and raised hopes for their increased participation in local decision-making structures[1].

This study, based on data from three villages in Meerut district of Uttar Pradesh (UP), argues that the impact of this measure on women's participation has been differential. In states where the social status of women has traditionally been better and levels of literacy, status in society, participation in the workforce and even, in local politics higher, women have been able to take advantage

*Sudha Pai, Associate Professor, Centre for Political Studies, JNU. This chapter is part of a larger study on the functioning of Ambedkar village panchayats in western UP and is funded by the SIDA, Sweden.

of the new measure. In Andhra Pradesh, Karnataka and Maharashtra, prior to the new legislation, women had contested elections, occupied reserved positions and contributed to the functioning of panchayats. In all women panchayats this was even, more clearly recognizable. Quite a few studies had pointed out the difference, that women members made to the nature of the decisions and the process by which they were formulated. Power meant giving priority to issues like drinking water supply, installation of pumps, construction of toilets, village wells and roads, appointment of teachers, closing of liquor shops, etc. There were instances, as in Vitner village in Jalgaon district (Maharashtra) where women got playgrounds built, land transferred to 127 women from their husband's share and toilets constructed in the SC areas. Conscious of their increasing housework and the need to have some free time and save energy, the women in Pidghara (Madhya Pradesh) went for a 27-point action plan that took up the building of educational and other community-based infrastructure. The experience and action agenda of the seven-member panchayat of Brahmanghar of Pune district has been similar[2].

In other parts of the country where women's position in the family and society and participation in public affairs has traditionally been low, the reservation measure has not caused much change. This is particularly true of states in the northern plains, such as Uttar Pradesh as is evident from the role played by the elected *'Pradhanis'* in the three selected village of Meerut district given below. It shows that reservation alone cannot change the status of women in the family and society and thereby ensure their participation in local bodies. The study also shows that rise in family income and improved life-style due to better educational qualifications, or investment in business by male members does not make a difference. The position of women and the perception that they have little knowledge about and are incapable of taking part in public affairs, even of independent voting, remains strong. The *pradhanis* in our sample villages are mere namesake representatives of the male members of their household[3]. The first two parts of the study provide a background to the study by describing the panchayat structure and position of women in UP. The third part presents the findings of the study while the conclusion discusses the factors determining participation of women in the new panchayats in UP.

I

Functioning of Panchayats in UP

UP is one of the states, where local institutions were established quite early, but their working has not been as satisfactory as in many other states, both in the colonial and post-colonial period.

Beginning with Ripon's famous resolution of local self-government, the history of panchayat institutions has been dotted with various attempts at increasing decentralization and people's participation[4]. The Royal Commission on Decentralization in 1909, after reviewing the working of local and district boards in the province realizing that they had not been a success, tried to give them a representative character. It recommended their resuscitation by the creation of a genuine electorate consisting of the members of the village panchayats, the provision for an elective majority on all the boards and a due representation of minorities through nomination. This led to the passing of the UP Village Panchayat Act, 1920, which sought to confer morepowers on the local bodies to look into local problems. However, enacted by British rulers in Delhi, it had number of defects: (1) It was enforced only in selected villages, (2) Sufficient freedom was not given to people to establish panchayats in their own areas, (3) There was no provision for election of members and (4) The financial position of the panchayats was so poor that they could hardly engage in any worthwhile activities[5].

It was only with the passage of UP Panchayat Act, 1947, that an attempt was made to remedy these shortcomings and establish panchayats in all parts of the state. These bodies were envisaged as purely a people's institution, free from official control and based upon adult franchise, with seat reservation for SC/STs and minorities. In UP, Gram Sabhas and Gram Panchayats were established in 1949, throughout the state much earlier than in any other state. In 1960, based upon the Balwantrai Mehta Committee Report, which led to the UP Kshettra Samitis and Zilla Parishad

Ahiniyam, there were changes introduced, which envisaged further democratic decentralization.

However, in spite of all these impressive provisions, the functioning of Panchayats in the post-colonial period has been disappointing. Elections to the panchayats were not held regularly and when held, the upper castes/classes in the village managed to capture power, leaving little room for representation for the lower castes and the issue of women's representation was never given a thought. Elections rather were a means by which the former were able to consolidate their power in the countryside[6]. The financial assistances provided were too little, the benefits were not evenly distributed and no major developmental works were undertaken by the panchayats. To remedy these defects the 73rd Amendment has given panchayats a constitutional position, i.e., they now form a third-tier below the state and elections must be held regularly unlike in the past. The finances available to these bodies and their responsibilities have increased. Reservations have been given to lower castes and women and it is hoped, an opportunity to play a role in local affairs.

II

Gender Inequality in UP

Much more seminal to our study, is the fact that UP seems to fare worse than most of them if not all other states, in the area of gender inequality. The position of women in UP and their ability to participate in public life, must be understood against the background that it is a region with exceptionally high levels of fertility, morbidity, undernutrition, illiteracy and social inequality and a slow pace of poverty decline[7].

A basic indicator of the disadvantaged position of women in UP is the female-male ratio in the population. In 1991, the number of females per 1,000 males was as low as 879[8]. The main cause of this was the considerable female disadvantage in survival from birth, until the mid-thirties. For the age group 0-4 the female death rate in UP is 16 times higher than that of male death rate. There is a direct link between excess female mortality in childhood and parental neglect of female children in this region. Female life expectancy is still below 55 years and the under-five mortality rate is as high as 141 per thousand. The number of maternal deaths in UP was estimated to be as high as 931, which is quite dismal compared to many other states. For example a new- born girl can expect to live 20 years longer if she is born in Kerala rather than in UP and the possibility of her death before the age of one is six times higher in UP in comparison to Kerala[9]. UP also has the highest birthrate among all Indian states, as well as the highest fertility rate.

Female literacy, an important factor promoting participation in local politics in other parts of the country, is strikingly low in UP being only 25 per cent. This verifies that only one woman out of four in the 7 + age group was able to read and write in 1991. Another vital aspect in our study is that female literacy rate is only 19 per cent in the rural and 50 per cent in the urban areas. The percentage is even lower among SC women in the rural areas being only 8 per cent—the segment to which our *Pradhanis* belong. If we consider the more demanding criteria of educational attainment such as completion of primary and secondary education, only 40 per cent of the literate females in UP had completed 8 years of schooling[10]. The most serious problem with female and to a lesser extent to male literacy in UP, is the persistence of high levels of illiteracy in the younger age groups. In the late 1980s, the incidence of illiteracy in the age group 10-14 was as high as 61 per cent and more than two-thirds of all rural girls in the 12-14 age group had never been to school. Gender differences in literacy rates are sharp in all income caste groups making women a disadvantaged section in society. There is also very low level of female labour force participation in UP. The 1991, census counts only 8 percent of women in UP as 'main workers' (persons involved in economically productive employment for at least half the year, apart from housework, which is excluded in the census)[11].

Low female participation in education and the labour force, is only one aspect of a general pattern of women's limited interaction with the world outside their households. A striking feature is the great resilience in the traditional patriarchical set up in UP society, which makes it difficult for women—specially rural women—to participate in politics. Even today, there are extreme social restrictions on women's freedom of movement and activities by physically confining them to the domain of the households, which even, diminish their ability to act effectively within that domain.

Improvement in the financial position of a household decreases, in fact, the mobility of women. Less than half of all married women in UP have regular exposure to any mass medium, compared to nearly 80 per cent in both Tamil Nadu and Kerala. Women's limited opportunities to acquire education and information, whether through schooling, social interaction, travel, mass-media, etc., is bound to affect their ability to play an informed role in local institutions such as panchayats.

Poverty is undoubtedly an important factor contributing to this state of affairs and it is true that UP has higher level of poverty than many other states. However, poverty alone cannot be blamed as the only reason for poor status of women in the state, a comparison between the eastern and western regions, makes it: clear. These two regions with roughly equal population sizes, account for about three-quarters of the total population of the state. The western region, which has enjoyed significant economic growth during the last three decades, is now considerably more prosperous than that of the eastern one. The head count ratio of rural poverty in western UP for instance, was only 26 per cent in 1987-88, compared to 43 per cent in eastern UP. Despite this, western UP fares no better than eastern UP in terms of the indicators of the well-being and status of women. While it is true that Haryana has a lower female-male ratio of 865, yet, western UP—with nearly three times the population of Haryana, more than 1/3 of the population of UP and in fact the more economically advanced region of the state has been described as the 'epicentre' of problem of low female-male ratio, which is only 0.84 percent[14]. In 1981, western UP had a higher child mortality rate than eastern UP, with a particularly large east-west gap for female children. Western UP also has higher fertility levels. It has failed to take advantage of its better economic position for taking a lead in the female education and the rates of female labour force participation are lower in western UP (2.5 per cent), than in Haryana or Punjab. The corresponding figures for north India and south India are 16 and 24 per cent, respectively. Keeping in mind this picture of the poor socio-economic position of women in UP, we now turn to our field study.

II

The Field Study

Socio-Economic Structure of Selected Villages

Meerut is one of the most prosperous districts in west UP and in the State, it reflects the socio-economic transformation taking place in this region over a period of time. The sample villages of Khanauda, Maithena Inder Singh (Maithena) and Uldiypur lie in Daurala block of Meerut district and within 15-20 km from Meerut city. Certain characteristics of the villages must be outlined to understand the impact of the new legislation.

These villages fall within the Green Revolution Belt of western UP, which since the mid 1960s, has been a prosperous agricultural region. Hence, the appalling poverty found in the eastern districts and Bundelkhand is not seen here. Jats and Rajputs form the dominant castes, the higher castes of Brahmins and Banias are in a minority and Dalits and the OBCs form the majority. In recent years the Dalits, particularly the Jatavs, have become socially aware and politically active due to mobilization by the Bahujan Samaj Party (BSP) and earlier the Republican Party of India (RPI) resulting in a process of 'Ambedkarization'. A significant development can be seen within all caste/class groups, but specially among the Jatavs, due to spread of education, since the 1950s and 1960s and resulting changes in the occupational structure, is the emergence of a new post-independence generation, which is politically conscious, socially aware, better educated and upwardly mobile. In almost all caste groups, families or individuals who emerged and who have diversified into various professions or businesses such as brick kilns, dairying, shopkeeping, transport, etc. The villages have also experienced the media explosion. Due to the invasion of cable TV and rise in newspaper reading in the 1980s, which has increased political knowledge and awareness. They are aware of governmental programmes implemented through the panchayats. Some of the problems agitating the villagers are lack of place for dumping garbage, adequate toilets specially in Dalit Mohallas, unemployment, law and order, electricity fluctuation, which affects farmers who own mechanical implements, etc[16].

These changes have improved the living standard of the *pradhanis* in the sample villages as income has risen, but have introduced little change in their family status or ability to participate in public life. All the *pradhanis* in our sample villages are about 45 years. As they belong to the better off families in the village, they do not work outside the home. The family income of the *pradhani* of Khanauda for example, is over 1 lakh annually and they own 90 *bighas* of land. On being questioned it was revealed that all of them had agreed to stand for election due to family pressure and the decision of their community and not because they were keen to do so. The reservations provided by the government had forced them to do so, as there was competition among Dalit families for the post of *Pradhan*. Regarding panchayat matters, they professed their ignorance and advised us to discuss with their husbands. All of them are illiterate and only able to put their signatures to official papers. All the *pradhanis* looked upon the panchayat as a government organization run by officials and participation by the villagers was seen as unnecessary. Interviewing them for understanding the working of the panchayat was of little use as they were ignorant of local affairs. The introduction of reservation and its impact on women must be understood in the context of the above situation.

New Panchayats in the Sample Villages

Two important measures introduced by the Uttar Pradesh Government in recent years have introduced a change in the functioning of the panchayats and made the post of *Pradhan* important in local politics. Firstly, the 73rd Amendment by providing reservation to Dalits has changed the social composition of panchayats in the sample villages, giving the lower castes a predominant position in these institutions. If the majority of persons in a village are Dalits or Backward Castes (BCs), then the *Pradhan* must be a woman from one of these communities, preference always being given to the former. In all the sample villages the *Gaon Pradhans* (i.e., *Pradhanis*) and the presiding officers of the Daurala Block Development Samiti at present are women from the Dalit community, the latter being from Maithena and Khanauda.

Elections for panchayat bodies were not being held regularly in UP prior to 1994. In Meerut district after 1970, they were held in 1972, 1982, 1988 and after the 73rd Amendment in 1995. Prior to the amendment, the *Pradhans* were the Jatavas, as Dalits form the majority in these villages and have been active in the *gram* and block panchayat, since the early 1980s. In the 1995, Panchayat elections, in all our sample villages women belonging to the Dalit community were elected to the post of *pradhan*. However, in reality to fulfill legal requirements they stood in place of their husbands, who presently carryout all the functions of the *pradhan*. Prior to the elections, in all the villages, at meetings in the Dalit Mohalla, prosperous and enterprizing Dalit families decided to putup their women in the election. The elections were hence, a contest between women from prominent Dalit families. The husband of the *Pradhani* of Maithena for example, is a big contractor and they are among the most prosperous families in the village.

In Maithena, which is a large village, there were 14 women candidates belonging to the Dalit community for the post of *Pradhan*, but only three gained a substantial number of votes cast, the rest being insignificant. In Khanauda there were six candidates and in Uldipur five, but in both cases the winning candidates won by large margins. The contest was in actuality between the leading Dalit families and not the women. Some respondents also held that the families, which putup female candidates were also approved and supported by the Jats and therefore, their election was the result of a tacit agreement among the powerful Jat families and the leading and prosperous Jatav families. A second reason for the post of *Pradhan* becoming so important in recent years is that Maithena and Khanauda in 1991 and Uldiypur in 1996, were identified as Ambedkar villages by the UP government as they have a large Dalit population. Under this scheme, existing governmental allocations for rural development/welfare programmes such as IRDP, JRY, Awas Yojanas, etc., in the case of selected villages were doubled for a period of two year and channelled through the block and *gram* panchayats. As a result much development has taken place in the village: link roads and toilets built, drains laid, handpumps installed, loans were given to the weaker sections for building houses, seting up small businesses, etc. Most of these benefits have gone to the Jatavs[17]. This has made the post of *Pradhan* very important as it gives him considerable powers of patronage. The villagers are dependent upon him for availing the benefits of various schemes, specially loans. Corruption is rampant at the village level and many villagers divulged that, they had to pay a bribe to the *pradhan* or official at the block level to obtain, even a small loan. Caste-based reservations and distribution of the benefits of welfare programmes, have therefore, been a more determining factor than reservations for women and local caste politics played an important role in the panchayat elections.

Role of the Pradhanis in Gram and Block Panchayats

The *pradhanis* play an almost insignificant role in the functioning of the *gram* and block panchayat level bodies. No statutory meetings of the *Gaon* Panchayat or *Samiti* have ever been held in these villages. The *pradhans* are expected to inform the Gaon Panchayat Samiti of the welfare schemes and funds available from the block for village development. At the *samiti* meetings various suggestions and demands for loans by villagers are expected to be discussed and decisions taken. However, in reality it is the *pradhan*, (actually the husband of the the *pradhanis*) and a few influential villagers, some of whom are members of the Block *Samiti*, who meet to take all decisions for the welfare of the village. The *pradhanis* have never attended any meeting or made any decision about allocation of funds to individuals or schemes. They merely sign on the papers sent to their houses after the decision has been made. The *Pradhani* of Uldiypur unlike the others, was however, quite knowledgeable about the various schemes, particularly those pertaining to women such as widow pension and women's health which were being implemented in the village, though she was not able to comment on the method by which the benefits were distributed, or on the numerous allegations of corruption.

At the BDS meetings held four times a year at the Daurala block office, attended by all the *Gaon Pradhans* and Block level officials, the problems of the area are discussed, information is provided by the BDO and other officers regarding the funds available. At this meeting, schemes are presented by the *Pradhans* for their villages and out of funds not earmarked for speciafic projects, allotments are made by the committee. The *pradhanis* of the sample villages attend the quarterly BDS meetings at Daurala block, as they are members of this committee[18]. On the occasions they are accompanied by their husbands or sons and remain silently seated throughout. At one of these meetings, attended by me, the BDO asked all those who are not members, i.e., those accompanying female members to leave. These persons then waited outside until the meeting was over. The requests for grants or detailed reports regarding progress of village schemes were presented by the male members from the villages, who are the elected members of the committee. At the end of the meeting the chairperson, who is the *Pradhani* of Maithena read out the decisions taken and put her signature.

III

Conclusion

Participation does not exist in the abstract, but is defined through the individuals involved, specific institutions, processes and ideological and cultural factors. Within any participatory structure, overall forms of social inequality and oppression are usually reflected and maintained. As the study shows the very low socio-economic position of women does not enable the *Pradhanis* of our sample villages, to participate in the functioning of panchayats. Their lack of education, low participation in the labour force or in activities outside the household, have limited their role to the household. They even, lack in knowledge about the various programmes in operation in the village and are unable to take part in decision making. Worse, it is not only the lack of requisite skills alone, but the existing patriarchal structures, which make this impossible. In the case of Uttar Pradesh, what we are witnessing is differential participation of men and women in the panchayats. While men due to their superior social position, literacy and knowledge of local affairs play a dominant role, women in spite of the provision of reservation are marginalized and play a minimal role.

The provision of reservations has not led to women participating in decision making in local bodies. However, standing for elections and becoming *pradhanis* has made a difference in the lives of these women. It has made them realize that it is their illiteracy, which prevents them from playing a more active and responsible role in the affairs of the panchayat. As a result of this perception, they pointed out that all girls below 15 years are attending the village school. The example of Mayawati, a Dalit lady who succeeded in becoming the CM, is often cited by them as an example, that women are capable of playing an active role in public affairs. The need is hence, to develop not only participatory mechanisms of empowerment, but also the means to overcome the structural inequalities of social power. Reservations together with education have the potential to transform the lives of women, but this will take considerable time in the male-dominated society of UP. Much needs to be done in terms of female literacy, independent voting rights, change in the status in the family and society, for women to fully participate in the public sphere.

REFERENCES

Dreze, Jean and Haris Gazdar, "UP: The Burden of Inertia", in *Indian Development Selected Regional Perspectives,* (eds.) Jean Dreze and Amartya Sen, OUP, 1997, pp. 33-179.

Kaushik, Susheela, *Panchayati Raj in Action Challenges to Women's Role,* Published by Friedrich Ebert Stiftung, New Delhi, 1995, p. 5.

Khanna, B.S., *Rural Local Self-Government National Perspective and State Studies in India,* Deep and Deep, New Delhi, 1994.

Mahipal, "Woman in Panchayat Experiences of a Training Camp", *Economic and Political Weekly,* January 24, 1998, pp. 150- 52.

Malviya, H.D., *Village Panchayats in India,* AICC Publication, New Delhi, 1956.

Mehta, Asha Kapur, "Recasting Indices for Developing Countries: A Gender Empowerment Measure", *Economic and Political Weekly,* October 26, 1996, WS 81. (Special Issue on Women).

Pai, Sudha and Jagpal Singh, "Politicization of Dalits and Most Backward Castes: Social Conflict and Political Preferences in Four Villages of Meerut District", *Economic and Political Weekly,* June 7, 1997, pp. 1356-61.

Records of the Block Development Officer (BDO), Block Daurala, Meerut District, UP.

Singh, Sural, "Status of Panchayati Raj in UP", *Journal of Rural Development,* 10 (1), 1991, pp. 57-79.

1. Asha Kapur Mehta, "Recasting Indices for Developing Countries: A Gender Empowerment Measure", *EPW* October 26, 1996: WS 81.
2. Susheela Kaushik, *Panchayati Raj in Action Challenges to Women's Role,* Published by Friendrich Ebert Stiftung Foundation, New Delhi, 1995, p. 5.
3. A similar experience is related in a recent study, "Woman in Panchayat Experiences of a Training Camp", *EPW* January 24, 1998, pp. 150-52.
4. B.S. Khanna, *Rural Local Self-Government National Perspective and State Studies in India,* Deep and Deep, New Delhi, 1994.
5. Sural Singh, "Status of Panchayati Raj in UP", *Journal of Rural Development,* 19 (1), 1991, pp. 57-79.
6. See the study on the first two panchayat elections in UP by H.D. Malviya, *Village Panchayats in India,* AICC Publication, New Delhi, pp. 323-25.
7. Jean Dreze and Haris Gazdar, "UP: The Burden of Inertia", in *Indian Development Selected Regional Perspectives,* (eds.) Jean Dreze and Amartya Sen, OUP, 1997, pp. 33-128.
8. Only four countries have a lower ratio. *Ibid.,* p. 45.
9. *Ibid.,* p. 40.
10. *Ibid.,* p. 43.
11. *Ibid.*
12. Interviewing women, whether upper or lower caste, on the functioning of panchayats, was very extremely difficult and not very productive as their knowledge and interest in local affair was very limited. On their own position in village society they were, however, after some prodding more forthcoming.
13. *Ibid.*
14. Very few countries have such a low ratio. *Ibid.,* p. 45.
15. *Ibid.,* p. 57.
16. For details see, Sudha Pai and Jagpal Singh, "Politicization of Dalits and Most Backward Castes: Social Conflict and Political Preferences in Four Villages of Meerut District", *EPW* June, 1997.
17. All details about the Ambedkar Village Programme are from the Records of the BDO, Daurala block, Meerut District.
18. The author attended the Block Meeting held on April 26, 1997.

7

WOMEN IN PANCHAYATI RAJ INSTITUTIONS: A CASE STUDY IN GOA

*Seema P. Salgoankar**

"Giving her equal opportunity would not solve the problem of inequality between the sexes. When a group of people is helddown by debility, physical and cultural, the only way to bring it up to equality with other is through conferment of preferential opportunities". —*Dr. Ram Manohar Lohia*

Since long, women have been deprived from decision making. Their potentials remain largely unrecognized and their contributions are often overlooked. Several factors are responsible for women's low participation, the most important are illiteracy, traditionalism, prejudices, economic dependency and the unfavourable political opportunity structure, with its high rate of predominantly male incumbency and slow turnover. The dire need today is to remove the disparity between women's formal political equality and their meaningful exercise of political power. Achieving the goal of equal participation of men and women in decision-making will provide a balance, that would more accurately reflect in the composition of the society. It will expand the range of human resources available to meet society's needs. At present, women's increasing political participation will be a source as well as a signal of social change[1].

There is a growing importance of role played by women at the grassroots level. Necessarily, the women should not merely be targets of benefits of development, but they should also contribute effectively in the processes of development. The entry of more and more women into the realm of rural politics suggests that their increased number will offer them equally increased opportunities to influence decision-making. The 73rd Amendment Act* was a milestone in this direction. It led to over one million women assuming the mantle of grassroots leaders. It led to the beginning of a Silent Revolution, contend George Mathew[2]. According to Srilatha Batliwala, it was a measure for the balance of power in rural politics, particularly for the empowerment of women[3]. Thus, being given the opportunity, are women able to assert themselves, is however still an open question.

Various research studies have been conducted to study the women's leadership at panchayat level in different states. The panchayat elections that took place in the State of Madhya Pradesh in 1994, brought forward a large number of women, many of who belong to the Scheduled Castes and Scheduled Tribes[4]. The study on role of women in Panchayati Raj in Madhya Pradesh by Rashmi Arun, found that a majority of women *Panchas* are housewives and are either illiterate or educated merely up to the primary level. In large number of cases the decision to participate in the election was not their own. If a seat was reserved for a woman, the men who were politically active convinced their wife, mother or sister-in-law to contest the election, in order to keep the family's presence intact in local politics. And in fact, it is the men who are exercising the power by proxy today. The institution of 'Sarpanch-Pati' or

*The 73rd Amendment has the following provisions relating to women:

(*i*) Not less than one-third of the seats will be reserved for women (including those for SCs/STs). These may be alloted by rotation to different constituencies of a panchayat.

(*ii*) There would be reservation for women in the seats that have been allotted to SCs and STs. Not less than one-third of the SC and ST seats may be reserved for women.

(*iii*) Not less than one-third of the total number of seats for the offices of the chairpersons at each level would be reserved for women. This would be rotated among different panchayat at each level.

'Adhyaksha-Pati' might not have any legal sanction, but it is thriving in many panchayat in the states.

According to Dr P. Jeyapal and K. Dravidamani, a study of the elected female representatives of Lalgudi Panchayat Union in Tamil Nadu, reveals that there is a predominance of the younger members among women Panchayat Presidents. Among them 80 per cent of them are inexperienced in political or social fields, and 87 per cent of them are found with low awareness on Panchayat Raj System[6]. UMA study group also noticed the same trend, that women in the child bearing age group are coming forward to join politics in spite of the domestic responsibilities[7]. The study of Maharashtra revealed similar features in one of the micro-studies of the state[8]. According to George Mathew, a study of women elected representatives to Karnataka Panchayati Raj institutions between 1987 and 1990, conducted by the Institute of Social Sciences at a time when the *Zilla Parishads* had just come into being, revealed that majority of the women elected members had no experience of active politics; usually a male member of the family had been instrumental in persuading these women to contest and in many cases women continued to devote all their time to household chores as usual, because the men in their families were involved in discharging the political responsibilities on their behalf. However, it was reported after two years when the same *Zilla Parishads* were studied, again that there were evident changes[9].

The Institute of Social Sciences, New Delhi, monitoring the performance of women Panchayat members in Orissa after the recent elections, revealed a mixed picture. While a woman *sarpanch* from Jagatsinghpur district, who although educated, took time to asert herself, while, other woman *sarpanch* from Rayagada district with no education whatsoever, tookup her job confidently from the beginning. AT the same time, both these districts had instances of women panchayat meetings, pointing to the need of proper training of the elected representatives, particularly women[10].

Sukla Deb Kanoongo, in his research on women's leadership in the Panchayati Raj with special reference to the State of West Bengal, found that many of them, in spite of being educated, in spite of having a tradition of political activity in the family and of having great support from their respective parties, are unable to participate in the whole process in a meaningful way. Many are finding the responsibilities very demanding, some are thoroughly engaged in their domestic responsibilities and some do not maintain good health. He also felt that the socio-cultural factors acted as a deterrent in many cases[11]. The work of UMA and of Indra Hirway on Gujarat's Panchayati Raj Institutions has repeatedly revealed the enhanced role of women from dominant castes such as the Vokkaligas and Lingayats, while *Dalit* and tribal participation has been muted. Male relatives usually coach women to speak at meetings, or actually do the necessary paperwork when the women are illiterate[12]. Alvathe studies of Gujarat, Kerala and Karnataka have shown that the effective female participants are those from the age group of 25-40 for whom child bearing and rearing responsibilities are less pressing[13].

Dr Ujwala Hiremath conducted a survey of 40 women members of ten village *Gram* Panchayat in Karnataka. Her studies show the same trend that is seen at the national level politics—members of influential families always seem to have an edge over the rest. Majority of the members were illiterate-thumb impression ones. However, it was interesting to note that all these women had a manifesto of development items for the village—shelter for the poor, electricity, toilets, roads, schools, water facility, doctors for primary health centres, sewing machines for young girls and many other things, including old-age and widow pensions, employment for youth, girls education, transport facilities, etc[14]. Sudha Pai cautioned, after brief study of three villages from Meerut district in Uttar Pradesh, that female literacy, independent voting rights and change in the status in the family and society are required for women to play active role in the village politics. The *Pradhanis* played an almost insignificant role in the functioning of the *gram* and block panchayat level bodies. They have never attended any meeting or made any decision about allocation of funds to individuals or schemes[15]. Manu Bhaskar, in her study of women Panchayat members in Kerala, found that only about 30 per cent of the members belonged to the forward caste/communities, while the bulk of them were from the backward caste/communities[16]. Mahi Pal opined that the role of women members was actually performed either by their husbands or any male member of the family[17]. In some of the villages in Haryana, it was observed that women representatives belonged to the family of the men panchayat leaders. It was also observed that in some places women leaders were so old that they could hardly move around[18]. However, according to Sweta Mehta women have asserted themselves in Haryana, after coming to power. Thus, one *sarpanch* of Rewari block removed the wine shop from her area, another told the SDO that if he did not get the water supply to the village she would drag him to the village[19]. In some states elected women have taken part in protest and rallies against wages and for drinking water. Some have reported to have participated in demanding better implementation of Government schemes and have communicated information of these schemes to the people for whom they were meant. In Arunachal Pradesh, some of the newly elected Panchayat leaders have even faced imprisonment in the process of persuading the Government to build a twelve-bed hospital for women. Women have raised many issues, like alcoholism, lotteries, drinking water, health facilities, etc. Panchayat women in Karnataka paved the way for the economy of women to flourish by arranging to impart floriculture training to women[20]. There are also recommendations made for the establishment of statutory women's panchayats at the village level to ensure greater participation by women in the political process[21]. This will provide greater opportunity to more women to gain experience and confidence in managing their own affairs. Medha Kotwal and Sinorcita Gopal Singh, who looked at all-women panchayats in Maharastra for *Aalochana* (discussion) felt that women here are working more effectively than the women *sarpanches* of other panchayats, because the former could get encouragement and strength from the fellow women. The members of all-women panchayats have shifted the developmental priorities of the village[22].

WOMEN LEADERS AT GRASSROOTS POLITICS IN GOA

Goa was liberated from the Portuguese rule in the year 1961. It has a long colonial history. While British ruled India for barely

200 years, Portuguese ruled Goa for 450 years. Thus, the impact of Portuguese domination, in political and socio-cultural terms has been deeper. The status of women in Goa is better off partly because of Portuguese rule. It brought in various legislations, which imposed ban on sati and child marriage, promoted female education and extended the Uniform Civil Code to Goa. The laws with regard to property, inheritance, marriage and divorce have given women legal equality on par with men.

The present State of Goa consists of 185 villages and has an area of 3,701 sq. kms. I consists of 11 talukas and two districts—North Goa and South Goa. Its small size has certain advantages in comparison with other states, the power asymmetric are not as sharp and hence the distance between the representatives and the voters is much less. This results in political accountability—an important aspect of democracy. The origin of the panchayats in Goa, can be traced back to the local self-governing institutions, which existed in the pre-liberation period, like the communidades, *juntas de freguesias* or municipal council. The ancient local self-governing unit were called as 'communidades', who owned the village land collectively. The residents of the village were called 'Gaonkars'. They got certain share, which was called as 'jonoirs' or 'jonn'. Communidades, though were essentially collective farming societies, also carried out certain socio-political and public functions. They looked after the affairs of temples and churches in their jurisdictions, built and maintained roads and performed most of the functions undertaken by the *gram*-panchayats of today. The *juntas de freguesias* came into existence after 1959, though they had been provided under the *Codigo Administrative* (Code of Civil Administration) of the 1933 Constitution of Portug[23]. It managed the public affairs in a village. It was a three-member body constituted for a term of three years. The president of this institution was appointed by the Governor-General on the recommendation of the municipal council of the taluka to which the village belonged. The municipal council, known as 'camara municipal], had ordinary jurisdiction over the taluka town, supervisory jurisdiction over all the villages of the taluka and was named after the taluka. The other two members of the *junta de freguesia* and their respective substitutes, were to be elected directly by the heads of the families in the village. The Portuguese

Government had full control over this body. In 1962, elections to the panchayats were held for the first time, followed by elections to the state assembly. In Goa, democracy had its roots right at its base. Thus, for the first time institutions were set-up, which represented people in the villages. Goa has a single tier system of Panchayati Raj located at the *gram* panchayat level. The strength of membership of the *gram* panchayats varies according to the population covered. Before the implementation of 73rd Amendment, one seat in each *gram* panchayat was statutorily reserved for women. All the village panchayats are grouped into taluka-wise blocks. Each of these blocks has a block advisory committee. These committees comprise the local MP, the local MLAs, *sarpanches* of all the *gram* panchayats within the taluka, representatives of the local institutions like the cooperative societies, government appointed representatives of SC and STs and government officials. In Goa there have been timely elections to the panchayats. The new Panchayati-Raj Act, 1994, has been brought into force through an ordinance on 20th April of 1994. The January, 1997, elections to panchayats in Goa, under the 73rd Amendment, saw a sizable number of women assuming the mantle of grassroots leaders. The cumulative representation of women in *Sarpanch* and Deputy *Sarpanch* positions came to 40 per cent.

OBJECTIVES OF STUDY AND METHODOLOGY

The study was conducted to draw socio-economic profile of women *panchas*. It looked into important questions like, whether women have become mere puppets in the power plays of men and politically vested interests ? Are these women mere proxies, or have power made them assertive ? Bardez taluka in North Goa was selected for the study of leadership of women *panchas*. It is the largest taluka in Goa. It is among the old conquestes and was ruled by the Portuguese for longer period of time, compared to other parts of Goa. The Uniform Civil Code, which gave socio-legal equality to women was first implemented in Bardez taluka. Today, it is a well developed taluka and has high female literacy ratio. This taluka has 33 village panchayats, with 88 women *panchas*. To study women leadership in this taluka, a sample of thirty-three women *panchas*, each from one panchayat, was chosen. The method of personal interview was adopted.

Table 1.1

Taluka	*Villages*	*Women Members*	*Total Members*
Pernem	17	37 + 2	119
Bardez	33	81 + 7	255
Tiswadi	18	46 + 2	142
Bicholim	17	39 + 2	123
Satari	12	24	84
Ponda	19	51 + 3	157
Salcete	30	72 + 9	223
Mormugao	9	27 + 2	79
Quepem	11	24 + 2	86
Sanguem	12	28 + 1	79
Canacona	7	17	55
11	185	446 + 30	1402

(446 women members are elected from the reserved, ward while 30 has won from the general category).

FINDINGS

The findings are into two parts: the first deals with the socio-economic status of the women *panchas* and the latter analyzed the political status of women *panchas vis-a-vis* the sharing of power in decision-making.

(A) THE SOCIO-ECONOMIC PROFILE OF WOMEN PANCHAS

Age

Age by itself can be a significant variable for the structural analysis of political leadership of women. The studies have divulged that most of the women enter politics in later years of their lives. This late entry rigidifies the existing male- dominated structures. In the survey, 51.5 per cent of the women *panchas* came from the age group of 31-40. However, a positive trend was observed where 21.2 per cent came from the age group of 21-30.

Marital Status

Data on marital status of women *panchas* show that a bulky majority of them are married. 90.9 per cent of them are married. Thus, unmarried women are less in politics. Goa is culturally different from other parts of India, it is a melting- pot of Indian and Portuguese culture, which has given a different status to women in Goa. There is a high female literacy in Goa and the mean age at marriage is 33.6 per cent. In spite of this there is absence of unmarried women in politics. These may be due to two reasons:

1. It is an indication of the continuing traditional attitude, which tends to keep them away from the public sphere in rural areas.

2. The political parties have failed to motivate women to take active role in politics.

Caste Factor

It is interesting to not that 61 per cent of the women *panchas* belonged to other castes. They belong to castes like artisans, carpenters, toddy tappers, fishermen, the agricultural labourers, etc. These castes are clubbed under what is called as *sudir* caste[24].

Caste Status

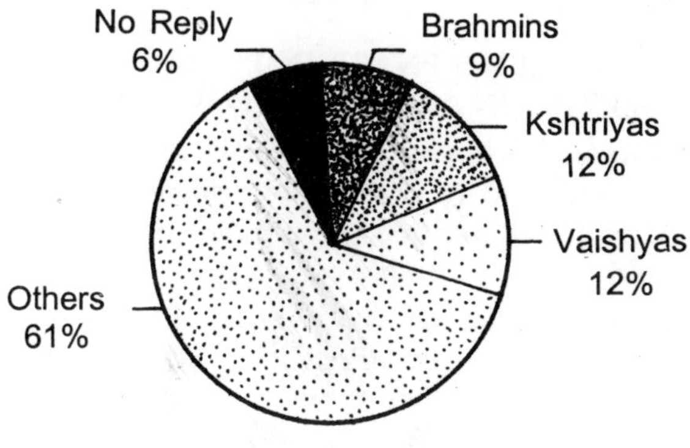

Fig. 1.1.

Occupational Status

The occupational status analysis shows that 63.6 per cent were housewives and 18.18 per cent supplemented their family income. They worked in fields, did tailoring and helped male members in business. 3.03 per cent were self-employed, while 15.1 per cent were in teaching and clerical jobs.

Educational Status

A positive trend is observed with regard to the educational status of women *panchas*. 66.6 per cent of them have completed middle or high school, which enables them to carry out the paperworks of the panchayat. Thus, compared to some other states, women *panchas* in Goa are better placed.

Educational Status

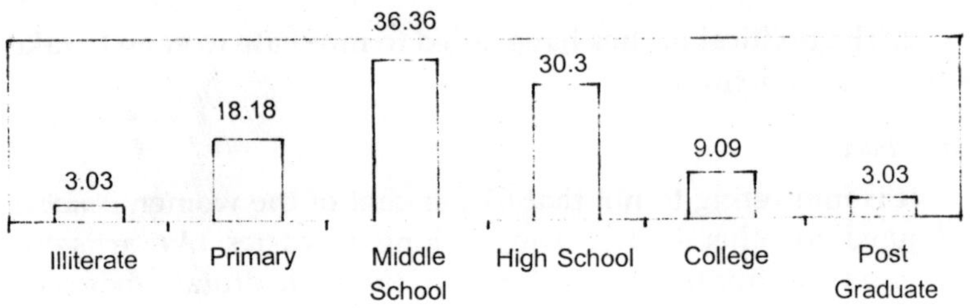

Fig. 1.2.

(B) HAS WOMEN'S ENTRY IN POLITICS MADE THEM ASSERTIVE IN ACQUIRING POWER?

It is commonly believed that women's increased presence in local politics will lead to their greater power and influence in policy-making. It was decided to examine women's participation in policy making and leadership experiences.

The survey revealed that 90.9 per cent of women *panchas* had contested and won for the first time. Being new entrants in politics, they were less aware and less informed about the processes of local politics. This acted as a major obstacle in their effective share in decision-making. When asked about the reason for their entry in

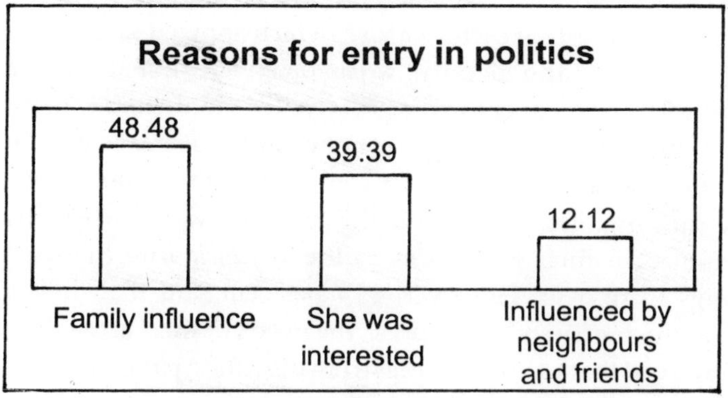

Fig. 1.3.

politics, 48.48 per cent replied that they were pushed into scene by their male family members. In this 9.09 per cent were the wives of the *sarpanches*. Their *sarpanch* husbands wanted them to contest as this would strengthen their panels. The canvassing for these women was fully done by their husbands. 15.1 per cent contested from the ward because now it was reserved for women. This was necessary to continue the hold of the family on the ward 6.06 per cent literally admitted that they contested because men told them that they would not have to do, an anything. However, interesting trend emerged when 39-39 per cent said that they contested because they were really interested in politics.

Statistics revealed that for 15 per cent of the women *panchas*, the decisions were made by the male family members. This reflects the disparity between shadow and substance of female power. It is necessary to bring about a qualitative change with women's participation in these fora, rather than bring it down further with women simply joining as puppets. 58 per cent were influenced by the male members in the family in decision-making. 39.3 per cent were influenced by their husbands, while 9.09 per cent were influenced by their brother-in-laws. Thus, it is necessary to look at two questions; do women want to remain in a male-dominated political set-up, or do they really want to participate in panchayat ? However 27 per cent answered that they took their independent decisions.

When asked about whether they were dominated by men *panchas,* an interesting picture arose, which showed 27.2 per cent being *sarpanches* and deputy *sarpanches,* were not dominated. Similarly 9.09 per cent of them were wives of the *sarpanches* of their villages, thus, the domination was not visible. 6.06 per cent did not go for meeting at all and 9.09 per cent said that they rarely spoke in the meeting. They preferred the informal ways, where they communicated their grievances to the *sarpanch* after the formal meetings were over. However, 48.4 per cent said that they did speak in the meetings and express the needs of their areas. It was also observed that women *panchas* from the ruling panel were more vocal and regular for the meetings than the others and again it was observed that those who were employed were more articulate than

Influence on decision making

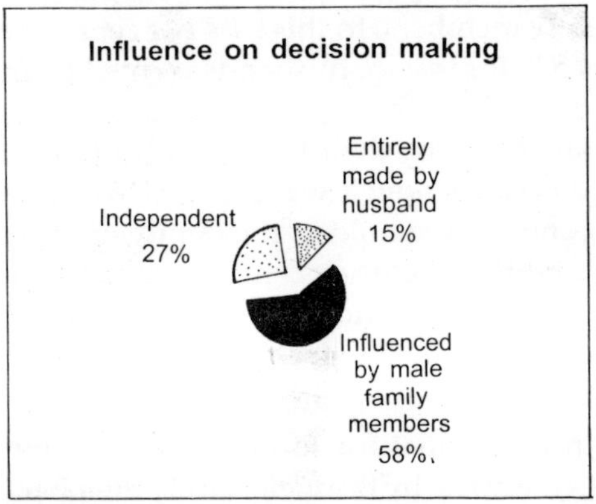

Fig. 1.4.

the housewives. The sense of economic independence, the exposure and awareness made these women more distinct. The change is evident. There is growing sense of responsibility and assertion among the women *panchas.* 39.3 per cent went regularly to the panchayat meetings. 30.3 per cent visited government offices for panchayat work and 6.06 per cent visited local MLA with their problems.

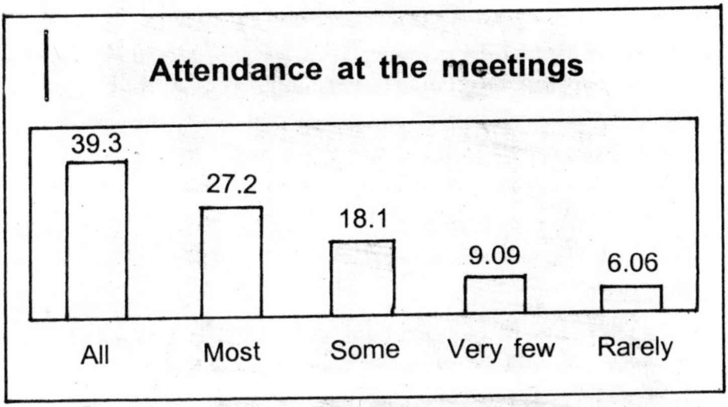

Fig. 1.5.

Future Prospects

The trends show that women have been able to assert themselves. The have started taking interest in their work. Certain measures beeds to be followed to help women to play their role effectively. Intensive training is necessary to train women in the intricacies of the process of decision-making and in administration. Thus, the NGOs should take the initiative to educate women in this regard. Societal attitude also requires to undergo drastic change. Women should be given more freedom and flexibility to encrise their powers. There is suggession recruitment of women officials in local bodies[25]. This will reduce the predominance of males, which will minimize the male hegemony in the administration. There is also need of structural and institutional reforms to neutralize the present power equation and make it more favourable for women. Some self-employment opportunities also needs to be created to help women gain more economic independence, which is a precondition for political empowerment of women.

(Ms Seema P. Salgoankar is a Lecturer in Political Science at the Government College of Arts, Commerce and Science, Quepem, Goa and is a research student in the Dept. of Political Science, Goa University. This article is based on her ongoing study.)

REFERENCES

1. Kathleen, Newland, December, 1975, Women in Politics; A Global Review, Worldwatch Paper 3, Washington DC, p. 19.
2. Mathew, George, 1994, Panchayat Raj: From Legislation to Movement, New Delhi, Concept Publishing House.
3. Batliwala, Srilatha, 1997, *Empowering Women*; Seminar.
4. Rashmi, Arun, April-June, 1996, *Role of Women in Panchayati Raj;* Vol. XLI, The Administrator, p. 115.
5. *Ibid*. p. 116.
6. Dr P. Jeyapal, K. Dravidamani, April, 1997, *Women Panchayat Presidents*, Vol. 44, No. 1. Social Welfare.
7. Mohanty, Bidyut, December 30, 1995, *Panchayat Raj, 73rd Constitutional Amendment and Women*, Economic and Political Weekly.
8. *Ibid*. p. 3349.
9. Dr Mathew, George, August-September, 1995, *Will Reservation Ensure Participation*, Vol. 42, No. 5-6, Social Welfare, p. 34.
10. Dr Mathew, George, August-September, 1997; *Women in Public Life*, Vol. 44, No. 5-6, Social Welfare, p. 24.
11. Sukla Deb, Kanoongo, January-March, 1996, *Panchayat Raj and Emerging Women Leadership*, Vol. 46, Social Welfare, p. 86.
12. Nair, Janaki, September, 1997, An Important Springboard, 457, Seminar, p. 44.
13. *Ibid*.
14. Dr Hiremath, Ujwala, May, 1997, *Women in Grassroot Politics*, Vol. 44, No. 2, Social Welfare, p. 13.
15. Pai, Sudha, May 2, 1998, 'Pradhanis in New Panchayats', Field Notes From Meerut District, *Economic and Political Weekly*.
16. Bhaskar, Manu, April 26, 1997, 'Women Panchayat Members in Kerala', *Economic and Political Weekly*, p. ws. 15.
17. Mahi Pal, January 24, 1998, 'Women in Panchayats', *Economic and Political Weekly*, p. 150.
18. Mishra, Sweta, January-March, 1997, *Women and Constitutional Amendment Act*, Vol. 47, Social Action, p. 22.
19. *Ibid*. p. 24.

20. *Ibid*. p. 25.

21. *Towards Equality: Report of the Committee on the Status of Women In India*, 1997, Seminar 457, p. 457.

22. Datta, Bishakha, 1998, And Who Will Make the Chapatis ? A Study of All-Women Panchayats in Maharashtra, Stree, Calcutta.

23. Mathew, George(ed.), 1994, Status of Panchayati Raj in the States of India, Institute of Social Science, New Delhi, Concept Publishing House, p. 4.

24. Xavier, P.D., 1993, Goa-A Social History, Prabhakar Bhide, Panaji-Goa, p. 36.

25. Khan, Tafzil M, July, 1996, *Women's Participation in Local Bodies: An Instrument for Emancipation*, Radical Humanist, p. 29.

8

TRANSFORMING WOMEN'S PARTICIPATION IN THE PANCHAYAT FROM THE BOTTOMUP: LESSONS FROM KALVA VILLAGE

Sandhya Gupta

Introduction

In the field of development and poverty alleviation, as well as in the natural sciences, chaos theory, and business management, a new 'bottomup' paradigm has emerged and is gaining popularity. Robert Chambers has described it thus: "On the new high ground, decentralization, democracy, diversity, and dynamism combine. Multiple local and individual realities are recognized, accepted, enhanced, and celebrated. Truth, trust, and diversity links"[1]. The new thinking rejects centralization, standardization, rigidity, and espouses principles of spontaneity, pluralism, and adaptability to explain the way systems are organized and work to maximize well-being. There is a growing recognition that these will be "greatest at the local level with an appropriate minimum of regulation to enable individuals to know what the rules are and what is happening, so that they can collaborate creatively".[2]

This idea can be said to be the spirit behind the 73 Amendment to the Indian Constitution—both its official sanction of Panchayat Raj and its 33 per cent reservation for women and SC/STs in panchayati raj institutions. If the pattern is extended to political organization, the logical system that emerges is a bottom-heavy federalist one, in which many local governments work autonomously and flexibly, engaging their citizenry's social energy, at the same time as they are in constant dialogue with other levels of government (including other local governments) and non-government. Internally and externally this local government structure, like any organization or organism, is in a state of flux, engaged with many different forces and actors, constantly shifting and negotiating its relations and processes on the basis of shifting identities, ideas, capabilities.[3] Such a vision for the local government structure in India (the panchayati raj) requires not only a devolving of funds and powers, but also the vibrant participation of its citizenry, including those previously excluded from public affairs. Hence the 33 per cent reservation for women and Scheduled Castes and Scheduled Tribes.

In fact, the participation of women in the *gram panchayat* can also be seen as an evolving, shifting phenomenon à la Chambers' paradigm. If we are concerned with the internal processes that are constantly organizing and reorganizing the village panchayat, then the reservation for women must be included as one important factor. Similarly, if we are concerned about the effective participation of women in the *gram panchayat,* we must look at and understand the reservation within the totality of rural development, not as an isolated attempt at political empowerment. This chapter attempts to introduce such an approach to women's local political participation. It endeavours to place the entry of women into the panchayat within a development paradigm that emphasizes fluid and bottomup processes. Focusing on the experience of Kalva village in Andhra Pradesh, it specifically highlights the influence of the self-help group on Women's Participation in the Panchayat—the ability of the Self-Help Group (SHG) model to raise the potential of women's leadership and the *gram sabha,* its process of formation as a model for improving women's participation in the panchayat and its structure as a model for a redefined panchayat. By looking practically at the interaction between women's participation in the self-help group and women's participation in the panchayat, the study attempts to grapple with the deeper question of the relevance of participation in formal *vs.* informal political institutions.

Research Methodology

A word on the methodology employed is in order, as it will explain the limitations of the study as well as reveal somewhat, how I espoused the idea of diverse, evolving, and flexible processes. This chapter is based on a qualitative study that has drawn on information gathered from a diverse range of field experiences. It draws on interviews of women panchayat members carried out with a formal, detailed and open questionnaire in ten villages of Kurukshetra district, Haryana in November, 1999. It further draws upon detailed case-studies of two villages in the same district, in which many different people of the village—including Anganwadi, ex-*sarpanch* and the Mahila Mandal members—were interviewed, besides Panchayat members. I turned to a case-study approach after I discovered that focusing only on women members, would give a fragmented picture of their participation at most. The bulk of the study is based on a visit to Kalva village in Andhra Pradesh in March, 1999, where I interacted with panchayat members as well as members of the village women's organization, Proddu. Field-work in Haryana and Andhra Pradesh was supplemented with visits to a range of non-governmental organizations (mainly working in south India) involved in motivating self-help groups and/or training panchayat members. Throughout, the literature research has supplemented the field-work.

The Paradox of the 73rd Amendment

If we are concerned with the phenomenon of women's participation in the panchayat—in fact the whole functioning of the panchayat itself the 73rd Amendment—as a bottomup people-centred process, we must begin by addressing an apparent contradiction in its very coming into being. Indeed, it is not immediately clear how Chambers' paradigm applies practically (though it does theoretically) to the case of local self-government empowerment in India. While the enactment of the 73rd Amendment constitutes a commitment to 'reversal' (that is, an upsetting of normal hierarchical power relations), it was not allowed to happen spontaneously, through a process of 'self-organization' with only minimal regulation. Instead, it was very much a top-down process. The amendment, instead of allowing for flexibility, outlines explicitly what the responsibilities of the panchayat are.[4] While these are not meant to be exhaustive and their very mention precludes the process the local body might have undergone to develop its own unique understanding of its responsibilities and functions[5]. Structurally, though not explicitly, the law contradicts the pattern (its own spirit). Moreover, it was imposed with no discussion at the local level, with those whom it would be affecting. It was passed without any sort of local consent or concurrence at all; neither did it make any provision for such local discussion. It gave full power to state governments for implementation as they saw fit and thus, made the mistake of classic top-down policy. As expected, most of the state governments have been slow to devolve down powers—most likely, because MLAs are unwilling to give up any amount of their power—and have allowed the bureaucracy to retain control over major local initiatives.[6]

In the case of women's reservation, it is a fair question whether such a provision would have emerged from discussion of villagers themselves, that is whether it could have emerged without such a push from above. This in not to assert that there would be no one at the village level with visionary enough to promote women's political participation. Certainly, some, if not many, women believe that they too should have a say in village affairs and development (and a few men, too). It only to suggest that the cultural, social and historical pressures at the local level might not allow women let alone men to espouse and promote such a thing, especially publicly. It is then, perhaps, worth asking whether affirmative action (such as a reservation for women) is compatible with the paradigm of diversity and democracy that it is supposed to be promoting. The relevant issue is not, whether the two are consistent, but rather, whether (if it is not a bottomup strategy) the affirmative action model can achieve the desired results—whether it can achieve the sort of thriving, creative and autonomous participation of women that is the point and that would, perhaps, even lead to a harmonious, democratic and local polity (besides its other, related goal of reversing historical and cultural injustices faced by women). Put another way, can such a reservation for women in an institution/structure entrenched in hierarchy (as the *gram panchayat* is) be effective? And to probe further, what is the place of the panchayat as a space for women's empowerment if all empowerment and development initiatives undertaken by NGOs done through civil society institutions, in bottomup fashion?

While these questions are not immediately answerable, Chambers does offer a clue to resolving the dilemma. Citing the collaboration of local knowledge and scientific knowledge, he promotes the idea of 'both-and' thinking, where something non-indigenous like technical knowledge can actually help 'make things better for those who are poor and weak'.[7] In this sense, an institution like 33 per cent reservation, while not a panacea, has its advantages. It does, after all, attempt to overcome, on a large-scale, historical and cultural injustice. In a feudal, misogynist, rural society where 'lowers' sometimes oppress other 'lowers' such a push from above can be of great help.[8] The key is to make the two—reservation and bottomup, gradual consciousness-raising—work simultaneously and synergistically. That means recognizing and enhancing the interaction of formal institutions (those with top-down sanction) and informal ones (those with bottomup sanction). There is, for instance, the possibility that an informal structure can help transform the formal one into something receptive to policy like reservation. What is needed now is a bottomup approach to make such a thing possible—to empower the women, change the panchayat and thereby effect the top-down dictum. Before discussing such interaction further, however, we first briefly discuss women's experience in the panchayat without the bottomup support.

Women in the Panchayat

That the reservation for women in the panchayat was very much a top-down imposition without a bottomup complement is evident in the experiences of women who have come into the panchayat since 1993-94. True, the reality of women's participation in the panchayat, since the passing of the 73rd Amendment in 1993, has varied with varying local conditions and personalities. Diverse, fluid and uncertain, it defies attempts to label or categorize it as one single experience.[9] Still, various studies have illuminated the many similar constraints that women panchayat members face in effectively fulfilling their responsibilities and constraints that were not addressed or removed before implementation.[10] These include both social/personal (direct) and political (indirect) pressures. In Haryana, for instance, illiteracy, *purdah,* lack of training and the male-oriented running of the meetings (e.g., often in the evening, at the home of the male *sarpanch,* amidst alcohol), not to mention the 'proxy- quality'—that is, the fact that, 'some women were merely putup as conduits for their husbands' indirect role in the panchayat— often prevent women members from speaking up or even attending the meeting.[11] Their husbands, instead, take on their responsibility for them. The political climate that prevails in some village—characterized by lack of unity, corruption, an incapacitated/fundless panchayat, and a heavily controlling bureaucracy, for instance—also prevents women's effective participation, even if they do go to meetings. In such an environment, women either get caught up in the conflicts themselves or their participation is moot.[12] They themselves also fail to see their own capability or that of the panchayat. Their male colleagues as well as the other villagers have an equally nonchalant and disillusioned view. And in general, if villagers have an unfavourable view of the panchayat, they usually do not see women's role in it as particularly useful. This only entrenches an already chauvinistic view, that women have no place in the panchayat, that on the whole, they are not capable of its demands.

The constraints women *panchas* have face (lack of confidence, experience, support and legitimacy in the eyes of the villagers) are entrenched within the society of each particular village. A top-down approach to activating the panchayat (through a law) without a bottomup component (on the ground discussion), however, exacerbates them. Various interests—politically ambitious male relatives or political parties, for instance—can use that law, then, for their own purposes. It is therefore, critical to embrace that bottomup aspect. An example of one village particularly successful in social mobilization efforts demonstrates how important that aspect can be, and how to improve women's participation in the panchayat can grow and learn from it.

The Panchayat and the Self-Help Group (SHG): the Case of Kalva Village[13]

If we are concerned about helping women's participation in the panchayat grow into its potential, then we must address its relation to another important forum for women at the local level—the Self-Help Group. A forum of between 8-15 women formed for purposes of micro-credit and income generating activities, the SHG usually has its goal economic and social empowerment of women. It is usually formed with the help of development NGOs and aims to have long-term effects on community development as well as women's empowerment, Looking critically at the relation between the SHG and the provision for women in the panchayat can illuminate what is necessary to make women's political participation effective and what forces are informing and reshaping that participation. First, I will look at how social mobilization efforts do (or do not) have an effect on political participation, by focusing on the case of Kalva village in Andhra Pradesh. Second, I will look at how the lessons of SHG formation can be applied to methods designed to improve women's position in the panchayat.

The lessons of the SHG experience for women's participation in the panchayat are, in some ways, rather obvious. If women are empowered economically and organized into groups, they are more likely to make more confident elected representatives. They are also more likely to hold their elected panchayat more responsible for its decisions. While thoroughly examining and analyzing such impact is beyond the scope of this study, it is worth recounting the experience of one village to illustrate the connections between women's civil society participation and their formal political role.

Kalva village, in Kurnool district, Andhra Pradesh, has gained particular fame for the social mobilization efforts of its women. Motivated by United Nation Development Programme project officer, Vijaya Bharati, over 300 women in this largely Muslim village are participating in SHGs of 10-15 members each. They meet and pool their savings every week, and have formed a larger, collective organization they call 'Proddu', which addresses larger loan grants, social issues and village development initiatives. Under the initial guidance of 'Vijaya Madam', these women identified and addressed the need for: an *ammawadi* for the children of working mothers (although there were already two government initiated anganwadis in the village, these were too far for many SC families living on the outskirts of the village); monetary relief and housing for destitute widows; organizing adolescent girls against child marriage; cleaning of a village irrigation canal (for this they contributed their own physical labour and were successful in their efforts, much to the disbelief of their male relatives). While these were all efforts an active panchayat might normally undertake, these women collectively agreed and undertook the works independently of any formal authority. In addition, they were able to change the attitudes of the village men from ridicule and resistance (sometimes physical) to respect and appreciation. The kalva men now speak of Proddu with praise and admiration. In fact, groups of men, inspired by Proddu's success, have also decided to form small savings/loan groups and have approached the women for advice on how to proceed. Some village have also been inspired to consider how to improve village public spaces. There has begun to appear in Kalva an atmosphere of possibility, responsibility and collectivity regarding uplift of the village, as if the spirit of the place had been revived.[14]

Effect on Women's Participation in the Panchayat: The Importance of Process

How does Proddu's success affect women's participation in the panchayat? The achievement of the Kalva women through Proddu portends their future participation in formal public affairs. The fact that the women have now had experience in doing social work (that is, work for the collective good and not for the family), dealing with block/district-level bureaucracy and upsetting resistance from the local men, means that they are prepared to undertake future task in village development. If any of them becomes a panchayat member in the future, she not only will bring with her personal qualities like experience, confidence and a heightened sense of social responsibility, but also is equipped with a support base in the form of Proddu and legitimacy in the eyes of the rest of the village—important tools for any public figure. In Kalva, the emergence of dedicated leadership among individual Proddu women is already visible. Vijaya Bharati, identifying their talent, has encouraged and developed it by having them train women in other villages and by taking them to various conferences, where they can represent Proddu.[15] These women—articulate, dedicated and popular—will, in a few years, certainly come to the fore of the village panchayat.

However, Proddu, is more than just a breeding ground for emergent leadership. There is a second, indirect, way which the social mobilization inherent in Proddu will affect women's participation in the panchayat—that is, via its effect on the *gram sabha*. Being a space where women come to recognize the power of collectivity and collective action, Proddu is, in fact, one aspect of a revitalized *gram sabha*, that collective body of villagers that holds its decision and policy-makers accountable and that actively participates in the implementation of policy. Proddu is itself something of a *gram sabha*, in that it is already a forum, where women are responding to and becoming involved in affairs of the village. It is also, through its positive influence on the mentality/consciousness of the other villager, a precursor to a much larger, formal village organization, including both men and women.[16] Such a village-wide, participatory *gram sabha* would be critical for a transparent, accountable panchayat and could be particularly helpful for the women *panches*. For, not only would qualified women candidates be supported: the more accountable and open the panchayat is required to be, the more likely just procedures will be carried out, in which women have an equal part.

The thing to note about this politicization is that it is, as in the paradigm articulated by Chambers, process-oriented, constantly evolving and influenced by other forces—including the process of SHG/Proddu-formation itself. None of the Proddu women is coming up into the panchayat on the basis of interest and competence immediately; it may take a few years for them to feel that they are in a position to contest (although, with the reservation, they may do so earlier). Also, their effective entry into the public realm is informed not only by the women's own confidence and competence, but also by the support given by the women and men of the village. Training a few women for positions of leadership without at the same time raising the consciousness of the women to support them, or the village men to realize their worth, would be fruitless, no matter how gifted those few women were to begin with. This is evidenced by the example of a woman *panch* in Ratgal,

Haryana, who, strong enough to contest the panchayat elections despite domestic resistance, soon became disillusioned by the local politics she faced in the panchayat and lacking real, widespread support from either a group of women or men, became just as ineffective as the others.[17]

Evidence in Kalva itself points of the fact that SHG-formation does not immediately or automatically mean inevitable change in the nature of women's claim in the panchayat. One would, perhaps, imagine that the women of the panchayat, though not necessarily 'enlightened' at the time of election, would be inspired by the work of Proddu and take on a new attitude towards their role in the panchayat—a 'can-do' attitude along with an attitude of solidarity with Proddu. This was not so in Kalva. The women of the panchayat were not necessarily forward-looking, despite the presence of Proddu. One of the women wanted nothing to do with Proddu, though she claimed to appreciate and admire the work it was doing. She also appeared to have had no change in attitude toward her role in the panchayat. She continued only to be the conduit for her husband's participation. The connection between the outcomes of Proddu—women's increased role in public affairs—and the purpose of the reservation were lost on her.[18] Clearly, the influence of her husband (as well as, probably, her own lack of confidence, interest and knowledge regarding public affairs) was a much stronger pull than the power of Proddu's example.

The case of Kalva's *sarpanch* is another example of the influence of forces working counter to Proddu's progress, of the fact that SHG-formation cannot immediately change the nature of women's role in the panchayat. Kalva's *sarpanch*, Fatima Bi, though motivated to fulfil her *sarpanch* duties after attending a training workshop at the behest of Vijaya Bharati, was none the better for Proddu, though the women called her several times to attend meetings and be involved in their work. Certainly, she undertook certain development activities in the village like building a new concrete road, fixing a water tank and expanding the school, commendable activities for a woman who had before sat behind *purdah* within the confines of her house. And she may have felt a push from the existence of Proddu, as certain women leaders of the organization did approach her and demand that she start acting like a *sarpanch*. However, Fatima Bi never consulted the women of Proddu regarding the development activities that she decided to undertake. She never asked for their input or their feedback. Despite Vijaya Bharati's urging, she never made transparent the account records of the panchayat and instead confined all public expenditure discussion to her family. She did, in fact, once or twice attempt to bar the efforts of Proddu. In general, though she has claimed much of Proddu's credit as her own, she has not cooperated and participated in Proddu work, much less done anything to promote or enhance it as a *sarpanch*.[19] In this case, personality (as well, perhaps, as family loyalties), has kept her from being the kind of visionary *sarpanch* one would have hoped, she could become with the support of an organization like Proddu and from creating the kind of link between the informal civil society institution of Proddu and the formal government institution of the panchayat that is potential of social mobilization.

It is difficult to tell exactly how much family pressures, rather than their own shortcomings, were preventing the above two women representatives from interacting with Proddu in a productive way. Certainly, family had overwhelming influence in motivating them to take up the position. Partly because of this, their position on the panchayat has much less to do with an individually felt desire to do something for the village and particularly for the women; it is much more connected to family obligation. These women, as members of the panchayat, still identify first and foremost with their husbands and their families, not with Proddu as a women's organization (though the *sarpanch* Fatima Bi is herself a member of an SHG), nor with the village as an entity. The key to Proddu and the SHGs in Kalva is that they begin to shift these identities and loyalties. They offer women a public identity that is not contingent upon family, but rather upon solidarity with other women (as individuals who experience similar problems to one's own). Such shift in identity has to do both with Proddu's process of formation and its structure. A look at the process of formation first shows why Proddu has been so effective at politicizing the Kalva women.

Perhaps the single most important factor in the formation of the SHG/Proddu, was the role of Vijaya Bharati, UNDP Project Officer and motivator from the outside. If we are considering effective politicization as a process that is ever fluid and influenced by the interaction between many forces, then this force can be considered as catalyst. Vijaya Bharati took months, going door-to-door in Kalva, addressing the needs and problems of the women, gaining their trust and becoming a confidante. As she herself describes it, she 'nurtured' the women in order to help them build up their own self-confidence. She was the probe, the gadfly, constantly guiding the women to fix their own problems through questioning and organization.[20] Significantly, she approached the women one-on-one, as individuals, not via family; at the same time she encouraged them to see the power of group organization. She thereby introduced to the women the possibility of another identity and loyalty.

Equally important to the motivational methods Vijaya Bharati employed were the methods of group formation she used. A United Nations International Children's Emergency Fund (UNICEF) report on SHGs in Madhya Pradesh has concluded that "participatory structures and procedures need to be developed that can be handled and managed effectively by the women themselves.... An indigenous leadership needs to emerge from the process of organizing and reflecting, to carry further the organizational tasks in the community".[21] Concurrently, Vijaya Bharati trained the women to hold certain rules for SHG formation and management that would promote commitment, participation and independent leadership: socio-economically homogeneous groups; Rs 30 saved per member, per month and weekly meetings; a leader selected by the members. But the credit activities of the SHGs, as she saw it, were merely a 'thread', keeping the groups together. The real purpose behind the organization was social mobilization.[22] To that end, the village level federation of SHGs (Proddu) that was suggested by her and formed by the women, provides the greatest demonstration of Kalva's success. For it is the amalgamation of the twenty or so SHGs that gives Kalva women their strength and solidarity, their bargaining power *vis-a-vis* the men in the village as well as the bureaucracy outside.

In fact, both the SHG and the Proddu groups point to another important aspect of Proddu's successful politicization of women: besides the process of formation, the structure itself. The process and the structure work in conjunction, in fact; the structure can be said to flow as a natural outcome of the process. The SHG, formed in its characteristic bottomup way, offers women a chance to come out of the house as individuals and be part of an alternative organization. In emphasizing the importance of group dynamics, communication and equality between members, the SHG shuns hierarchy and stagnancy. It encourages all women to participate and speak up assertively on their own behalf as well as on the behalf of others in need. With its self-help philosophy, it offers the women an alternative identity—not as 'wives' or 'mothers', SHG but as women who draw on experiences of being wives and mothers, women as economic subjects, women who are also citizens of the village and are concerned about it. The panchayat, because of its hierarchical pattern and lack of empowering space for women, cannot offer such an alternative identity, although it, too, offers a public identity. In its present form and idea, it parallels, rather than gives an alternative to the family. The power in the SHG/Proddu model in Kalva is its potential effect on that panchayat structure. In fact, by applying the lessons of Kalva's social mobilization (including shift in identity, the vigilant and socially conscious Proddu and also the changed attitude among the village men) to the process of improving women's role in panchayat, the panchayat may itself be able to change from a hierarchical, elitist structure to a diverse, participatory one.

Applying the Lessons of Kalva to the Panchayat

Apart from the gradual effect social mobilization is likely to have on women's public participation, how can the example of Kalva's Proddu be applied to the process of improving women's claim in the panchayat? If we are talking about holistically changing the nature of that position from one which is passive, dependent on husbands/family and dismissed by much of the village, there are four things to keep in mind: the motivation of the women, networking, involvement of the village and redefining (thereby transforming) the panchayat in the minds of the villagers.

First, the SHG experience, particularly in Kalva, shows that the role of the outsider as catalyst is crucial. How that an outsider interacts with the villagers is especially important. Vijaya Bharati showed that raising the political consciousness of individual women is effectively done with individual, prolonged interaction and often on a one-to-one basis. This applies as much to elected women representatives as to women forming micro-credit groups. The women must be given an idea of their role as individuals in the public service, not as conduits of their families. Agencies (particularly non-governmental organizations) working to improve women's participation in the panchayat should therefore move beyond simple, one-time training programmes to embrace a more interactive and participatory approach to preparing women members for their roles. This includes going to the village itself, meeting the women 'on their own ground', engaging them in a dialogue, all over a prolonged period of time. Where organizations are working on such participatory techniques,[23] they have generally adopted one or more of these tactics, but not all.

The second lesson that efforts to improve women's participation in the panchayat can take from the experience of Kalva and SHGs in general is the importance of networking. In Kalva, no single SHG could have undertaken the work that Proddu undertook as a collective of over 300 women. It could neither have had the widespread effect on the attitude of the men of the village, nor been so successful in the work. It may not have been able to mobilize the courage of its individual members, either. (Lone SHGs in other villages, made up of a total of 20-40 women, are sometimes able to undertake village development work. These, however, are generally not able to mobilize the support of the majority of the village women and generally confine themselves to work they can do in the specific area of their members' residence.)[24, 25] Networking women panchayat members is especially important because of their small number per village. Networking can give otherwise isolated women representatives a feeling of collective strength and expose them to the experiences (similar to their own) of women *panches* in other places, making them feel they are not alone. It can also, like the SHG/Proddu, offer previously home and village-bound women an opportunity to come out of the house and village and form an identity with an alternative forum.[26] Participating in this forum can also give them the bargaining power (as, say, a lobbying group) *vis-a-vis* bureaucracy and other sectors that they would not enjoy as individual woman panchayat member.[27]

Applying the lessons of Kalva, agencies should, thirdly, focus on raising the consciousness of the rest of the villagers. In Kalva, women were indeed able to undertake development activities without the active support of their menfolk; however, they were working collectively, not individually. Evidence in other villages shows that an individual woman often succeeds in a traditional and repressive environment when at least one 'enlightened' male family member offers space and leniency.[28] The attitude of the men is therefore important. In Kalva. once the men began to appreciate Proddu's work and cooperate, women's public participation became legitimate; the entire village then came into a better position to move forward, plan for its own uplift, through a sense of self-help and collectivity. In villages where social mobilization may be slow to effect such an attitude change towards women's public entry, the outsider can act as catalytic agent. My own experience as a researcher interacting with a group of men in Ratgal village, Haryana, revealed that an outsider working through dialogue (not one-way training sessions) can prod previously held assumptions about women, make men articulate and own their views, make them realize that they themselves are complicit in gender oppression.[29] While mindsets cannot be immediately changed, such two-way dialogue can generate active thought that can be continued in the future.

Involving non-panchayat villagers (particularly men) in consciousness-raising serves another important purpose: beginning to redefine the idea of the panchayat as an institution of participatory local governance (and at the same time, 'energizing' the gram sabha).[30] This is possibly the most prescient lesson of the SHG experience. The SHG is successful in raising a level of social and political awareness among the women partly, because it offers a space for women to participate as equal individuals and in this participatory way, discuss issues of concern to the village itself. The panchayat at the moment does not offer an empowering space. It is an old institution, entrenched in ideas of elitism, hierarchy/patriarchy and stagnancy. In order for women to participate effectively, the accepted notion of the panchayat, both among the panchayat members and in the village as a whole, must change. It must be redefined in the village psyche as a democratic, dynamic and diverse institutions whose existence is not a given, but dependent on the input and wishes of the villagers. In the most democratic way, it is what its constituents make of it. In such a transformed forum, women's voices can come out and be heard. For such a redefinition to occur, however, trainers or implementing agencies interested in improving women's political participation must interact with all the villagers, at varying levels and to varying degrees, discussing with them in dialogue the purpose of democracy and their own role in promoting the uplift of the village. Villagers should also be encouraged to discuss such things with each other, in order to shape the most effective representative institution for their needs.[31] Besides changing the notion of the panchayat to make it more conducive to women's participation, this would be the beginning of a vibrant *gram sabha* that, if it served its purpose, would hold its elected members accountable and support them in undertaking the work of the village. Besides being important in its own right, such a *gram sabha* would also support women elected representatives, as mentioned above.[32]

To undertake such a process of changing the concept of the village panchayat as part of the process of improving women's participation in the panchayat is to recognize the inter-connectedness of the various institutions and phenomena at work in the village, the fact that no one of them works in isolation, but is constantly affecting and being affected by the others. To recognize this is to begin to break down old assumptions, old hierarchies and open a space for women's effective participation in the *gram* panchayat.

Conclusion

Women's role in local governance is thus itself a shifting and evolving phenomenon. The affirmative action nature of the 33 per cent reservation is, in the terminology of Chambers, a move toward 'reversal', that is, reversal of power relations an attempt to change the status of here to fore disempowered 'lowers'. With the cultural history of India being what it is and political parties slow to allow effective participation of women, such reservation may be necessary to allow women entry into public affairs.[33] The 73rd Amendment, however, is only a framework, only a rule. It should be seen as a factor triggering a process of change and undertaken in a variety of ways, all locally based. In that case, the process of empowerment and capacity building that occurs 'from the bottomup' is critical. This process includes not only focusing on the formal institution of the *gram* panchayat, but also focusing on informal institutions like the SHG. It means recognizing the interaction between the formal and the informal as well as the important role of all the villagers in the development and functioning of village affairs. Working sometimes in collaboration, sometimes in dialectical fashion, the village institutions together can achieve a transformed panchayat and effective participation of its women members—the sort of participatory and non-hierarchical governance envisioned by the 73rd Amendment's reservation and by the paradigm articulated by Chambers. That would not only be redefining women's role in public planning and politics, but also redefining the panchayat and thereby, the nature of local democracy. That indeed would be the breaking of a new high ground.

NOTES

Sandhya Gupta is a 1998-99 American Fulbright Scholar to India studying Women's Participation in Panchayati Raj. She has completed her AB from Princeton University, in Princeton, New Jersey. The original version of this paper was presented at a seminar on Women' Studies organized by the Mumbai office of the United States Education Foundation in India, 27 April 1999.

REFERENCES

1. Robert Chambers, *Whose Reality Counts: Putting the first last*, London: Intermediate Technology Publications (1997), p. 188.
2. *Ibid.*, p. 195.
3. While this is in line with post-modernist thinking, it is not really a new idea; Gandhi, for instance, had a similar idea of 'village republics'. See M.K. Gandhi, *Panchayati Raj*, Ahmedabad: Navajivanor Publishing House, (compiled 1959). Gandhi also articulated his vision for an India of self-governing villages in *Village Swaraj* and *Constructive Programme*. It may even be possible to extrapolate such philosophy from Hindu scripture. For a discussion of the political philosophy of the *Bhagavad Gita*, for instance, see Satya P. Agarwal, *The Social Role of the Gita*, Delhi:

Motilal Banarsidass, (1993), or A.V. Rathna Reddy, *The Political Philosophy of the Gita*, New Delhi: Sterling Paperbacks, (1997).

4. Eleventh Schedule (Article 243G), *The Constitution 73rd Amendment Act, 1992*.

5. The argument can be made, however, that regardless of what was written in the act, villagers could have gotten together to discuss such responsibilities themselves. But it does not seem that, anyone was there to facilitate such a thing, or to motivate the villagers to see such a thing as important. That is, the idea of the panchayat had not changed.

6. For discussion on the effect on this in Haryana, see Mahi Pal, 'Centralized Decentralization: Haryana Panchayati Raj Act, 1994', *Economic and Political Weekly*, (July 16, 1994), pp. 1842-44.

7. Chambers, (1997), p. 205.

8. 'Lowers' is the term Chambers uses to denote people who in a particular context are subordinate to others.

9. Mukta Banerjee, in her article 'Women in Local Governance: Macro Myths, Micro Realities', *Social Change*, (March, 1998), pp. 87-100, does a particularly nice job of demonstrating how divergent the experiences can be by presenting four case, studies of diverse women in diverse circumstances.

10. See, for instance, Multiple Action Research Group (MARG), *They Call me Member Sahib*, (1998), Ekatra, *Women in Panchayati Raj in Madhya Pradesh and Rajasthan*, (1997), Susheela Kaushik, *A Study of Panchayati Raj in Haryana*, (1998).

11. Personal observation and interviews with members of Chhapra and Ratgal villages, Haryana, January, 1999.

12. *Ibid*.

13. All information obtained about Kalva was through: personal observation and interviews with Kalva villagers, including the *Sarpanch* and other panchayat members, conversations with Vijaya Bharati, conversations with UNDP officer K. Raju, newspaper clippings on Kalva and a UNDP (unpublished) report put out on Kalva. Where there is no citation, the source is one or a combination of these. I have found it easier on the reader to state this at this point rather than cite every other sentence.

14. Personal observation and communication with a range of Kalva villagers.

15. personal communication with Vijaya Bharati and Zubeida Bi, a Kalva woman active in Proddu.

16. SHGs, in general, seem to help build up more effective *gram sabha* by increasing the managing and questioning capacity of previously marginalized members of the village.

17. Interview with woman *Panch*, Ratgal, Haryana, January, 1999.

18. Personal observation and interview with woman *panch*, Kalva, March, 1999.

19. Personal observation, interview with Fatima Bi, personal communication with Vijaya Bharati, Zubeida Bi, and the women of two SHGs in Kalva, March, 1999.

20. For instance, she trained the women to themselves undertake a survey of the village to assess how many destitute widows there were.

21. UNICEF, *Self-Help Groups in Madhya Pradesh*, (1997), p. 47.

22. The report also contends that the groups should be formed for more than just credit purposes.

23. For instance, the Institute of Social Studies Trust (ISST) in Bangalore makes a point of carrying out three days participatory/interactive training for women members in the village itself, but the organization has been weak on followup. As a consequence, it is not clear whether the women members are able to sustain the kind of motivation they receive during the initial training.

24. The experience of Village Action Group, in Auroville, Tamil Nadu and of Mahila Samakhya, Karnataka, both organizations attempting to organize women on the basis of social action (and not micro-credit) first, speak to this.

25. Extensive research done by Sangeetha Purushothaman on grassroots women's movements in Maharashtra also points to the effectiveness of networking in accessing government resources. See Sangeetha Purushothaman, *The Empowerment of Women in India*, New Delhi: Sage Publications, (1998).

26. One organization in Bangalore called Search has undertaken such networking; it has organized 'conventions' for women *panches* representing twelve Karnataka districts (and including other prominent women, like SHG leaders). The results have been favourable, with women articulating a heightened sense of confidence, responsibility and commitment to the work of women and the village. Search has been careful enough in their facilitator role to allow the women themselves to organize and run the next convention.

27. If we are acknowledging the importance of women's organization in raising the confidence and political consciousness of women, particularly for future political participation in the formal sphere, then one lesson to come out of Kalva may be to organize women into groups for that specific purpose alone. This is certainly one possible lesson, but I have chosen not to elaborate on it. However, the idea has been taken up by at least one NGO—Sayahi in Kerala. As part of Sahayi's efforts to build the capacity of future elected women representatives (and in general to make the women more informed members of the *gram sabha*) it is motivating groups of women to form on the basis of political mobilization.

28. The case of the first Mahila Mandal leader in Ratgal, for instance, who was supported by her husband to head the groups, but had to sneak comrades to meetings secretly because their husbands were more resistant.

29. For a bit more elaboration on this particular instance, see my article, 'Panchayats as Vehicles of Participatory Democracy', *Politics India*, (April, 1999), pp. 13-14.

30. *'Energizing the Gram Sabha'* is a term used by Tapas Datta, UNICEF Delhi (personal communication, 4th April, 1999), to describe motivating the village as an integral part of building the capacity of the *gram* panchayat.

31. One method to be considered in (PRA), Participatory Rural Appraisal—adapting it for discussions on the panchayat and governance. For an explanation and discussion of PRA, see Robert Chambers, *Whose Reality Counts: Putting the First Last*, London: Intermediate Technology Publications, (1997).

32. However, such a group would have to be truly inclusive of both men and women; if only a group of men, it could also potentially try to sabotage the work of women.

33. For discussion on the failure of political parties to effectively incorporate women, see Abhilasha Kumari and Sabina Kidwai, *Crossing the Sacred Line*, New Delhi: Orient Longman, (1998).

9

ISLAMIC FUNDAMENTALISM AND WOMEN IN PAKISTAN

Uma Singh

Both in India and Pakistan, there has emerged a vast corpus of literature on gender location and construction. Particularly, in Pakistan, much of the debate on gender has revolved around what has been termed as Islamic resurgence or fundamentalism. The concrete reasons for this explanation lie in the basic ideology on the basis of which Pakistan came into being in 1947 and the issue of gender in an independent Pakistan cannot be understood apart from struggles over the state. Immediately after independence, Pakistan had to deal with establishment of a state machinery, constitution, foreign exchange shortage, weak infrastructure and lastly resettlement of refugees, who had migrated to Pakistan at a tremendous material and personal cost. The first two and last two factors had far-reaching implications for women in Pakistan. The question most pertinent facing the ruling elite was as to how Pakistan's Muslimness or its identity as distinct from a common Indian culture was to be expressed and concretized. Further compounding the problem was the fact that, some ulama (Muslim religious scholars and teachers concerned primarily with Islamic laws) who had been staunch opponents of the idea of Pakistan including Maulana Maudoodi, later migrated to Pakistan and were demanding the construction of Pakistan as an Islamic state. During Jinnah's lifetime this took the form of a nod to Pakistan's Muslim heritage, through the official inclusion of the term in referring to the state. Immediately after his death, Liaquat Ali formulated the Objective Resolutions of 1949, which sought simultaneously to appease the population by promising that Pakistan would be a democratic state, in which minority rights would be guaranteed and one in which, "all Muslims would be able to build their life in accordance with the teachings and injunctions of Islam". Ulama were employed as advisors to the legislatures. Islam was made the state religion and gradually the role of the Council of Islamic Ideology was strengthened. Rather than go directly to the people for support, those in power decided to use religious ideology as a political crutch, whereby, they could garner support. The roots were thus, laid for theocracy rather than democracy. Once again, Pakistan's religious leadership was by no means united. Individuals like Ghulam Ahmad Parwiz and Maulana Shabbir Ahmed supported and provided theological justifications for Pakistan's credentials. Others including Maulana Maudoodi initially opposed it. All agreed, however, that Pakistan should have an Islamic 'Character', which meant giving primacy to particular (albeit divergent) interpretations of religious laws at the levels of the state. Indeed it was the Jamiat-ul Ulema-i-Islam that led the call for a formation of a Board of Talimat-i-Islamiya (Islamic teachings) a demand granted by the Constituent Assembly's Basic Principles Committee. This board recommended: "The Head of the State should be a Muslim with ultimate powers... government should be run by an elite of pious Muslims chosen for their piety by the Muslim electorate... the community of Ulema should decide what legislation was repugnant to the injunctions of Holy Quran and the Sunna and was therefore, invalid... a Legislative Assembly, which they identified with the Islamic... in fact, Arabian Shura or Tribal Consultative Assembly should be empowered to demand the resignation of the Head of State in certain circumstances".

These recommendations, although turned down are significant in terms of the politics of the time and of the struggle over state ideology and its institutional framework. Critical as well is the distinction between religious elements lately co-opted by the state and those who continued to oppose it. A schism arose within those adhering to a scripturalist position an Islam with Maudoodi and the Jamaat-i-Islami taking the most extreme positions. The fact remains that historically the struggle for women's rights in

Pakistan has been one of consistent opposition from the religious orthodoxy. Beginning in 1949, just after the country's creation, with the protest over the presence of two women parliamentarians in the Constituent Assembly of Pakistan, any movement for even, minimal rights for women has encountered opposition from these forces.

"The decade of the 1980s, has truly been a decade of women of Pakistan", wrote Hamza Alavi. His reference was to the women's resistance to Zia-ul-Haq's military regime and its proclaimed Islamic measure that in effect downgraded women. The eighties were significant for the crystallization of Anti-Women's Rights Movement in urban Pakistan, which strongly challenged on both religious and political grounds the government's so-called Islamization process. However, the same period also saw the entry of heavily veiled women on the public scene, who projected themselves as defenders of Islam and denounced those women questioning state initiated measures—a point, which will be elaborated later in the chapter.

Gender and class politics frame the current debate on women's role and position in Pakistani society. Essentially located in urban centers it has been a debate between obscurantist men from the lower middle class and the newly rich middle class with aspirations for political power and women's rights activists belonging to the professional middle and upper middle class. Initiated by men, the debate reflects, their perception of middle and upper class women as threats to the existing order. It has led to the politicization of gender, whereby, those advocating women's emancipation are viewed as modern and as such opposed to Islam. The debate manifested through opposition of women on the basis of religion remained marginal until 1977. Led by a small group of Ulema and Maulvis, dispersed over a number of religiously defined political parties, it failed to make much impact on the evolutionary process of women's emancipation. But it intensified after 1977, with the military government's use of religion to legitimize its rule. With the government's patronage with them, the position of male antagonists of women's rights was bolstered as were their efforts for cultural hegemony. The implementation of Hudood ordinances provided an additional avenue for expressing social and familial conflicts. The fact, that over 50 per cent of the cases appealed to the Federal Shariat Court (FSC), were overturned, warrants the conclusion that many cases filed are brought to the courts for the purpose of exerting social control alone. Added to the normal social control mechanisms available to them, parents, husbands and guardians have been empowered by the introduction of the Hudood ordinances with the real or implicit threat of bringing criminal charges against their children and wives. Finally the implementation of the Hudood ordinance has been disproportionately skewed towards Pakistan's lower socio-economic strata. Very few middle or upper class Pakistanis have been charged with the commission of Hudood crimes. Neither outcome is the fault of the courts nor of the laws, but rather is reflective of the inegalitarian structure of Pakistani society. Charles H. Kennedy in his study, "Islamization and Legal Reform in Pakistan, 1977-1987", has argued that Islamic reforms (Nizam-Mustafa) promulgated by General Zia-ul-Haq have had only a minor impact upon the legal, social and economic institutions of the state. This observation, definitely marks a departure from the conventional interpretation, because the politicization of the process of Islamization has played a very significant role in the political environment of Pakistan during the 1980s. Zias government perceived the reforms as leading Pakistan in the direction of becoming 'truly Islamic'. Opponents of the reforms argued that the reforms were reactionary, anti-democratic and discriminatory to women. Charles Kennedy in his study, further contends that it was just rhetoric and political noise with little significance, as they were very seldom implemented. The continued vitality and relevance of the Nizam-i-Mustafa despite its 'non- implementation' can be gauged from the fact, that none of the governments, since Zia's death have made any sincere effort to repeal these laws. The PPP election manifesto in the 1988, election pledged to eliminate inequitable practices by promising to become a signatory to the United Nations Convention on the Elimination of all Forms of Discrimination Against Women (a promise not kept); improve working conditions and prospects for women including the establishment of maternity leave (nothing was accomplished in this regard), repeal of all discriminatory laws against women (another broken promise), reform personal law to bring it in line with the demands of contemporary socio-economic realities (again a broken promise) and to take special measures to promote the literacy of women. Again, in this regard, except for foreign donor efforts not only could the PPP government achieve any success towards promoting literacy, it had not even, made any significant effort in this direction. In 1988-89, groups such as the Women's Action Forum (WAF), Pakistan Women lawyers Association (PWLA) and a transformed All Pakistan Women's Association (APWA), lobbied the state to introduce new laws, which would empower women. Within few months of the PPP coming to power, however, they became disillusioned as they realized they were still fighting an uphold battle.

While Benazir's government had been able to prevent the implementation of the Ninth Amendment and the Shariat Bill during its tenure, it was less successful in its attempts to repeal some of the earlier legislation passed during Marital Law, owing to the Eighth Amendment restrictions introduced in 1985, by Gen. Zia. Importantly, while the platform on which the PPP had won favoured women's empowerment, most members of the provincial and national assemblies remained entrenched in patriarchal views on women's place in society. However, Benazir government took some steps for empowering women by releasing Report of the Pakistan Commission on the 'status of women', fulfilling her promise that Pakistan would become a signatory to the United Nation's Convention on the Elimination of all Forms of Discrimination Against Women and ensuring the continued reservation seats for women in Parliament, which had expired in 1988, though none of these were finally taken.

The existence of sharp gender disparities in access to resources is usually attributed to cultural and social constraints on women's mobility. A patriarchal system continues to prevail in Pakistan, giving males power over females through control of property and household income. Rigid cultural precepts separate the sphere of activity of men and women. The typical division allocated roles within the household to women and those outside the home to men. The cultural restraints imposed on women vary considerably by ethnicity and class. In terms of ethnic group, for example, Pathans, who live mostly in the North-West frontier province and Baluchis tend to observe a more rigid division of labour between the sexes than any other groups and to impose greater social restrictions on women. In general, however, women in the upper echelons of society do have considerable access to education and to modern sector jobs. In some way, such women have more in common with their counterparts in the developed countries than with women from the rural areas of Pakistan. An example of this distinction can be provided with an illustration of national elections held in October 1993. The federal government had mandated separate polling stations for women, throughout the country. In cities like Lahore, Rawalpindi and Faisalabad, this was apparently enforced and women exercised the right to vote. But, elsewhere, local officials took it upon themselves to assume that women would not come to vote and the separate booths were not set up. Anita Weiss, an expert on gender studies witnessed this phenomenon, while observing the election in District Pishin in the province of Balochistan. This district is inhabited largely by Pushtun tribesmen who conform to rigid codes of conduct particularly concerning gender relations. Women observe strict Purdah. The psychological state of women themselves was more pathetic then the lack of polling stations. The blank looks on their faces underscored the lack of involvement with domains outside their homes. In every instance when she spoke with a woman, waiting to vote, she invariably related that she had been brought to the polling station by a man in her family (usually a brother or father, occasionally a husband), because he wanted additional votes cast for a particular candidate. In District Pishin women's identity card, necessary to show before being allowed to cast one's ballot, had no picture nor the woman's own name on them, in deference to local concerns regarding female seclusion. Many of the women, she observed trying to cast their votes, even did not know the names of their fathers or husbands as they used honorific terms to address them at homes. Those who could not state the name of their father or husband as listed on the identity cards were not allowed to vote. Thus, these women were not exercising their own electoral franchise, but rather being provided another ballot to be cast for the choice of their family's men. Women's conventionally limited access to anything or anyone outside their kin group, underscored by their lack of access to education and related process that enable them to gain an understanding of the ways in which external events have an effect in their lives as the status of women virtually deny them their suffrage in a democratic election. This, of course, is a larger issue that is related both to literacy and economic transformation. This example is indicative of the degree to which many women in Pakistan live very differently and certainly in an inferior legal, social and economic status from men. This also illustrates credible evidence about sex discrimination and deep rooted social prejudices against women. There is a wide gulf between what is prescribed by religion for the protection of woman and what she gets in practice.

While about four-fifth of the rural women participate in farm activities, such as binding of wheat sheaves, thrashing, or cleaning of grains and they are usually reported as non-working members of the household. In the usual census and labour force survey data, about 5 to 10 per cent of the women are reported to be members of the civilian labour force. One reason for such underestimation by respondents, particularly males is that the Pakistani culture defines the role of the man as the prime bread- winner and provider of food and shelter. One other factor, that seems to have a strong negative association with work participation is the practice of Purdah the (the seclusion of women). There is a major conflict between norms prescribed by the Islamic Religion and cultural deviations from these norms. Cultural deviations are not uniform across the whole country. They vary by such factors as the socio-economic status of the family in which a woman is born and lives, the rural urban setting, caste group, etc. Regional group studies aimed at redefining the roles and status of women need to take these conflicts and the patterns of deviation into account. Table 1 illustrates some situation in which the actual norms and behaviour differ or even, contradict the prescribed norms (they are taught by Islam) because in the present day emphasis on revitalization of the Islamic way of life in Pakistan, it is important to understand the discrepancies, between the Islamic prescriptions about women's role and status and the actual situation.

Table 1
Conflicting Prescriptions, Values and Perceptions for Seven Roles of Pakistani Women

Role	*Prescriptions (Islamic)*	*Values*	*Perceptions (actual behaviour)*
Parental role	1. A woman must be paid *haq mehr* before divorce. 2. If infants/young children are to be cared for by the woman, then father must provide compensation/maintenance to her.	In many cases the family of the divorced woman considers the demand for maintenance to be below their dignity.	Few divorced women are actually provided maintenance for themselves and their children.
Occupational role	A woman has the right to do work other than housekeeping.	Female work beyond household work is generally perceived as status reducing and thus, not a preferred role.	According to census data, only 5 per cent to 10 per cent of the women aged 10 + are in labour force. Female work is under reported because of the negative value it generally carries.
Conjugal role	A woman has the right to divorce her husband under specified circumstances.	Divorce for a female is considered shameful. Some women spend their entire lives in a separated state rather than sue for divorce.	Divorce is strongly discouraged. Less than 1 per cent of female are reported to be divorced at any age.

**Haq mehr* refers to the dowry, that a husband agrees to pay the wife at the time the marriage is contracted.

Table 1 Continued

Role	*Prescriptions (Islamic)*	*Values*	*Perceptions (actual behaviour)*
Domestic role	A woman has the right to manage household matters and make the necessary decisions related to such matters.	In some cases, husbands or other family members actually control the finances as well as making decisions.	In cases, where women do not have any income of their own, they are completely dependent on their husband for sustenance.
Kin role	A mother-in-law and daughter-in-law should treat each other with affection and respect.	In many cases, the daughter-in-law is expected to give unconditional obedience, while the exportations about reciprocation from mother-in-law are less rigid.	Quarrels between mother-in-law and daughter-in-law are commonplace.
Community role	A woman has the right to appear as witness and express opinion on community-related developmental issues.	Cultural values strongly discourage the appearance of women in a court of law, as it is considered dishonourable.	Very few women actually appear as witnesses.

Table 1 Continued

Role	*Prescriptions (Islamic)*	*Values*	*Perceptions (actual behaviour)*
Individual role	A woman has the right to receive education; own and dispose of property and approve/disapprove the mate chosen for her.	Some girls believe they are not smart enough to receive education; parents in some cases discourage education and have lower aspirations for the education of daughters than for sons.	Only 11 per cent of the Pakistani women aged 10 + are literate; less than half of the urban; and one-tenth of the rural school age girls are in school.

Despite some progress in the past decades Pakistan's performance in the area of female education, as reflected in literacy and enrolment rate remains extremely poor. Over two decades the primary school enrolment rate for boys rose, gradually from 59 per cent in 1985 to 61 per cent in 1985, while the rate for girls increased from 20 to 32 per cent. At the secondary school level the gender gap is considerably wider as reflected in the 1985, ratio of 34 females per 100 males. The female drop-out rate at the primary level is as high as 50-60 per cent. Gender disparities in school attendance vary widely by province and area of residence. They tend moreover to be greatest in rural parts of the country where female enrolment rates are particularly low. According to data from the 1981 Census, the relative difference between males and females in rural areas was lowest in Punjab, but much larger in other provinces, particularly the NWFP. Even, in Punjab only three per cent of rural girls in the relevant age groups were enrolled in secondary school, while elsewhere, the comparable enrolment rates were about one per cent. The 1991 Census indictates that 72 per cent of the population of Pakistan resided in rural areas a fact that should be taken into account while considering the implications of these extremely low female enrolment rates. The large gender gap in schooling in rural areas has been attributed to lack of appropriate facilities for girls and in particular, to the non-availability of female teachers. Given the cultural restrictions that hold in various degrees across all regions, segregated schools with female teachers are an important prerequisite to make female education more acceptable. Where financial resources are limited, there is usually greater economic pressure to educate sons, since schooling would lead to better employment prospects for them. Daughters are expected to stay at home rather than to seek jobs. The outcome is that in Pakistan, only a small elite ordinarily from urban areas provide their daughters with the opportunity to acquire higher education. Women belonging to professional classes of the dominant elite have over the years managed to expand themselves and present a dilemma to men. These women have also ventured the spheres of activity considered to be solely male dominated—they are in politics, engineering, town planning, banking and computer programming and are as competent as men in their work. This explains why the discourse in Pakistan over women's rights and their position in society has been between 'fundamentalist' men and 'non-fundamentalist' women. This perceived threat has become an imminent reality with spiralling inflation and what Hamza Alavi calls the, "crisis of the middle and lower middle class household economy". While for the poor sections of society the division between the male-female space of operation is blurred, because of the exigencies of survival (in rural areas in any case the agricultural economy cannot be sustained without joint inputs of male and female members of the household) for the urban lower and middle classes, it presents a major problem. Both men and women are placed under stress. Men have to cope with the sense of failure emanating from the inability to fulfil their primary responsibility and the concomitant psychological loss of masculinity, in other words, their identity. Women have to assume roles they are neither conditioned nor prepared coming from highly segregated cloistered households. They have to deal with an unfamiliar and often mixed environment as the 'outsider' in both alien and insecure world. They need a reassuring anchorage and religion provides this. Thus, if women join obscurantist fundamentalist movement, it is because the latter do respond to some of the women's needs and allay some insecurities.

This, however, is only partial explanation of 'fundamentalist' women visible in Pakistan today, a point, which has been briefly mentioned earlier. An important factor was the resistance to Zia's Islamization by women and women's organizations from the platform of Women's Action Forum (WAF). It appears that WAF's questioning of the distorted interpretation of Islam to justify legal measures, rejection of *Maulvis* as self-styled guardians of Islam and challenging of the patriarchal structures underlying subordination has had a greater impact than warranted by their numbers. The obscurantist have felt compelled to promote a vocal women's lobby of their own to counter WAF's activities. The Jamaat-i-Islami had responded in a similar manner in 1974- 75, when a group of left wing women students formed the Women's Front (WF) in Lahore's Punjab University. The WF was perhaps the first instance of feminist expression of women's rights, that questioned patriarchal norms. Within a short period, the Jamaat had set up a women's section of its students' wing. That was the first time that women students in the *burqa,* associated with 'fundamentalist' women made their appearance. The women students' section called Islami Jamiat Talebat is now a permanent subsidiary instrument of Jamiat-i-Islami. Its activists use aggressive strong arm tactics typical of the male students wing of the Jamaat-i-Islami (Jamiat-e-Tuleba) against liberal women students. The Islami Jamiat-e-Tuleba has the dubious distinction of introducing firearms in campus and using violence in student politics.

It was therefore, not a coincidence when Majlis-e-Khawateen, a women's organization unheard of before came out with press statements against the progressive women's demonstrators in Lahore protesting against the law of Evidence in 1983. That the Majlis has the support of Jamaat-i-Islami and the President herself became obvious over the years. Nisar Fatima, the President of Majlis was elected member of the National Assembly of 1985, on the reserved women's seat with Jamaat-i-Islami support. She was also nominated with Jamaat-i-Islami's support and nominated by Zia to the council of Islamic ideology (an advisory body responsible for examining existing laws for their Islamic content and proposing new laws), as well as the 1984, Commission on the Status of Women. The Commission was composed of 13 women and three men besides *ex-officio* members. Of the women at least ten belonged to the professional elite class. Despite hand- picked by a military government, the Commission came out with an excellent report on women's oppression. It examined the prevalent social and cultural norms, critically reviewed the proposed and promulgated Islamic laws concluding that the latter has been a setback to women. Nisar Fatima, the only 'fundamentalist' representative of the Commission wrote a dissenting note. Her basic disagreement was with the commission's perspective. For instance, she felt that the discussion on legal issues be undertaken by religious scholars only and that instead of demanding equal opportunities emphasis should have been on the importance of the family, responsibility of the male as earner, head of household and decision maker, women's place in the house as obedient wife and caring mother, strict segregation and women's exclusion from professions that do not need them. The unexpected candidness of the report and its obvious variance from the official policies resulted in it being shelved, the only part that received publicity was Nisar Fatima's dissenting note. In June 1990, *Khawateen Nifaz-e-Shariah Mahaz* (Women's Enforcement of Sharia Front) was formed with the blessings of the movers of the Sharia Bill following its adoption in the Senate in May 1990. A Nifaz-e-Shariat Conference was organized by the front in the same month, where 'fundamentalist' women rejected democracy as an imported ideology and made women's rights activists as well as the then Prime Minister Benazir Bhutto targets of its attack. Any action or statement of WAF or any non-fundamentalist women's organization had invited an immediate and vitriolic response from women of the religious right accusing the former of being westernized, alienated and non-religious.

The exploitation of Islam for political gains is not a new phenomenon in Pakistan. Successive rulers have repeatedly, used religion in an attempt to win political legitimacy and mobilize public support. But, such moves have never worked. Nawaz Sharif, like a true successor of Zia pursued the same retrogressive course, which served to fuel religious fanaticism. Religious minorities feel that with the enforcement, of the shariat laws, they would become the targets of widespread discrimination and persecution. The worst dangerous aspect of the government's. Islamization policy is that it could fuel religious fanaticism and sectarian conflict, which will further fragment the social fabric. Women's right's organization and minorities particularly have vehemently opposed the Shariah Bill.

Now, it remains to be seen what is the new dictator Purwez Musharref's policy on religious freedom in the country. However there is little likelyhood of soft peddling on religious matters by Musharref, since he is closely associated with different religious fundamentalist groups.

10

STATUS OF WOMEN IN THE ISLAMIC REPUBLIC OF IRAN

S.J. Havewalla

Islam is one of the younger religions of the world spread over all the continents and almost in each and every country of the world, with large following. It has been adopted as the State Religion by several countries. It is very interesting to note that the interpretation of the Holy Quran varies from person to person and country to country in the context of their cultures, traditions, society and politics. Iran, Afghanistan and Saudi Arabia are three typical examples of Islamic States having lots of contradictions and contrasts among themselves over various issues based on Shariat, although they also share a few similarities and common traditions.

The most controversial subject in the Islamic society has always been The Status of Woman. The Prophet has clearly and extensively stated about women's right and status which have been established by the holy Quran, yet the norms for woman vary a lot from society to society in the Islamic world. A special particular titled "Surat-un-Nisa" (سورة النساء) in Quran defines the rights and status of women in a Islamic society. It is indeed surprizing that in spite of such clear instructions given by the God in the Holy Quran in reality most of the Muslims have been denied many legal rights to women, which were otherwise supposed to be given to them according to the Islamic law. (شريعت)

Paying the highest tribute to Woman the Prophet of Islam has proclaimed (الجنت تحت الاقدام الامهات) (Paradise lies under the feet of Mother). This clearly shows that out of the two genders the highest kind of spirituality and goodness are attached to women.

From the administrative point of view man seems to be gaining more as a head of family with the responsibility of running the house financially—because as far as inheritance of the property is concerned man gets double, the share of woman.

SECTION 2

11. Allah (thus) directs you
As regards your children's[516]
(Inheritance): to the male,
A portion equal to that
Of two females: if only
Daughters, two or more,[517]
Their share is two-thirds
Of the inheritance;
If only one, her share
Is a half.
For parents, a sixth share
Of the inheritance to each,
If the deceased left children;
If no children, and the parents
Are the (only) heirs, the mother
Has a third: if the deceased
Left brothers (or sisters)
The mother has a sixth.
(The distribution in all cases
Is) after the payment
Of legacies and debts.
Ye know not whether

يُوصِيكُمُ ٱللَّهُ فِىٓ أَوْلَٰدِكُمْ ۖ لِلذَّكَرِ مِثْلُ حَظِّ
ٱلْأُنثَيَيْنِ ۚ فَإِن كُنَّ نِسَآءً فَوْقَ ٱثْنَتَيْنِ فَلَهُنَّ
ثُلُثَا مَا تَرَكَ ۖ وَإِن كَانَتْ وَٰحِدَةً فَلَهَا ٱلنِّصْفُ ۚ
وَلِأَبَوَيْهِ لِكُلِّ وَٰحِدٍ مِّنْهُمَا ٱلسُّدُسُ مِمَّا تَرَكَ
إِن كَانَ لَهُۥ وَلَدٌ ۚ فَإِن لَّمْ يَكُن لَّهُۥ وَلَدٌ وَوَرِثَهُۥٓ
أَبَوَاهُ فَلِأُمِّهِ ٱلثُّلُثُ ۚ فَإِن كَانَ لَهُۥٓ إِخْوَةٌ فَلِأُمِّهِ
ٱلسُّدُسُ ۚ مِنۢ بَعْدِ وَصِيَّةٍ يُوصِى بِهَآ أَوْ دَيْنٍ ۗ
ءَابَآؤُكُمْ وَأَبْنَآؤُكُمْ لَا تَدْرُونَ أَيُّهُمْ أَقْرَبُ
لَكُمْ نَفْعًا ۚ فَرِيضَةً مِّنَ ٱللَّهِ ۗ إِنَّ ٱللَّهَ كَانَ
عَلِيمًا حَكِيمًا ﴿١١﴾

An-Nisāa, or The Women.
In the name of Allah, Most Gracious
Most Merciful.
1. O mankind ! fear
Your Guardian Lord.
Who created you
From a single Person,[504]
Created, out of it,
His mate, and from them twain
Scattered (like seeds)
Countless men and women;-
Fear Allah, through Whom[505]
Ye demand your mutual (rights),
And be heedful of the wombs[506]
(That bore you); For Allah
Ever watches over you.

سُورَةُ النِّسَاءِ

بِسْمِ اللَّهِ الرَّحْمَٰنِ الرَّحِيمِ

يَا أَيُّهَا النَّاسُ اتَّقُوا رَبَّكُمُ الَّذِي خَلَقَكُم مِّن نَّفْسٍ
وَاحِدَةٍ وَخَلَقَ مِنْهَا زَوْجَهَا وَبَثَّ مِنْهُمَا رِجَالًا كَثِيرًا
وَنِسَاءً وَاتَّقُوا اللَّهَ الَّذِي تَسَاءَلُونَ بِهِ وَالْأَرْحَامَ
إِنَّ اللَّهَ كَانَ عَلَيْكُمْ رَقِيبًا ﴿١﴾

The 'Surah' clearly points out that man is given double the share, because he is entrusted with the administrative responsibility of looking after woman who has great share in creating the human-world. Unfortunately, the 'Surah' is misinterpreted and some of the religious preachers for various selfish reasons have given their verdict that according to Islam, woman is less intelligent and two women are equal to one man. The 'Suras' divine ideal distribution of work between man and woman, *i.e.*, the administrative responsibility and spiritual responsibility, is deliberately overlooked by such hypocrites.

The Prophet of Islam appears to be one of the most liberal-minded man in the world, who had no inhibitions in marrying a woman almost twenty years older than him (Khadijah), who by profession was a trader and his employer earlier. He did not stop his wife from working outside, even after their marriage. The Prophet's biography indicates that he had treated his wife with great respect and dignity.

The Prophet's daughter Fatima holds a very special and high position in the spiritual Islamic world. Her name appears as one of the five prime members of the Prophets 'Holy' Family (Ahle Bait) and she commands equal respect and dignity like other family members of the Holy Family. She is acknowledged as a very intelligent lady participating in all important deliberations and meetings organized by her father. She used to participate in various discussions actively. The Prophet was extremely fond of his daughter Fatima.

The Polygamy in Islam has almost lost its original noble purpose of giving shelter to orphan, penniless or downtrodden women giving them the legal social status of being a dignified wife. The uneven ratio between men and women in Arabia during the life time of the Prophet might have been a major factor. There were certain preconditions for polygamy, *i.e.*, seeking permission from the first wife, taking oath of loving and treating all the wives equally and making no distinction amongst the children of different wives.

3. If ye fear that ye shall not
Be able to deal justly
With the orphans,[508]
Marry women of your choice,
Two, or three, or four;
But if ye fear that ye shall not
Be able to deal justly (with them),
Then only one, or
That which your right hands posses.
That will be more suitable,
To prevent you
From doing injustice[509]

وَإِنْ خِفْتُمْ أَلَّا تُقْسِطُوا فِي الْيَتَامَىٰ فَانكِحُوا مَا طَابَ لَكُم مِّنَ
النِّسَاءِ مَثْنَىٰ وَثُلَاثَ وَرُبَاعَ ۖ فَإِنْ خِفْتُمْ أَلَّا تَعْدِلُوا فَوَاحِدَةً أَوْ
مَا مَلَكَتْ أَيْمَانُكُمْ ۚ ذَٰلِكَ أَدْنَىٰ أَلَّا تَعُولُوا
﴿٣﴾

In fact, the permission of polygamy was also granted in order to share the pathetic plight of helpless widows who not only financially but also morally needed man's support. In fact, marrying a widow and giving shelter to her and her children was highly appreciated by the Prophet. Polygamy was allowed in a case where a woman was unable to bear a child; again with the pre-condition that the children of the second wife should treat the first one like their own mother and the second wife should also treat the first one with respect and dignity

The prophet was very careful about the Law of Inheritance and prescribed the following :

11. Allah (thus) directs you
As regards your children's[516]
(Inheritance): to the male.
A portion equal to that
Of two females: if only
Daughters, two or more,[517]
Their share is two-thirds
Of the inheritance;
If only one, her share
Is a half.
For parents, a sixth share
Of the inheritance to each,
If the deceased left children;
If no children, and he parents
Are the (only) heirs. the mother
Has a third: if the deceased
Left brothers (or sisters)
The mother has a sixth.
(The distribution in all cases
Is) after the payment
Of legacies and debts.
Ye know not whether
Your parents or your children
Are nearest to you
In benefit. These are
Settled portions ordained[518]
By Allah: and Allah is
All-knowing, All-wise.

يُوصِيكُمُ اللَّهُ فِي أَوْلَادِكُمْ لِلذَّكَرِ مِثْلُ حَظِّ
الْأُنثَيَيْنِ فَإِن كُنَّ نِسَاءً فَوْقَ اثْنَتَيْنِ فَلَهُنَّ
ثُلُثَا مَا تَرَكَ وَإِن كَانَتْ وَاحِدَةً فَلَهَا النِّصْفُ
وَلِأَبَوَيْهِ لِكُلِّ وَاحِدٍ مِّنْهُمَا السُّدُسُ مِمَّا تَرَكَ
إِن كَانَ لَهُ وَلَدٌ فَإِن لَّمْ يَكُن لَّهُ وَلَدٌ وَوَرِثَهُ
أَبَوَاهُ فَلِأُمِّهِ الثُّلُثُ فَإِن كَانَ لَهُ إِخْوَةٌ فَلِأُمِّهِ
السُّدُسُ مِن بَعْدِ وَصِيَّةٍ يُوصِي بِهَا أَوْ دَيْنٍ
آبَاؤُكُمْ وَأَبْنَاؤُكُمْ لَا تَدْرُونَ أَيُّهُمْ أَقْرَبُ
لَكُمْ نَفْعًا فَرِيضَةً مِّنَ اللَّهِ إِنَّ اللَّهَ كَانَ
عَلِيمًا حَكِيمًا ﴿١١﴾

12. In what your wives leave,
Your share is a half,
If they leave no child,
But if they leave a child,
Ye get a fourth; after payment
Of legacies and debts.
In what ye have;
Their share is a fourth,[519]
If ye leave no child;
But if ye leave a child,
They get an eighth; after payment
Of legacies and debts.
If the man or woman
Whose inheritance is in question,
Has left neither ascendants nor descendants.[520]
But has left a brother[521]
Or a sister, each one of the two
Gets a sixth; but if more
Than two, they share in a third:
After payment of legacies
And debts : so that no loss[522]
Is caused (to any one).
Thus is it ordained by Allah;
And Allah is All-knowing.
Most Forbearing.

۞ وَلَكُمْ نِصْفُ مَا تَرَكَ أَزْوَاجُكُمْ
إِن لَّمْ يَكُن لَّهُنَّ وَلَدٌ فَإِن كَانَ لَهُنَّ وَلَدٌ
فَلَكُمُ الرُّبُعُ مِمَّا تَرَكْنَ مِن بَعْدِ
وَصِيَّةٍ يُوصِينَ بِهَا أَوْ دَيْنٍ وَلَهُنَّ
الرُّبُعُ مِمَّا تَرَكْتُمْ إِن لَّمْ يَكُن لَّكُمْ وَلَدٌ
فَإِن كَانَ لَكُمْ وَلَدٌ فَلَهُنَّ الثُّمُنُ
مِمَّا تَرَكْتُم مِّن بَعْدِ وَصِيَّةٍ تُوصُونَ
بِهَا أَوْ دَيْنٍ وَإِن كَانَ رَجُلٌ يُورَثُ
كَلَالَةً أَوِ امْرَأَةٌ وَلَهُ أَخٌ أَوْ أُخْتٌ فَلِكُلِّ
وَاحِدٍ مِّنْهُمَا السُّدُسُ فَإِن كَانُوا أَكْثَرَ
مِن ذَٰلِكَ فَهُمْ شُرَكَاءُ فِي الثُّلُثِ مِن بَعْدِ
وَصِيَّةٍ يُوصَىٰ بِهَا أَوْ دَيْنٍ غَيْرَ مُضَارٍّ
وَصِيَّةً مِّنَ اللَّهِ وَاللَّهُ عَلِيمٌ حَلِيمٌ ﴿١٢﴾

Thus, mother, wives, daughters, sisters and daughters-in-law all of them have their share in the property of man.

There is quotation in Hadith (Sonan Abi Daud, Kitabul Adab, Vol. p. 354):

"من كان له انثى فلم يئدها ولم يهنها ولم
يؤثر ولده عليها ادخله الله الجنة."

(Only the father of a girl, who would not bury his daughter alive, who would not neglect or insult her and who would not prefer his son over the daughter will be permitted by God to enter the heaven).

At another place in Hadith, it is indicated that: (Tirmiji, Kitabul-Bir, Vol. 4, p. 281)

"لايكون لاَحدكم ثلاث بناتٍ اوثلاث اخواتٍ

فيحسن اليهن الاّ دخل الجنة"

(If a man has three daughters and three sisters and he treats them well, then God will permit him to enter the heaven).

The marriage in Islam is basically a social contract between a man and woman. According to the contract, the woman who surrenders her own self and her services to her husband and his family, in return is entitled for 'Mehr' *i.e.*, a sum of money, a man has to provide to her for her future security. The *Mehr* is supposed to be paid on the very day of the marriage, but later on it was decided that, since, it is the money for the future security of Woman, it is to be paid in the case of divorcing her. Divorce also is not a simple matter as it is made out today. The Law of Divorce differs from country to country, but the fact remains evrywhere that the contract money is to be paid to wife as future security at the time of divorce.

Amongst all the Islamic states and nations, Iran enjoys a quite different status and follows different norms. Perhaps Iran is the only 'Shia' state. In contrast to the other middle eastern Islamic states, Iran is an Aryan nation and society. Iran has accepted a religion of semetic people, but (unlike Egypt and Syria, the other two great nations with rich cultural heritage), has refused to give up its Aryan character. Iran rejected the proposal of accepting Arabic as mother tongue or state-language. Arabic was respected only from the religious point of view.

Time and again Iranians have been taking up the task of purifying the Persian Language, whenever, they felt that the Arabic words were entering into their language beyond the desired proportion. Where the two great ancient countries, Egypt and Syria proclaimed themselves Arab nations losing their ethnic identity, Iran is very proud, even, today for being an Aryan country.

The status of woman in Iran appears to be quite controversial, in some way the woman of Iran are politically and socially, quite free nonetheless they also have to face some restrictions springing out of the Iranian clergy's orthodoxy.

Following the Shia tradition, Fatima becomes an important symbol of perfect womanhood amongst Iranian women. As against some countries like Afghanistan, where women are denied the right to study and take up a career or profession under the orthodox Taliban Government, the Iranian Constitution gives full right to the Iranian women to be educated and pursue the career they like. Acknowleding women as good teachers who can influence young minds in a better way, they are also advocated to take up teaching as job on a very large scale. Iranian government had protested against the Taliban government, clearly mentioning that Islam never prohibits women from learning and acquiring knowledge. In fact, it is obligatory on their part to be educated. Thus, Iranian women, who in the medieval Iran was not appreciated for writing poetry and recite them in public, are free today to express their innermost sentiments and emotions and publish it or recite it. The Land of Poetry has welcomed the women, but, there is a restriction. The European type of Feminism and Feminist Movement are not only criticized but also condemned and prohibited.

During Shah's regime a special bill was passed in the Parliament under the title 'Kanoon-e-Khanewadeh' (Family Code). According to which the right of divorcing one's husband was granted to Muslim women who were ready to forgo *Mehr* or the contract money for her future security at the time of her marriage. Needless to say, condemning this as the European practice, the present Islamic government did not continue the act. Today divorce is only man's prerogative.

Holding Fatima at the highest spiritual level and accepting her as one of the five prime members of the Prophet's Holy Family (اهل بیت) it is surprising that the highest political post Rahbar is only reserved for men. The political rights to women in the beginning of Islamic Republic of Iran were not at par with men. On one hand, when they were not denied the right to be the members of the Iranian Parliament, they were not supposed to argue vehemently. They could not hold the post of a Judge in the courts.

Fortunately, with the passage of time, there is less orthodoxy and a lot more liberal attitude towards women in the recent past. A couple of them have come forward to contest for the election of the Presidential post and now they are given more representation in the Parliament. Since, Refsajani's government day by day women are marching forward in the political fields too. There seems to be no objection amongst Iranians to accept a Lady President, if she wins election, or her holding high office in the government, but the *Rahbar's* post is still not meant for them.

The fundamental right of voting in election is enjoyed by the Iranian women. There is no bar of class, caste or financial position. Women too are quite enthusiastic about it and participate in a very large scale in building up their nation. They also enjoy full freedom to launch any political protest or participate into demonstrations like Iranian men. They are free to choose any profession including Engineering Medicine. They are sent outside the country as political representatives too. Numbers, of them have visited India in that capacity too.

The, enforcement of 'Hejab'[1] for Iranians and also for non-Iranians residing in or visiting Iran is no doubt an overdone act, but for Iranians themselves it has a great political motive behind it Reza Sah Pahlavi by passing a bill in the Parliament prohibiting 'HeJab', enforced the Act very strictly. Reza Shah was inspired by Ata Turk to do so with that idea of modernizing Iran. No woman was allowed to walk on the streets with Hejab even if she wanted to do so. While protesting against the Pahlavi regime and fighting for the personal freedom, the freedom-fighting young women as a symbol of protest to the Pahlavi regime accepted Hejab willingly. Later on (almost one and half years after the Islamic government took over) Hejab was made compulsory for all women in Iran. It was given national as well as religious colour. At the beginning women (foreigners) working in the Iranian offices outside the country were also forced to take up Hejab. Same was the case with women visiting offices, but later on, foreigners were exempted from it, although the Iranian government insisted on decent dressing *i.e.*, not wearing short and provocative clothes for the visitors outside Iran. Even, today for foreigners staying or visiting Iran Hejab is compulsory.

Inspite of Hejab Iranian women, mentally, physically and politically seem to be more independent than many other women behind veil anywhere else in the world. Unlike many Islamic states Iranians (woman) can drive cars, come outdoors and do their work, take part in deliberations, meetings with men, can discuss and give opinions have a major say in the final decisions etc. There is no restriction for them to go abroad and study or travel outside the country alone. They might have been prohibited from going to discotheque and walking in the parks holding husband's or any other man's hand, but they certainly enjoy much more freedom than women of the other Islamic states in the west Asia and the middle East[2].

REFERENCES

1. The practice of covering all parts of the body leaving the face open.
2. Quoranic quotations have been taken from Holy Quoran printed at Al-Madinah A1-Munawarsh under the auspices of the Ministry of Hajj and Endowments, the Kingdom of Saudi Arabia, 1413 H.

11

Gender Gap and the Changing Women's Vote in American Elections: 1980-1996

K.P. Vijayalakshmi

In every recent American election, significant attention has been paid to divergent political traits of men and women. The emergance of political differences between men and women, however, was concretely recorded during, the 1980's Presidential Election. Eight percent fewer women than men voted for Ronald Reagan. Historically, such a difference in a national election was unprecedented. The eight-percent gender difference in voting came the same year, and a second historic precedent was set. For the first time since women won the suffrage in 1920, a higher proportion of women voted than did men.

During next two years, the voting difference based on gender in presidential elections came to be linked with the Presidential performance approval ratings. At the same time, the increasing preference of women voters for Democratic Party in Congressional and Presidential races began to be focussed upon. Subsequently, these differences became indentified as the 'gender gap'. To many observers, this 'gender gap' perhaps seemed a forerunner to the fulfilment of suffragists, dream that women would vote as a unified bloc.

The Emergence of Gender Gap

The term 'gender gap' refers to difference between men and women in political attitudes and voting choices. Although this gap has historical roots, political differences between women and men have increased in scope and shown greater persistence in recent years. As one expert points out, it has become an 'enduring feature' of American politics. It is now accepted that a gender gap is apparent in :

(*a*) voting behaviours,

(*b*) party identification,

(*c*) evaluations of Presidential performances and

(*d*) attitudes towards various public policy issues.[1]

From when did this gap emerge?

Many analysts have pointed out that the differences in the voting patterns of women and men that were evident in 1992, were a continuation of trends that first emerged in 1964. It solidified by 1980.[2] In the elections of 1952, 1956 and 1960, women generally voted Republicans. However, in 1964, Senator Barry Goldwater's rhetoric and his attacks on welfare state led to the very first gender gap. It appeared that women were more likely to vote Democrats than Republican. This pattern has been repeated in every Presidential Election except in 1976. Both in 1964 and 1972, gender gap was substantial and continued to climb about 6 to 9 per cent in 1980, 1984 and 1988' races. But, in both 1968 and 1976, elections, women were found to be only slightly more likely than men to vote for Democratic candidates.[3] The 1992 and 1996, elections have only continued the gender gap, which was points four points for the former and 11 for latter.

Evolution of the Gap

The significance of women voters in these years and particularly after 1976, prompts us to look into the major factors that led to it. Arguably, it was the record number of women who voted in the 1980, elections (more than 50 per cent), than the men that computed the gap. Women's voting turnout was an irrefutable factor in arresting the decline of women voter's influence as perceived in 1976. For instance, it was observed that from the original estimates of a 30-40 per cent turnout difference in the 1920s, it had declined to 10 per cent by the 1950s, when the University of Michigan's Centre for Political Studies began its election studies. By 1964, the gender difference in voting turnout had dropped to 5 per cent by 1969, it was 4 per cent and by 1976, it had all, but disappeared.[4]

The other historical impetus to the turn around of the 1980s, in which women's turnout was 1.5 per cent higher than that of men (1984), was the cumulative impact of Voting Rights Acts of 1965 and the numerical growth of women in the overall population. By 1984, women made up of 53 per cent of voters, 7 per cent more than men, (US Census, 1986). While one may pointout, why it was that the anticipated emergence women's bloc immediately after the passage of Suffrage Amendment in 1920, did not seriously materialize as a starter for the study, it would perhaps be noteworthy to look at some of the analysis.

From the early attempts to explain the suffragists, disappointments to the recent research, there has been an evolution in the scholarly views. From explanation of eternal biological differences to those based on differential access to resources like, education, income, race, ethnic and marital status, the significance of gender-based groups amongst voters has elaborated the framework of voter behaviour and its analysis. Studies by Herriam and Gosnell (1924), found that low voting rates among immigrants and less educated women pointed to the importance of women's nature. The identification of subgroups among women gained prominence in later studies. Focussing on the socialization aspects as the basis for gender differences, Lane (1959) and Greenstein (1965), elaborated the theme of women's training of passivity. Significantly, it was Campbell and his associates (1960), who identified in his classic, *'American Voter'* the strong relationship between education and voting (in women as well as men, however). They attributed the closing of the voting gap to women's sense of civic responsibility rather than any intrinsic interest or knowledge about politics.[5]

This has prompted analysts to pointout that, "there has been little evidence from 1940s to the 1970s, that gender plays a role in determining issue positions, candidate evaluations or candidate preference". The studies that did document voting was marked by the absence of gender based statistics that might have identified as women's voting block and merely showed that women participated less than men and were slightly more Republican than men (A. Campbell, 1960).

Since then many studies spawned by a new generation of scholars looked more seriously at the consequences of the massive changes occurring in women's lives as they left the domestic sphere for higher levels of education and paid employment. (Hynn & Flora, 1973, Anderson, 1975, Hensen, Franz & Netmeyer Hays, 1976).[6] These studies basically formulated a new argument. Lower turnout reflected women's restricted access to the same critical resources that account for different rates to voting for men: namely education and income.[7]

The rapid growth of the contemporary feminist movement during this time called the assumption held by political scientists into question, that women had no policy interests distinct from those of men. During the late 60s and 70s, many women organized to push for concerns, which had been overlooked by the political process. Labelled 'Women's issues', these were defined as those where policy consequences were likely to have a more direct impact on a large number of women than men.[8] Indeed, the emergence of feminist movement was itself cited as pluralist proof that many women perceive their interests distinctly from men.[9]

Many studied the representation of women's interests in the governing bodies. Starting from 'Equal Pay for Equal Work' issue in the World War II years, Gallup Polls of 1942, 1945 and 1954, showed women overwhelmingly in favour of such a legislation. But it was not until 1963, that the Congress finally passed the Equal Pay Act.

Similarly, the Equal Rights Amendment ERA, was first introduced in the Congress in 1923 and was reintroduced in almost every subsequent legislative session. However, both houses passed it only in 1972. A Gallup Poll taken in 1974, showed that 73 per cent of females were in favour of such an amendment. Subsequent polls continued to point to a plurality of women favouring the ERA. The amendment eventually fell by three short of the states necessary for ratification.

Finally, as early as 1970, a CBS News Poll found 78 per cent of women in favour of the establishment of day care centers to oversee children of working women. Yet, this was not taken up by federal or state governments.

As these examples illustrate, the responses to the female interests or constituents in policy to benefit women were negligible or inadequate. Hence, the question: How to attain a more adequate representation of the interests of women on policy issues dealing with women ? At least three conventional strategies came into use along with unconventional tactics such as boycott or demonstrations: one, use of lobbying tactics to influence representatives; two, organizing women to vote for representatives, who will safeguard their interests and three, engage in an effort to elect women to political offices to represent the interests of women. While this paper assumes that the process of change in women's vote is linked to all three, the second strategy of organizing women to vote for those who represent their interests has significantly contributed to the 'gender gap' that emerged in the 1980s ; it also became pronounced in the area of Presidential evaluation.

Despite the obvious difficulties in the pursuit of this strategy given the influence of party identification candidate image on voting decisions and the diversity among women, the 'gender gap' of the 1980, Reagan Election led women's organizations, such as NOW, (National Organization for Women), or National League of Women Voters or EMILY's List (Early Money is Like Yeast 1985), to continue to build on the legacy of the 70s in which a ... "quiet revolution... that encouraged women to think about politics. Bella Abzug's slogan, that a "woman's place is in the house—the House of Representatives" because a national slogan. ... "Make Policy not Coffee" touched the chords of confinement many activist women felt over organizational roles that diminished their contributions".[10] In effect, the assertion of legitimacy of public roles for women became the 'epigram of an age'. The decline of the collective influence of the suffragists began to slowly be reversed. Nowhere, was this particularly visible as in the voter turnout. Women's turnout in elections is thus a key factor is explaining the 'gender gap'. The other two components derived from this are partisanship or party identification and vote choice.

Women's Voting Turnout and Participation

Many attempts to explain the suffragists, disppointments in anticipating the growth of women's voting bloc in the 1920s, pointed to a prominent feature. Significantly, women voted at a lower rate than men (about 10 per cent), largely due to differences in sex roles. However, it was also pointed out that changning role definitions might lead to increased participation by women. Other findings pointed to the following :

— Gender differences were greater in South and non-metropolitan areas, than, in other sections of the country.

— Older women and women with younger children were less likely to vote than their counterparts.

— Gender differences were slight or less in turnout between college educated men and women.

— Younger people without chlidren and single women were likely to vote, more than males.

— 'Sex differentials' may diminish as women became more educated and new sex role definition became widely diffused in rural areas and among those with lower level of education.

Figure 1 shows the percentage of women and men, who reported to have kept on voting in Presidential elections from 1964, to 1992, according to Census Bureau surveys. These data indicate that turnout rates for both women and men have generally declined, since the 1960s. However, turnout rates for women have not declined as sharply as those for men. As a result, women voted at higher rates than men, since 1980. The table also indicates that, while voter turnout rates increased for both women and men in 1992, the percentage increase was slightly higher for women than for men. Because women comprise a larger proportion of the population than men, the increasingly higher turnout rates for women relative to men take on even, greater significance. The combination of more women in the potential electorate and a higher rate of voting among women meant that in 1992, 53 per cent of the electorate were women, and 47 per cent were men. These figures indicate that there were 6.3 million more women than men in the electorate in 1992.

Thus, the combination of being majority of voters and being likely 'swing voters' have made pollsters and pundits look at women voters as a new viable group in elections.

The 1980s, emerged as the decade of women voters, who cited significant policy differences for their voting behaviour. Reagan pollster Richard Wirthlin in fact, said that, he used the phrase 'gender gap' during his extensive polling of female voters in the late 1970s.[11]

It appeared clearly that women were distinctly favouring Democrats and that the Republican Party would be pursued by this gap in years to come. The important lesson was and continues to be the fact that women are 53 per cent of the electorate and they can determine the outcome of elections.

The 1990s, elections (Congressional and Presidential) voter turnout recorded by the Center for American Woman and Politics at Rutgus showed that in every election, since 1980, the proportion of eligible females who voted has exceeded the ratio of eligible males who voted. In all Presidential elections prior to 1980, the voter turnout rate for women was lower than the rate for men. In 1988, 54.5 million women cast their voters as against 47.4 million men, by 1992, 60.5 million women as against 53.3 million men and 1966, 56.1 million women to 48.9 million men voted.[12]

The voter turnout in Congressional electiosns in the 1990s, has marked the continuation of this trend. While in 1990, 43.3 million women hold their tranchise against 38.7 million men and by 1994, 44.6 million women voted to 40.4 million men. Women also outnumbered men among registered voters. In the 1992, 1994, 1996 and 1998, elections, the women voters continued to turnout in more numbers than the men and the gender gap was sustained despite the Republican Congressional victory in 1994. An October 1995, survey conducted by Times-Mirror Center for the People and the Press showed that older voters and a majority of women disapproved of GOP led Congress and were more likely to vote for Clinton in 1996, than any Republican challengers. Underscoring a widening gender gap on social issues, women were increasingly distrustful of the Republican agenda, borneout in 1996 Congressional elections.

The main reason cited for the GOP victory in 1994, was that 16 million women did not turnout to vote in 1994, of which 13 million fell into the demographic segment of 'non-college educated' women.[13]

Thus, the 'Year of the Woman' (1992), may well have given place to the 'Year of the Woman Voter' (1996). Women voter's significance to both parties was highlighted in the campaigns of both Clinton and Dole, signalling widening party margins amongst men and women.

It became evident that President Clinton's lead among women voters was so large (between 20 and 30 points over Senator Dole), that any challenger would face on question of affirmative action, deficit and taxes. Indeed, by September 1996, 42 per cent of the women polled had an unfavourable opinion of Senator Dole, while just 29 per cent of the men polled had such an opinion.[14]

The Reublican strategy was broadly to mobilize and persuade younger, single women and women entrepreneurs in small businesses that the Reyublicans advocate regulatory relief, fight for tax reform and resist compulsory health care coverage. It also concentrated on issues of (1) crime: viz. death penalty, personal security abolition of parole, etc. (2) economic job security, financial issues affecting the family and the impact of spending cuts.

But in mobilizing women to turnup for voting in favour of then the Republicans had a mixed reception. On the one hand, their politics had some agreement with the concerns and expectation of women, on the other hand, their perceptions of the party were much more negative. So, many advisors and party pollsters advised the GOP to "... not to change the message, but to refine it and combine it with most effective messengers and delivery style.[15] Others pointed out that Republican must actively court the Black vote. As Republican Senator of Georgia Paul Coverdell put it, "they 9 the blacks have gotten into a situation, where one party takes them for granted and not the other party does pay attention",[16] The Republican attention was fuelled probably by the polls held by *Joint Center for Political and Economic Studies,* (a Washington based think tank) which showed that blacks were as conservatives as whites on social issues and more likely than whites to be churchgoers and to favour school prayer.[17]

In an effort to mobilize women further, the Republican in the Congress setup an Advisory Committee on the Gender Gap, which will help the party bridge this gap and advise more 'femalefriendly'.[18]

The Republican polling firm, American Viewpoint, pointed out that women voters were distinctly uneasy about the party's position on the environment and education. Even, more importantly, voters showed greatest concern on the role of government and porviding the base for the gender gap to widen. Recognizing that the Republican rhetoric went too far in the case of downsizing the scope of the government was thus, crucial to win back the women voters.[19]

Gender and Partisanship

It has been widely noted that until the 1970s, women and men had remarkably similar attitudes on most political issues and exhibited almost the same pattern of voting and partisan attachment.[20] Some notable exceptions such as greater concern for morality issues of opposition to the involvement of the United States in violent conflicts were highlighted as significant departures.

Over the last two decades, however, differences expanded in areas pertaining to women's social and political roles, 'social compassion', support for minority rights, protection of the environment and basic economic issues augmenting the previously limited attitudinal gap concerning peace and morality. This in turn, promoted a growing partisan and ideological gender gap of 6 to 10 points during the 1980s. Moreover, this gap remained fairly stable when measured in Presidential voting and party identification.

The growing divergence between the attitudes of women and men 'almost certainly' stemmed from changing role of women in American society as denoted by higher education and entry into work place, growth of the women's movement, women's increased social insecurity due to growing divorce rates and shrinking welfare budgets. Thus, as women moved away from traditional roles, their attitudes towards broad range of issues such as supporting racial equality, helping the disadvantage and demanding equal rights for women begen to echo a 'gender consciousness' and 'feminism'. The impact of such differences was significant in the late 1980s and 1990s, on partisan identification for women and men.

According to the data available from the American National Election Studies, changes in partisan identification for women and men from 1952 through 1992, women were slightly more likely to identify as Republicans than were men in the 1950s and 1960s, and this trend continued through 1980. However, since 1960, women have consistently been more likely then men to identify as Democrats, since 1960 and that the gap has widened. This seeming inconsistency, that women in 1970s, were both more Republican and more Democratic than the men is possible because women were less likely to consider themselves independents. The following table shows these changes.

Table 1 shows the changes in partisan identification for women and men from 1952 through 1992, according to data available from the American National Election Studies. As some of the early studies of voting behaviour suggested, women were slightly more likely to identify as Republicans that were men in the 1950s and 1960s, (see, for example Campbell et al., 1960) and this trend continued through 1980. However, these data also show that women have consistently been more likely than men to identify as Democrats, since 1960s and that the gap between women and men has generally widened. This seeming inconsistency—that women in the 1970s, were both more Republican and more Democratic than men-is possible because women were less likely than men to consider themselves to be Independents.

Table 1
Gender Differences in Party Indentification 1952-1992

		Women	*Men*
1952	Democrats	49	48
	Independents	20	26
	Republicans	30	26
1956	Democrats	45	46
	Independents	21	28
	Republicans	34	26
1960	Democrats	51	46
	Independents	18	26
	Republicans	31	28
1964	Democrats	54	51
	Independents	21	25
	Republicans	26	24

		Women	Men
1968	Democrats	48	43
	Independents	28	31
	Republicans	24	26
1972	Democrats	44	38
	Independents	32	39
	Republicans	24	23
1976	Democrats	43	37
	Independents	31	42
	Republicans	26	21
1980	Democrats	45	38
	Independents	32	40
	Republicans	23	22
1980	Democrats	41	33
	Independents	32	39
	Republicans	27	28
1988	Democrats	40	30
	Independents	32	41
	Republicans	28	29
1992	Democrats	40	32
	Independents	37	40
	Republicans	23	28

Source: Center for Political Studies, American National Elections Studies, 1952-1992. Independents who lean toward parties are coded as Independents.

The net partisanship gender gap became much wider during the 1980s, as men defected from the Democratic to the Republican Party at higher rates than women. (Bolce, 1985, Wirls, 1986, Miller, 1991). According to one Democratic pollster, these aggregate patterns mask some of the interesting differences among women, who were and are far from monolithic in the 1970s and 1980s. The allusion was to the opinion that older women, home makers, evangelical women became increasingly Republican while younger, working women and college educated women maintained Demcoratic preferences.[21]

Form this perspective, the gender gap should have exacerbated in 1992, because of the events centering around the election, such as Lawyer Anita Hill's fight against sexual harassment in front of an all male Senate, Republican convention's insistence on 'Culture Wars' Hillary Clinton's attraction as a role model for feminists. Yet, the gender gapinstead of expanding. As pointed out, by a Centre for American Women and Politics Study, (Rutgers University, New Jersey), (CAWP), women were more likely than men to support Bill Clinton by 4 points Voter Research Surveys showed that Bill Clinton received 45 per cent of women's votes as compared to 41 per cent of men's votes.[22]

The exit poll also showed that the gender support for Ross Perot was 17 per cent by women as compared to 21 per cent of men. There was not a gender gap vote for George Bush, 38 per cent men to 37% of female voters voted for him. The gap between Clinton and Bush was, however 45 per cent to 37 per cent, i.e., 8 points. The increasing scope and persistence of this gap was strikingly visible in 1996, elections. As CAWP Fact Sheet 1997, points out, the 1996, elections was marked by a 11 point gender gap 54 per cent to 43 per cent largest ever recorded with women favouring Bill Clinton and men voting for in Bob Dole. In both 1992 and 1996, women were less likely to vote for Ross Perot than men. The following table illustrates these points.

Table 2

Presidential Candidates	*Voter News Service*	
	Women	*Men*
1992		
Bill Clinton	45%	41%
George Bus	37%	38%
Ross Perot	17%	21%
1996		
Bill Clinton	54%	43%
Bob Dloe	38%	44%
Ross Perot	7%	10%

In 1992, Presidential Election, the size of the gender gap was affected significantly, by cross pressures felt by many women on issues concerning abortion and other social and moral issues. As some suggested, the growing prominence of the gender gap of the 1980s, may have "diverted attention from the fact that the gap between traditional women and feminists were growing as well, as denoted by the surprising lack of gender gap on abortion and Equal Rights Amendment".[23]

Testing the hypothesis that clash of opinion between feminists and traditional women has eroded the gender gap, Clark and Clark provide stimulating findings. Confirming the image of women as more liberal than men, where women were 8 per cent less likely to vote in comparison to men to identify themselves as Republicans on the economy are better than the Democrats and less supportive of Republican Foreign Policy (about 11 per cent).[24] Thus, while, there are some indications that the 'perfumed cleavage' between feminists and traditionalists may have attenuated somewhat the gender gap in 1992, it was still live in most issue areas.

The 1996, election again highlighted the persistence of the gender gap in Presidential Election, which was about 11 per cent between Clinton and Dole. It continued to be pointed on the following.

- General ideological and partisan attachments,
- Soical and welfare spending,
- Role of the state (government),
- Women's issues,
- Mornal and cultural issuses,
- Civil Rights,
- Militarism and foreing policy,
- Crime and
- Environment.

The gap, according to observers was a poweful tool by which women were able to make gains in high level elected offices.

The 1998, Congressional elections deserve a special mention as it followed the Presidential scandal involving Monica Lewinsky, a young White House Intern and President Clinton. In the ensuing bitter war, which was both moral and partisan, gender gaps were recorded on whether President Clinton should be impeached. The CNN poll immediately after 17 August, 1998, statement of President Clinton found a 20 per cent gender gap with 63 per cent of the women saying they were satisfied with the statement ot 43 per cent of men. Gallup Poll 1998, put it more moderately 60 per cent males approved of Clinton to 65 per cent females and 62 per cent females and 62 per cent men wanted him impeached to 68 per cent women, while 65 per cent of all adults did not want him impeached.[25] Most women favoured reprimand and censure of Clinton, but not removal from office and his approval ratings remained high.[26]

By September 1998, leading feminists argued that the opponents of the President have a political agenda that will harm women long after the scandal has faded.[27]

Highlighting the then speaker Newt Gingrich as partisan warrior with puritanical and fundamentalist views on women's issues, feminist leaders pointed out that by supporting the opponents of the President, women can invite the riske of losing the gains of "the year of the women in 1992", in the 1998, Congressional elections as well as years of reactionary control in both Houses of Congress and "... perhaps, even, the Presidency itself" (referring to the Republican attacks on Vice President Al Gore, who is under investigation by the Justice Department for possible violations of Campaign Finance Laws). The results of November elections have again provided fillip to the issue of gender in American politics. The Republican gains predicted by many failed to materialize. While the Repulicans retained the majority in both Houses, they did not gain any seats in the Senate and lost five seats in the House. However, it did not translate into major gains for women in public ofice as well. A net gain of only two women in the Congress and Governorships was rather disappointing. Several positive trends have been noted though. One was that more women are running for office. Far more women are winning their primary races (73 per cent of female House Candidates won their primary race from 57 per cent in 1996 and 48 per cent in 1992). Most importantly, both major parties are more actively courting female candidates who have proven they can wage a strong campaign. These indicate that the positive gains are expected to continue. Consider the following table from the 1998, National Survey.

Table 3

Percentage of Growth	*Data of Decision*	*Gender Composition*		*Women's Congressional vote*	
		Male	*Female*	*GDP*	*DEM*
8%	On Election Day	61%	39%	38%	57%
9%	Weekend before	54%	46%	43%	53%
19%	Last two weeks of October	58%	42%	38%	58%
10%	First two weeks of October	50%	50%	53%	43%
11%	In September	50%	50%	45%	52%
40%	Prior to September	46%	54%	48%	51%

Despite a President plunging in an impeachment crisis, another pre-1998, Congressional elections survey calculated a Democrat margin of + 12 per cent (*i.e.*, 50 per cent women for Democrats to 38 per cent for Republicans).[28]

The widening party margins have thus, become an increasing factor in reinforcing the gender gap.

Gender, Vote Choice and Outcomes

Although a wide range of variables contribute to election results and margins of victory, success among women's groups has proved decisive in American election in the 1990s. Starting from Clinton's victory in 1992, women voters have gained importance in the eyes of politicians, parties, pollsters and political analysts in their bid to analyse the winners and losers.

Yet, women's vote went beyond their preferences determining the winner. Their vote choices are seen as connecting private concerns of home and family to the political agenda. From, 'Soccer Moms' who typified the erosion of support to the Republicans to Enily's List (a Political Action Committee PAC), from non-educated working women to college educated women, older women, and women of colour, there is growing recognition that the choices made by women are based on the basis of issues, party and candidate evaluation.

It as also heped in identifying the fact that minority women, union households, urban and 'twenty something' women compose the democratic base.

Gender, like age and party identification has become a usefully broad measurement by which to examine voter's attitudes and choices. Most importantly, as women comprise 53 per cent of the electorate, they if united can determine the outcome of elections, forcing both parties to remain mindful of their concerns. What motivated the women on their vote choices ?

Data from Voter Research and Survey Exit Polls suggest that women voters were motivated by different issues and yet another research shows that women often view the same issues from a different perspective.

While issue agenda do not differ dramatically, women and men tend to see their own economic situation differently. Women and men worry differerntly about :

Women: Health Care, education, helping the poor and homeless, protecting American jobs, etc.

Man: Deficit, taxes, energy and defense policy, etc.

Women and Men and National Policy

Women:-Social problems and Policy: As women tend to feel economically more vulnerable, they adopt a broader view of the economic agenda. Hence, women are more sensitive to price rise, medicines, care for the women are much more concerned about work, wages and family. So in a sense, the stand on economic issues contributed to the vote choices of women after the 1982, recession. The issue of balanced budget thus, became central in legislative elections especially.

On issues of energy and environment, war and peace and social and political issues including the role of the government, public safety and crime control, women tended to bring home different priorities as well.

While abortion was one of the issues, that women considered more central to their vote choices than men, they were also likely to support candidates who favoured equal rights. Many suggest that women consider ending discrimination as an important government goal and tend to feel that they are discriminated against.

Conclusion

Gender gap represents an important change in American political system. It has a direct impact on electoral out comes, when the differences between men and women's perceptions, priorities and agenda are so pervasive and significant that translate into a margin of support for a particular candidate from amongst any one sex that more than offsets the opposition's support.

Men and women may share their dissatisfaction with the current state of the government, but as the gap shows, they have divergent views on what should be done about it. More importantly, the women are likely to favour a social safety net, less cuts in social programs from the budget cuts and in consequence were less likely to favour a party that was seen as extreme right.

In many respects, the policy agenda of women's movement may be difficult to find in the campaign rhetoric adopted. In the short term however, many organizations argue that choosing Democrats has advanced policies which help women. Any long term prospects for political gain may not depend only on the clout they muster from a gender gap that determines who wins, but on what these candidates offer comprehensively to the problems that women face.

BIBLIOGRAPHY

Andersen, Kristi, (1975) "Working Women and Political Participation, 1952-1972". *American Journal of Political Science*, 19: pp. 439-453.

Andersen, Kristi, (1979) "Generation, Partisam Shift, and Realignment," pp. 74-109, in Norman H. Nie, Sidney Verba and John R. Petrocik, eds., *The Changing American Voter*. Cambridge, MA: Harvard University Press.

Baxter, Sandra and Marjorie Lansing, (1983), *Women and Politics: The Invisible Majority*, Ann Arbor: University of Michigan Press.

Blondel, J. (1970), *Votes, Parties, and Leaders*, London: Penguin.

Campbell, Angus, Phillip Converse, Warren Miller, and Donald

Stokes, (1960), *The American Voter*, New York: John Wiley.

Carroll, Susan J., (1985), *Women as Candidates in American Politics*, Bloomington: Indiana University Press.

Greenstein, Fred I, (1965), *Children and Politics*, New Haven, CT: Yale University Press.

Hansen, Susan B., Linda M. Franz and Margaret Netemeyer-Mays, (1976), "Women's Political Participation and Policy Preferences," *Social Science Quarterly*, 56 March: pp. 576-90.

Lane, Robert, (1959), *Political Life*, New York: Free Press.

Shapiro, Robert Y. and Harpreet Mahajan, (1986), "Gender Differences in Policy Preferences: A Summary of Trends from the 1960's to the 1980's", *Public Opinion Quarterly*, 50: pp. 42-61.

Bolce, Louis, (1985), "The Role of Gender in Recent Presidential Elections: Reagan and the Reverse Gender Gap", *Presidential Studies Quarterely*, 15: pp. 372-86.

Miller, Warren E., (1991), "Party Identification, Realignment, and Party Voting: Back to the Basic" *American Political Science Review*, 85: pp 557-68.

Wirls, Daniel., (1986) "Reinterpreting the Gender Gap" *Public Opinion Quarterly*, 50: pp. 316-30.

REFERENCES

1. Centre for American Woman and Politics, (Eagleton Institute of Politics, Rutgers University, New Jersey), 1997.
2. See *Gallup poll*, 1964.
3. See Voter Choice through *CBS/NYT Exit Polls* for actual break-up. In fact, the 1976, Voter Polls indicate that there was no gap in vote choice.
4. Carol M. Mueller, "The Empowerment of Women: Polling and the Women's Voting Bloc", Carol M. Mueller ed., *The Politics of the Gender Gap: The Social Construction of Political Influence*, California, Sage, 1988, pp. 22-23.
5. For all these citations see biliography.
6. See bibliography.
7. Mueller, No. 2, p. 23.
8. Susan J., Caroll, *Women as Candidates in American Politics, Indiana University Press, 1985*, p. 15.

9. *Ibid.*

10. Linda Witt, Karen M. Pagett and Glenna Matthews, *Running As a Women: Gender and Power in American politics, Chap. 5*, pp. 110-11.

11. *CO Researcher*, Vol. 7, No. 8, 28 January, 1997, p. 183.

    Richard Wirthlin had divided women into 64 categories and found that President Reagan had different strengths and weaknesses with each group. The Republican Party conducted extensive research on women and had polled 45,000 by election day.

12. *CAWP*, "Sex Differences in Voter turnout", July, 1995.

13. EMILY's List, *Women Can Lead Democrats Back in 1996*, (1996), See also Celinda Lake, "The Democratic Puzzle" *Elections and Campaigns, October/November, 1995.*

14. *Congressional Quarterly*, "Dole must Close 'Gender Gap' to avoid Clinton Landslide", 26 October, 1996, p. 3085.

    See also *Congressional Quarterly, "Democratic Clout is Growing As the Gender Gap widens", 17 October, 1992*, p. 3265.

15. Celinda Lake and Kellyanne Fitz Patrick, "Gender Gap Politics" in *Campaigns and Elections*, Vol. 16, pp. 22-26.

16. Kirk Victor, "Duking it out in Dixie" in *National Journal*, 13 December, 1997, p. 2501.

17. *Ibid.*

18. *Roll Call Politics*, 1 December, 1997.

19. Linda A., Divall, "Keys to expanding G.O.P. Majorities" in *Polling Report*, 9 December, 1996, pp. 5-6.

20. Cal Clark and Janet Clark, "Whither the Gender Gap ? Converging and Conflicting Attitudes Among Women", in Love Lace Duke ed., *Women in Politics: Outsiders or Insiders*, 2nd edition; Prentice Hall, New Jersey, 1996 pp. 79-80.

21. Mary E. Bendyna and Celinda C. Lake "Gender and Voting in the 1992, Presidential Election", in Elizabeth Adell Cook, Sue Thomas and Clyde Wilcox, *The Year of the Women: Myths and Realities Boulder, Westview Press, 1994*, pp. 243.

    See also Robin Toner, "Women in growing Numbers say they favour Democrats", in *New Yourk Times*, 21 April, 1996.

22. CAWP, *News and Notes*, Winter 1993, W/9, No. 1, p. 5.

23. David, Seans and Leonie Huddie, "On the origin of Political Disunity Among Women", in Louise Tilly and Patrica Gumin eds., *Women, Politics and Change*, NY: Russel and Sage, 1990, pp. 249-77

24. F.n. 10, p.13.
25. Gallup Polls, "Clinton Views Among Basic Demographic Groups", 1998.
26. Statement of Eleaner Smeal President of the Feminist Majority on the Possible Impeachment of the President.
27. *Feminist News*, 25 September, 1998, see also *Washington Post 24 September, 1998.*
28. *Women's Monitor*, "The Gender Gap and the 1998, Congressional Vote", October, 1998.

12

POLITICAL SOCIALIZATION OF SOUTH ASIAN WOMEN IN BRITISH POLITICS

Yamini Gupta

In order to understand political socialization, I feel it is important to define and explain as to what we understand by socialization as Political Socialization is only one form of socialization. By Socialization I mean, a developmental process by which an individual learns or gains the necessary skills, knowledge, attitude and dispositions which enables him or her to function more or less as an effective, though not as an inevitably competent, member of a society, e.g., Barrie Stacey in his book *'Political Socialization in Western Society : An Analysis from Life-span Perspective'* (1978), says that:

> "Socialization refers to the development processes whereby each person acquires the knowledge, skills, beliefs, values, attitudes and dispositions which enables him or her to function as a more or less effective, though not inevitably complaint, member of society. Through these developmental processes, the individual learns how to live with others, even though values, beliefs and patterns of behaviour may vary from one generation to the next. While induction into society during childhood and adolescence is crucial, adulthood brings its own socialization processes. Experiences and activities associated with employment, the labour market and the

economy, marriage and in parenthood, government and political events, ageing the retirement make their mark along the lifecycle, as may dramatic events such as war, economic depression, migration on a massive scale, and major political realignments. In any event, the training received in childhood and adolescence cannot be fully adequate preparation for what is demanded in later years.

Socialization does not necessarily result in civilized values and behaviour or necessarily contribute to the maintenance of political stability. Dispositions towards hostility and violence can be effectively transmitted between generations. This is well illustrated by community relations in Ulster, a place where intergenerational socialization seems to be especially effective. Given the conflicts, disturbances and barbaric elements in society (particularly as they appear in class, religious, sex and race relations), and the conflicts between states in international relations, socialization not infrequently contributes to uncivilized values and conduct, prejudices and hatred, disorder and violence. It follows that any realistic view of socialization should allow for the possibility of interplay with both conflict and social change.

To view socialization simply as the widespread inculcation of traditional norms, values and attitudes or the shaping of vast numbers of people so that they fit into and perpetuate a given social order, is clearly inadequate. In modern societies every generation contains people who growup to reject or depart from many conventional norms, values and behaviour patterns, and to contribute to social change. Further, wherever there exists more than one important agency of socialization, there is some potential for developmental inconsistencies and conflict in experience. What the person experiences in one setting may jar with his experience in other settings. Thus, in class divided, ethnically mixed, culturally varied societies, socialization into particular subcultures could well affect the relationships of substantial numbers of people to the dominant elements in the society."

In the book, *Introductory Sociology*, (1990), whose general editor is Anthony Giddens, socialization is defined as:

> "The process by which we acquire the culture of the society into which we are born the process by which we acquire our social characteristics and learn the ways of thought and behaviour considered appropriate in our society is called socialization".

It is apparent from the definitions presented above that socialization processes help an individual to internalize values and behaviour patterns of the society in order to become an accepted member of the society, although it is not always the case as has been pointed out by Barrie Stacey in the book mentioned above.

There are various approaches to studying socialization. Some of the approaches will be discussed here, and the first approach that I will discuss here is the psychoanalytical approach. According to this approach various activities of the learner are conceptualized in essentially irrational and behaviouralist terms, the individual is perceived as responding more or less in an automatic and stable way, as a consequence of prior experiences, to configurations of stimuli coming both from the external environment and from within the learner himself. Theoretical explorations of the dynamics of behaviour changes vary, considerably from writer to writer, but in most cases emphasis is on an individual responding to, rather than initiating, social interaction and concomitant learning experiences.

This approach is influenced by the Freudian School of Thought. Freud's position regarding the relative importance of innate and environmental influence is a mixed one. Although the basic driving forces of behaviour are assumed to be inherited, many of the manifest forms of action are acquired through associations during interpersonal situations. The importance of these external events in the development of social behaviour was especially recognised by Freud, who maintained that early familial influences could determine later personality characteristic. Freud was primarily interested in dynamic, complex motivations and how these dynamically interrelated forces account for the manifest social behaviour of an individual. But in his early writing he addressed himself explicitly to the question of the basic mechanism accounting for these later complex associations. The key to this system, he proposed, is the reflex arc. Basic responses of personality are conditioned by early experiences. Clearly, then, the early experiences of each individual will be paramount in shaping his social development, according to this theory. But an individual needs different kinds of socialization, depending on the stage of development he[1] she is at in terms of age and social context, e.g., Orville G. Brim Jr. in his article on 'Adult Socialization ', which is published in the encyclopedia said:

> "The socialization that an individual receives in childhood cannot be fully adequate preparation for the tasks demanded of him in later years. As an individual matures, he moves through a sequence of statuses corresponding to different stages in the lifecycle. In addition, his interpersonal environment may change because of geographic or social mobility, with consequent demands for new kinds of behaviour. Even though some of the expectations of society are relatively stable through the lifecycle, many others change from one position to the next."

(International Encyclopaedia of the Social Science, 1968)

The other approaches to the study of socialization have given importance to genetics and environment being the basis of social development of an individual, e.g., Gassell (1946), was one of those who made a contribution to the genetic position according to which external factors were not so important as the genetic endowment for the development of the individuals. Piaget, (1923), too laid emphasis on the inherited developmental tendencies of an individual. Piaget's schemata portray definite stages, of levels, or orderly progression, each stage occuring at a particular age, supporting the position of a genetically determined sequence in the developmental process.

A similar position, but wiu important differences, was earlier proposed by Baldwin (1897), to account for both the mental and social development of children. He posited that children have an inclination, apparently innate, to imitate and that this imitation occurs in specific stages. This position was further developed by G.H. Mead (1934), in his description of the processes whereby one learns to assume the role of another person. Although Baldwin and Mead seemed to assume an innate tendency to imitate, their presentation makes external events crucial in determining much of social behaviour, since the child cannot imitate a model unless it is there to copy. Similarly, Pavlov (1927), who investigated the established and the important variables, involved in the acquistion of conditioned reflexes, did not directly study social development. It was with Watson that conditioning became all important in accounting for social behaviour as well as for almost all other behaviour. Watson proposed that a person's actions aside from a limited number of innate reflexes completely the product of conditioning experiences. With this theory, the pendulum had swung to the far extreme, recognizing the importance of the rate of the external and social factors in the study of the social development of an individual. The author, Roger, V. Burton of 'Socialization in the encyclopaedia, states that:

> "Future theorists would have to acknowledge the role of environmental events no matter what assumptions or positions they take regarding genetic contribution of behaviour".

The above mentioned view is similar to the views held the sociologists like Anthony Giddens, whose definition of socialization in the book edited by him, which is already mentioned above. David A. Goslin (1973), supports Anthony Gidden's point of view and writes about sociologists' positions and says :

> "Sociology concentrating on characteristics of specific groups of institutions in which socialization occurs and on the common social skills required in varying contexts."

Emile Drukheim is one of the sociologists who talked about consensus and importance of social factors in two different kinds of situations where individuals were socialized to accept the norms and values of their respective societies in order to perpetuate that society. First of all, primitive society, he said, divided into small segments consisting of aggregates madeup of kin group, class and tribes where those larger groupings had little real cohesion, since each segment or local unit could be self-sufficient as hunters or agriculturalists. Hence, even if these small segments were severed from one another, they could still survive. Even within these 'segments' social cohesion is depended upon the power of rigid collective norms governing behaviour in every detail, so that the total conformity was maintained. If any transgression did occur then revenge would be the basic social response. The primary source of confirmity, however, was the shared consensus of norms and values, the conscience collective, which was absorbed and reproduced by every member of the society. For Durkheim, mechanical solidarity was a phrase which conveyed this rigidity and crudity of social forms. It shows that even in primitive society individuals were socialized to maintain and perpetuate the existing social order if they deviated, they were dealt with by the punishment considered appropriate by the society.

On the other hand, he talks about the modern societies which are not conceived of as the fragmented breakdown of community, as the evolution of societies provides an underlying potential for more stable and sophisticated social cohesion. The key to this potential is the process of social evolution which takes the form of increased social differentiation, whereby society develops specialized institutions which deal with particular distinct areas of social life, e.g., religion, production, Just as evolution of animals produces more specialized and sophisticated organs to perform particular functions for the whole creature, society comes to develop a range of distinct institutions which deal more adequately with particular needs of the social whole. Just like the anatomical organs, they are mutually dependent for their survival and correct functioning depends upon the healthy functioning of each of other and the maintenance of correct interpretation of all the organs. The potential, then, built into modern society is for organic solidarity. He says that if lively sentiments can be aroused for the mutual dependence of each of these parts of the society, then conflict and crises, so prevalent can be swept aside. Once again, a new moral consensus must be constructed to bring forth order, unlike that in primitive society, this moral order is flexible and adaptable to allow it to cope with the diverse social roles and positions in a complex society the individual has more freedom within the social constraint. A prime task for contemporary sociology is therefore, the construction of a new central civic morality which will be disseminated efficiently by a state education system.

The most important point about Emile Durkheim's views on the maintenance of social order, that I wanted to make was the point that supported our position that every society, whether primitive or modern, socializes its members to follow the norms and the values of that society in order to maintain the order in the society and perpetuate it. Durkheim has presented views on various other issues, but we do not need to throw light on all the work that Durkheim has done, as my purpose to include Durkheim's views was to demonstrate how societies socialize their members to follow the traditions, norms and values of that society, in order to maintain social stability and perpetuate the social system. Although I have to say that Durkheimian views are not devoid of criticisms. They are criticized for not laying sufficient emphasis on the importance of individuals in societies. The other criticism is that they lay too much emphasis on consensus and social order in society as opposed to the role of conflict in society. They are also accused of comparing society with biological organisms which the critics feel cannot be applicable or comparable to any society, or the social changes that take place within it. They are further criticized for not presenting a correct picture of social development as Durkheim, being an evolutionary, talks of social development in a linear fashion and does not give sufficient credit to the role of the importance of diffusion in social development. I will not go further into the critical assessment of the work of Emile Durkheim, as this is not the purpose of the paper.

The second sociologist that I have included here has spoken about the social order and importance of social factors in a somewhat similar manner to Durkheim. He is Talcott Parsons, and his views will be relevant for the work on Socialization. T. Parsons was very much influenced by the functionalist school of thought but as his work developed, the functionalist themes were supplemented by cybernetics (the theory of making of systems in general) to produce his most abstract and formalistic theory in The Social system. Here, T. Parsons argues that any system of action (a society, an institution, a small group, etc.) has general features, for in order to operate successfully as a system certain functional prerequisites have to be fulfilled. These are, in ascending order of importance: (*a*) adaptation, (*b*) goal attainment, (*c*) integration and (*d*) pattern maintenance. Correspondingly, within the social system as a whole, the most basic need is for, (*a*) adaptation to environment through economic activity, but this only provides for the 'higher' aspects of social life. Actors pursue (*b*), socially shaped goals in ways that are governed by (*c*), the norms and sanctions institutionalized in society, ultimately these norms and goals derive from (*d*), an overreacting cultural system of values, on which there is consensus. He further says that, thus, cultural system controls other aspects of society and if we wish to explain social change, then we must look first at changes in cultural systems, e.g., T. Parsons explains the Black Civil Rights in terms of the 'core American values' equal citizenship rights,equal opportunity being mobilized by the majority. The disparities of economic benefit and political power are systematically underplayed as features of the social world which can cause conflict. Even, when T. Parsons discusses power, it is not portrayed in terms of domination of oppression. Instead it is portrayed as necessary resource which members of society collectively agree to allocate to particular authority and it is assumed that the people so appointed use their power selflessly for the collective needs.

T. Parsons clearly gives priority to the 'problem of social order' which can be achieved by conformity of the actors, which is maintained by socialization, (e.g. by the educational institutions) and social control. His account of the personality places great emphasis on internalization of socially given norms and values, rather than suggesting any more active process of negotiating or defining roles by the actor. Deviance is dealt within society by the social control agencies. But he assumes that occassionally deviance, in the form of innovation, may aid the survival of social system.

T. Parsons further says that, any action system needs adaptive mechanisms to bring it back to equilibrium and this need for structural integration is T. Parsons solution to the problem of order. It is argued that the social system operates in such a way as to ensure that its functional needs are fulfilled and that social and system integration are sustained, which is maintained by the institutions of socialization, such as the education system and family, etc., which supports the position that has been taken by various sources of information in literature on socialization to a great extent.

T. Parsons views have their fair share of criticisms too. The work of T. Parsons shows the classic strengths and weaknesses of positivist organism. He does not hesitate in looking at society as a structured, interrelated whole or to attempt to reveal aspects of the operation of that social whole which are opaque to the actors making up the society. Such a perspective can be criticized in two ways. Firstly, it can be criticized for being too wholistic and presenting a derogatory and inadequate account of social action, and secondly, it can be seen as constantly underemphazing social conflict.

Here, I would like to say that some other aspects of the work of T. Parsons have been left untouched only because our purpose is to demonstrate that T. Parsons lays emphasis on the socialization of individuals through various institutions for socialization for the maintenance of the social system. It is not our purpose to present every aspect of Parsonian views.

It will be interesting to find out how within the framework of Durkheim and Parsonian points of views, which preaches social cohesion on the basis of the following of the general norms and values of that society, which may or may not be sympathetic to the causes of the minority people in Britain' for example, particularly South Asian women in this case, when it comes to the matter of employment, housing and high political ambitions. (As this case deals with political aspirations for South Asian women in Britain). How the interests of the white majority, as opposed to the interests of minorities as a whole, or interests of South Asian women as opposed to interests of white women, either in politics or any other social spheres are prioritized? Are there problems in policy making and its implementation? Are the supporters of the Parsonian and Durkheimian views going to satisfy the thirst for reply to the questions, i.e., South Asian women, want to pose to the government of Britain and the quest for justice of the South Asian women in terms of policy making, poor implementation of policies with no real significance to the lives of the South Asian women? Is Britain ready to see South Asian women as Cabinet Ministers and in other powerful positions to which these women may aspire? Will it be considered as deviance and threat to the cohesion and integration of society as it is considered so by the National Front Party of Britain and dealt with strongly by what the Durkheimians and Parsonians call the institutions of social control, i.e., by the police force and other such measures? Will black women and the South Asian women who are already suffering in job market due to sexism and racism, have to face the same prejudices in their political ambitions? Do they (South Asian women) need to be socialized not to aim higher, despite the potential being there? (See Donald R.Young (1973) and Goslin (1973). Should the majority be socialized to accept South Asian women in power and not treat them as a threat and create a new equilibrium? Is there a need for mutual socialization for a new social order and equilibrium in Britain? Or, does Britain need to socialize for socialism and not capitalism for the sake of giving justice to all? Why South Asian and black candidates only succeed in ethnically dominated areas and not in the areas which have predominantly white areas? Answering to such rebellous views, T. Parsons states that the black riots of America of the 1960s, as being compatible with the values of equality between mankind in America. Similarly, the quest for justice of the South Asian women in Britain will be part of the values system promoting equal opportunity for all in Britain according to the functionalists.

It is also important to mention that, I am fully aware of the situation that various political parties have tried, and are trying to deal with the issue of racial discrimination in politics, as it is very much clear from various successful black and South Asian Labour Party Candidates, who have been elected as MPs, such as Mr Grant, Mr Keith Vaz and Mrs Abboit, etc. Many women are in higher positions in the judiciary and have been elected as councillors at local levels, e.g., Mr Keith Vaz's mother was a Councillor in Leicestershire when I last spoke to him. Although this gives some hope to women who are South Asian and are in British politics, the fight for power is a audacious one for a South Asian than a white woman in Britain.

Now, I will talk about the anthopologists, who have studied socialization too. Anthropologists are somewhat different from the sociologists in their definition of socialization. David A. Goslin writes in the book, edited by him, titled 'Handbook of Socialization Theory and Research, (1973), about the anthropological definition of socialization and says:

> "......anthropology viewing socialization from the standpoint of the broader culture, which helps to determine the overall boundaries of socialization experiences".

Some of the approaches used to study socialization by the anthropologists are the psychoanalytical and the cultural approaches. Anthropologists too, used the psychoanalytical approach, often being influenced by Freud. Margaret Mead was the first anthropologist who was engaged in the study of an aspect of socialization. She did use Freudian psychoanalytical approach, but not at first, as she was not strongly influenced by this approach and as she was not mark any significant in her report on the life of adolescent girls, talk about the Oedipal complexes and oral fixations, but rather about the everyday life of these girls, paying particular attention to the ways in which their lives contrasted with those of American girls of the same age. Her description of getting grown up in New Guinea was also more anthropological than psychoanalytical in its conception, but her later study of three contrasting cultures in New Guinea clearly showed Freudian influences.

Two psychoanalysts, Geza Roheim and Erik Erikson (*International Encyclopedia of Social Sciences*—1968), did fieldwork in non-western societies. The former mainly in Australia and Melanesia and the latter studied the American Indians. Both of them have reported about child rearing practices and interpreted some of the rituals, values, and customs as being the consequence of unconscious conflicts engendered by these practices. Roheim was so arbitrary and dogmatic in his interpretations that he antagonized many anthropologists and gave the study of socialization a bad name among the more conservative, members of the profession. Erikson's interpretations were, by contrast, sensitive, illuminating and non-dogmatic a fact which did much to counteract the influence of Roheim.

Abram Kardiner, Edmond Sapir and John Dollard, Ralph Linton and Cora DuBois *International Encyclopaedia of the Social Sciences* (1968), published work and psychoanalytical writings on rearing toilet training, control of sex, dependence and aggression as part of the areas in which some of the specialists in the studies if socialization are interested in J.W.M. Whitting says that, studies in anthropology using psychoanalytical approaches concentrated on the practices of child rearing which were even used to interpret the "national character" of modern nations.

Learning theory has been used in various studies of socialization. Learning and behaviour theory was developed in the laboratory rather than on the "couch" or in the "field", and therefore, the method used was experimental rather than descriptive and interpretive. The staffing of hypotheses so that they can be tested or jeopardised is crucial to laboratory science. Although the procedures of the controlled experiment are inappropriate for the study of socialization, correlational studies, both within and across cultures, are quite feasible. The effect of work by the experimental learning theorists was to introduce hypothesis testing, case counting, and the use of statistics to the study of socialization. John W.M. Whitting and Irvin Child expressed this development in their cross-cultural study of socialization:

> "Most previous work in culture and personality has been oriented primarily towards seeking concrete understanding of specific cases. Our work in contrast is oriented toward testing generalized hypotheses applicable to any case. The difference is not between interest and lack of interest in general hypotheses. The student who is primarily oriented toward full interpretation of the individual case inevitably makes use of general hypotheses as on interpretive device. But he is inclined to take their validity for granted and use them simply as tools, which contribute to the understanding of the concrete case. We are not willing to take the validity of a hypotheses for granted until we can see adequate evidence to support it, and we are willing to leave it to the future task of applying validated hypotheses to the interpretation of specific cases." (1953, p. 5)

Learning theory, as we have seen, is not particularly suitable for interpretive research. When used by J. Whitting (1941), in the study of Kwoma society of New Guinea to study socialization process, it was so literal that it was almost a *tour de force*. This exercise by the anthropologists was not later repeated. Certainly the Kwoma data were in no sense the test of a theory, but they did provide a vehicle for presenting a view of certain aspects of socialization process.

An analysis of the method by which supernatural beliefs were transmitted in Kwoma society was also presented. This analysis was intended as an antidote to both the exaggerated Freudian interpretations, which seemed to imply that the so-called projective system of the culture was reinvented by each generation from the neurotic fantasies of its members; and to the bizarre 'racial unconscious' hypotheses, which held that religious beliefs were genetically transmitted.

Since learning theory was not specially useful as an interpretive device, the Kwoma example was not followed. However, as one of the basis for developing the so-called complex mechanisms of social learning, it was invaluable. Another and more profound influence of learning theory was methodological rather than substantive. Although I have to state that the procedures of controlled experiment are inappropriate for the study of socialization, as we have already demonstrated. But I agree with Daniel Bertaux who says in his book *Biography and Society—The Life History Approach into Social Sciences* (1981) that biographical research can counter-attack the positivists who claim that qualitative research is not reliable, by producing better data using larger sample based on selection criteria used by the positivists for sample selection, i.e., sample may be of 100 and the biographical method will be more valuable for the understanding of social problems because of the rich data that it produces, although it will be expensive and time consuming. Other limitations of the qualitative research can also be made limited by the deliberate efforts of the responsible researchers.

All the three approaches mentioned above, i.e., the psychoanalytical, sociological and the anthropological approaches, encompass many theoretical issues, among them (1) the relative influence of early as opposed to later experiences on behaviour, (2) the relative emphasis to be placed on the individual drives, motives, and needs as energizer of behaviours, as opposed to the influence of social apparatus (groups, institutions, culture as a whole), (3) the relative importance to be placed on the process as opposed to the content as basis for predicting and understanding social behaviour; (4) the extent to which one focuses on the unique aspects of socialization, as opposed to their common properties, (5) whether one's primary aim is to study the courses of deviation from the behavioural norms, with the measurement of the extent of the duration or with forces that tend to produce conformity to the normative expectations.

Since the domain of socialization is a very wide one, which encompasses all the above five areas, which concerns social scientists, it is not possible for me to cover every area that can be of interest to all social scientists in this small article, although I will throw some light on some of the areas that interests the social scientists, while studying socialization, I must further state that, only the bird's eye view of these areas will be presented, as it is impossible to turn a small article into a book. Besides, it has to be mentioned that a researcher chooses an area of socialization, which interests her or him, e.g., some might deal with the child socialization, others may choose adolescent socialization or, like myself, one can also be interested in political socialization.

Since the research is to be on the political socialization problem among South Asian women in British politics, I will like to define it first so that, while the purpose of explaining various dimensions of socialization is undergoing, I will like to discuss alongside the subject of politicization, so that the aspects that can be relevant to this kind of project can be brought to light. Let me first define what I understand by politicization or political socialization. Greenstein talking about political socialization says:

> "Narrowly conceived, political socialization is the deliberate inculcation of political information, values and practices by institutional agents who have been formally charged with this responsibility. A broader conception would encompass all political learning formal and informal, deliberate and unplanned at every stage of the lifecycle, including not only explicitly political learning, but also nominal non-political learning that affects political behaviour, such as the learning of politically relevant social attitudes and the acquisstion of politically relevant personality characteristics".
>
> (Quoted in *Berrie Stacey*, 1978)

Similarly, David Easton, Robert Hess and Jack Dennis and others have stated that:

> "No system is able to maintain itself from any length of time without educating its young politically. Each new generation emerges upon the political scene as a tabula rasa upon which political system must seek to imprint its images if it is to persist".
>
> (Quoted in *R.M. Kelly* and *M. Boutilier,*1978)

Since my research deals with South Asian women and their political socialization, it is only appropriate to talk about the nature of socialization and the issues involved in the study. I have not come across information on ethnic minorities and their political socialization in Britain. But, I did find some information on American minority people and socialization in the book edited by David A. Goslin (1973), which is mentioned above. I felt it was relevant to this work because like Britain, even America is predominantly white, developed, urbanized and industrialized nation and since it is South Asians, who fall within the minority section in the western countries, it will have some relevance for this research. Donald R. Young, who is the author of the article titled 'The Socialization of American Minority People', in the above mentioned book, has spoken on various issues that are involved in the problem of socialization of black minority people in a white nation. Basically he highlights their poor and deteriorated psychological, economic status, (not so much, economic, though, as he states that, their economic status is better in the USA than what it was in their country of origin) and minority status and the impact it has upon their education, employment and morale, e.g., he said:

(1) "Regardless of whether we are considering a form of social class or a caste-like element in the social culture, the primary socialization relevance of minority groups' inferior status lies in its restrictions on the economic, political and social roles of minority individuals and evident unhappy personality problems.

(2) "Aspirations are the individual's conception of the role in the social order which he find's most

> satisfactory. One thing minority individuals are practically certain to have in common is an awareness of their special social status. This, they learn about early in life and are reminded of as long as they live."

I must add here that since South Asian women not only have minority status, but suffer from racism, sexism in Britain and America particularly in the job markets (see A. Phizacklea 1983; Eggleston Report 1986; J. Rex and S. Tomlinson 1977-78), although they have successfully participated in picketing against the factory management (see S. Westwood 1984), but in the field of education, the performance of young South Asian students have been particularly good (S. Tomlinson 1980, 1984, P. Bhachu 1984-85, etc.).

Most of the literature published on South Asian women in Britain shows them as intelligent, hard working and politically aware individuals. South Asian women whether Sikh, Muslim or Hindu women have fought against racism, ill-treatment by the management as stated above, for better working conditions by foundry workers and against cruelty on some immigrants by the immigration officers, etc.

South Asian women wherever they have immigrated from, have brought anti-British feelings with them and are still dominated by the nationalistic propaganda done by their nations of origin. The various programmes celebrating India's and Pakistan's independence from Britain is a humiliating experience for the Britishers on their own soil but Britain has never suppressed such celebrations by its immigrant population and has instead sent congratulatory notes to the nations who sought freedom from British rule. This is the greatness of Britain's governments and its monarchs which has not been mentioned to the immigrant population by the researchers on the ethnic experiences in Britain. The land that teaches them to be free, to fight for human rights on its own soil as well as the soil where it rules or ruled, shows the greatness of the British nation which has been undermined by the inhumanitarian nationalistic movements of the nations where Britain once ruled. South Asian women have this imperialist past which they hate (yet they are in Britain), they face racism in employment, but have been furiously participating in British politics. All the political parties in Britain have encouraged all the minorities to send their representatives at all the levels of political activities and South Asian women are working here as Heads of Race Relations Departments, as councillors, chairpersons, vice-chairpersons, obtained candidatures as MPs, are represented in House of Commons as MPs and in House of Lords in senior capacities and as advisors to the British world leaders with whom I spoke while I was doing my research on South Asian women in British Politics. They may not be palpable to the naked eyes, but South Asian women are working as political activites in the British hinterlands in the main political parties, trade unions and pressure groups are fighting for the rights of minority and majority people in Britain collaborating on some common issues. The educated women have done better than the less educated women in politics. Published reports on Britain shows that minority women more than their men, are active in politics. A researcher studying the socialization of South Asian women in British politics will have to take these factors into account. They also have to study gender bias, the caste and classes of these women and its influence on the political participation, e.g., you have to study whether Kshatriya, the caste of the rulers and the warriors, is still trying to capture the power in Britain, the blind and the disabled South Asian women in politics (see the list for other trade unions and pressure groups in Britain provided by Birmingham Trade Union Head Offices in Midlands). There is a lot of literature on the gender bias, caste and class of South Asian people but not so much information on the blind and disabled political activists of South Asian backgrounds, so I will now highlight the issues involved in working with the blind and the disabled political activists who may be having the South Asian background.

Let me take the case of a blind woman (may be South Asian) or a girl in politics first. Rt. Hon. Mr. David Blunkett of the Labour Party, who was the Shadow Health Secretary, is blind. He has this disability although he is not a woman, yet, his standing in world politics is an important example of a blind person's success as there can be many South Asian women in politics in Britain who may have these problems and who may need immediate attention. Therefore, it is important to understand the problems they may encounter in politics and in their real life. It has been indicated, e.g., that all blind people have difficulties which are common to them.

Robert A. Scott (1973), writing about blind children, said that the understanding of the blind children of the real world is very different from that of the sighted children. They have not only the sounds and the touch of various objects of this world to give them some partial understanding of the real world, but quite often coordinating the two has not been possible. Blind children often in various schools, he suggests, were reacting wrongly at the wrong time (it is obviously from the point of view of a sighted person), which makes a sighted person wonder as to why a blind person would behave the way she/he does at the time when it is not appropriate. It is only because they tend to associate certain sounds with what they imagine to be happening, according to their interpretation, which probably seems right to them, but not to us. He also cited an example, when a teacher gave her blind students a tree with a squirrel on top of it and explained what it was. Then she withdrew the tree and gave the squirrel to the students and asked her students to feel and tell her what it was. They confused the squirrel to be the tree and not the other way around. Even by touch, they could not identify the object, so it is obvious that what this world means to sighted person is very different from what it means to a blind person. They speak only from their memory of what they hear from others and they actually do not have understanding of the reality itself, unless they were not born genetically blind and were sighted some time in their lives, but only went blind due to some reason. They obviously need special books to read and they write in a different way, using braille language. Their understanding of gender division is also negligible due to the difficulty that one feels because of the social stigma attached to letting a blind child feel the sexual organs in order to make him/her realize what the difference in the sexes actually means.

The most intensive interpersonal relationship that a blind individual has are those with his close family, and only those friends who are either in the same position, social rejects, or people with very idealistic outlooks in their lives. They also suffer from the fact that they often as children have a tendency to confuse and fail to make distinction between themselves and the others, as was the case of Helen Keller, who confused somebody else's story to be hers, although later she remembered that she heard the story in one summer of her childhood from her teacher, as she was haunted by this incident for a long time in her life (Robert A. Scott, 1973).

Realizing the kind of difficulties a blind woman faces, it surely will be difficult for women to succeed in politics, if there were to be any woman in the research project who happen to be South Asian and blind. The prejudices that an ethnic woman has to face in a predominantly white society, on top of that, her problem of blindness is a third cause of stigma that they can suffer from, i.e., besides gender and sexism. What will be the fate of such women and their political aspirations in a predominantly white nation? I feel that mutual socialization for both of the blind, black and South Asian women candidates and the majority society should take place, if there is to be any realistic and meaningful chance in politics for blind and South Asian women in Britain. Rt. Hon. Mr. David Blunkett as a blind British Cabinet Minister has all the assistance in is work and so will the South Asian blind political activitsts in Britain. Britain being a developed nation, its programmes for all the sections of its society are very progressive and sympathetic and various facilities to aid such activists exists, if they wish to benefit from them. News coverage on TV, radio and newspapers of such incidences acts as a source of encouragement for those who are working for blind people's and for blind South Asian political women activists.

The second category of people I want to look at are the physically challenged. This category faces numerable problems in their everyday existence and it is not only they who need special socialization to cope with their disability, but also those who care for them. Many times parents or carers have to face embarrassments in front of the people due to their disabled child and they need to be trained for such unpleasent situations. E. Goffman (1963), said that the perosn who is disabled and stigmatized in society always holds the same opinion about himself as we do, and I quote him:

> "....tends to hold the same beliefs about his identity as we do".
>
> .....he may perceive... that whatever others profess, they do not really 'aspect' him and are not ready to make contact with him on 'equal grounds'". (1963)

Stephen A. Richardson states in his article, which is included in the book edited by David A. Goslin (1973), titled *Handbook of Socialization of a Child'* , in which he says that it is a general tendency among the people to treat disabled individuals as sick and always feel that feebled people are in such an unhappy situation that it is necessary to be extra warm and careful with them in order to save them from being hurt. People also think that it need too much commitment to be friendly with a disabled person, and such relationship are also avoided because it probably might become difficult to get out of such relationship.

He compares the situation of a disable person with the situation of a minority, i.e., they both are up against the majority of the society. But he further makes clarification by saying that there are major differences in the situations of the two categories, such as a minority individual has many members in his group in society with whom he can exchange views and seek help and advice, but a disabled person does not. In his home or in the society, he cannot find many people who are in his situation to exchange views and find the understanding she/he is looking for.

Disfigurement of the body is one of the aspects which brings pain and limitation for those who are disabled. People find it hard to hide their feelings looking at the disfigured bodies and through their expressions on their faces and their anxiety that they feel after witnessing this disability, which is not commonly found among the people, they make the disabled person feel unwanted.

He further says that despite their painful experiences, there are efforts made to bring various disabled people together with their families, so that they can develop their understanding of their situations and find sympathy and understanding from people who really perceive their situation. Many disabled people, particularly blind people, marry each other too, which brings them some happiness.

Many of the disabled people also try to use artificial devices in order to compensate for the absence of their real limbs or any other part of the body. Many diabled people use artificial legs or arms and many blind people wear dark glasses to hide their blindness, which gives them much better chance of being accepted by the general public. This certainly relieves some of the pain and psychological suffering that they have to go through.

Along with all the prejudices they have to face due to their disabilities, they also have to face other prejudices from which even able-bodied men and women are not safe. The situation for South Asian women in white society with disability makes it even more difficult, as they face additional prejudices of sexism and racism too. It will be interesting to find out how do disabled South Asian women cope with their disability and political ambition, if such opportunity does arise in their lives. It has to be stated that Britain's programme for people is very good and there are constant developments in this field in order to help out these people.

Age and education are other aspects which affect the political participation for South Asian women in our case, which obviously is the outcome of the socialization by family and state apparatuses. Education plays an important role in political socialization and political participation. Sandra Baxter and Marjorie Lansing (1980), too support this point when they say:

> ".....that women and men with higher levels of education vote at higher rates than people with less education".

Janne Jaquette (1974), Dean Jaros (1973), Vijay Agnew (1979) and Rita Mae Kelly and Mary Boutilier (1978), have made similar comments in favour of the argument that their education has a favourable influence on the political socialization and political participation, particularly of women, although Jane Jaquette has also pointed out that black women who belong to working classes in America tended to be politically more active than their white counterparts and more active than their men (1974).

Age, as I have already stated, plays an important role in political participation as is also pointed out by Jane Jaquette (1974), who found in her research :

> "..... the political participation ratio of younger and older women are surpassed by the rate of their sisters aged thirtyone to sixty. This pattern holds true when we look...at involvement in partisan and non-partisan community organizations. Only 15 per cent of the league members and 25 per cent of the party women, were relatively young or old, but 42 per cent of the registered

voters fell into those categories. Further evidence that political participation changes with age is available in many studies (Verba and Nie, 1972; Milbrath and Goell, 1977)".

Various studies on the impact of age on political participation, has been confirmed that women of younger and older ages tend to be politically less active, but more active in middle ages, i.e., between 30 years and 50 years of age.

Similarly, age has great significance in terms of socialization and political socialization. As the sociologists know, that at different age levels a different nature of socialization is required depending upon which stage you are in the lifecycle.

In infancy and childhood, a different nature of socialization is required, i.e., Harriet L. Reingold (1973), in Goslin's book, points out :

"The infant then may be thought of as a socializer of his parents. He instructs them in the behaviour they must display to evolve his normal growth and development. He is an effective member of society to the extent that he fashions his caretakers into parents; he organizes a family out to separate individuals".

"To correct any over-emphasis on the socializing effectiveness of the infant, the socializing effect of the parents on his behaviour must also be pointed out. The parents provide the physical, and especially the social environment, that will provide the standard by which the infant will discriminate future events. In this social environment he develops the emotional bound that forms the basis of the parents' ability to instruct him in the way of his culture".

At the stage of infancy, most parents and the infant will have some bond with each other, except for some exceptions based on culture, racial and sexual differences and differences based on class and caste of these families. At infant level itself, the issues of gender, sexism, class and racism are applicable and accordingly, will be the outcome of social relationships that an infant would enter when it grows older, of course not undermining the creativity of an individual's mind and its ability to structure and restructure her/his own life, which equally is important. Political aspects may too influence the lives of childrens. e.g., what government policies for childcare and unbringing are made, childbirth facilities which are the outcome of decisions made by various political bodies. This probably is the beginning of the contact a future politician in the form of an infant may have with politics. The respondents themselves might be from a politically active family and hence their politicization will be at a faster rate.

Childhood, adolescence, youth and old age need its own kind of socialization, which has to be interpreted in terms of once again, the respondents' backgrounds, gender, class, whether the families want and aim for integration by mixing and submerging into the social life of the majority, or whether they want to maintain their own cultural segregation, i.e., favour pluralism in social life, the role of parents, mass media, unheavals education system, and politics (see Goslin 1973; S.Tomlinson 1984; G.K. Verma and C. Bagley 1975,1979, 1980, 1982, 1984, 1985, 1986; S. Shaikh 1987; Eileen M. Byrne 1978; S. Delamont 1978 and 1980, etc.).

It is very clear from the literature that is published on South Asian people that despite emphasis on gender distinction within their families, there is also a tendency to give morale support to daughters for good educational achievement as it is very clear from various research reports that the South Asian girls tend to perform much better than South Asian boys and the majority of students till the age of sixteen (particularly Hindu and Sikh girls) which is indicative of the fact that women are encouraged to achieve good education on equal basis if not more. This probably is an indication of the continuity of the culture of their parents, who were broughtup in the society whose culture has given reverence to female deities and worshipped women as Goddesses, which persists among many of the Hindu families even today. These arguments can be supported by the works of Maria Mies, 1980, Tara Ali Baig 1976; S. Wadley 1977; G. Khanna 1978; Y. Gupta 1989. My own research in the north of England produced evidence that the Hindu tradition of giving importance to female Goddesses, who are still worshipped in Hindu temples in Britain, and the continuous existence of Shudra caste in Britain has maintained the link between today's Hindus and the matrilineal Hindus of the 11th century BC, of whose descendants are these Shudras.

Matrilineality which has given importance to female heads of the family, still persists in various disguises among Hindus, particularly among the Shudra caste, and indeed, in the minds of the Hindu migrant people of the subcontinent who have felt the powerful existence of the majority Hindu rule and its traditions of worshipping women in power and see them as role models to imitate.

Besides the cultural histories of these South Asian girls in Britain, they are also the products of urbanized, westernized, capitalistic regime, industrialized and modernized Britain which has got its own culture, educational and employment policies, its emphasis on sexual and racial equality, the feminist influence on the society, particularly through the educational institutions, experiences of racial discrimination, peer groups and families, and constantly shrinking job markets and social benefits for those who want to give up jobs to be in full-time politics, are some of the factors which will determine whether these women will like to aspire and achieve their political ambitions in this country (see Goslin 1973; A Kelly 1981, 1978; E. Kelly 1981; H. Kenithar 1979; A. Phizaklea 1983, 1987; P. Bhachu 1984-85; A.G.D. Bradney 1987; J. Brennan and P. McGeeror 1987; E. M Byrne 1978; C. Juliet and S. Watt 1987; A. Dale 1987, etc.).

It has to be mentioned that all of the above-mentioned factors will be relevant in all the stages of the lives of the respondents, whether in their childhood, adolescence, youth or in old age, as these aspects of their family life and their society will be important institutions of socialization and possibly assist them in the achievement of their political goals. Donald R. Young, writing about the socialization of American minority people, pointed out the existence of pressure groups for political actions due to the comparative feelings of insecurity among the minority people, which could help the minority people fight for their pride and interests. He also pointed out that the voluntary organizations of the blacks, such kind that exists among the Hindus who have come from various parts of the world in Britain, who offer support to their members and act as agents for socialization, e.g., various Swaminarayan Hindu Temples and community centres exist all over the country, *i.e.*, Britain, who teach the old and the young Hindus about the inculture and religion.

Donald R. Young has also indicated that the minority people should not only ask for equality and success in all the social spheres, but also try to socialize and mutually prepare their communities for such success, so that when the opportunity arises they are prepared for it, e.g., talking about the lack of preparation among the black Americans, he stated that :

> "No doubt the position that a high proportion of Negroes are not yet ready to take advantage of the opportunities they demand frequently has been taken for obstructionist purposes, but that does not change the fact that preparation for change is needed and that it takes effort and time", (1973).

In conclusion I would like only to say that political socialization plays an important role in assisting a women to achieve her political ambitions, but in order to understand the role of socialization in it, it is important to take gender division, role of upheavals in life, church or religion, feminist influence, caste, class, racial aspects, cultural, political and educational aspects of the family into consideration and those of the society in which they are socialized, its social and economic development and its educational policies, political institutions, particularly in relation to women, needs to be looked at too. In British context in order to understand the position of South Asian women in its political sphere, one must study, the American and the position of EEC rulings in this context as Britain works as one of the allies of America and European nations and what happens in America and European nations has a great bearing on what will happen in Britain in all the social spheres.

NOTE

South Asian women: All the women who have migrated from the Indian subcontinent, i.e., from India, Pakistan, Bangladesh and Sri Lanka to Britain are studied under the term South Asian women. These women may have migrated to various nations in Africa and from there to Britain or from elsewhere to Britain, but if they have their origins in the Indian subcontinent, then they are given the term South Asian women.

These women who migrated to Hong Kong or Africa in the first instance and then immigrated to Britain, are given the term Twice-

Migrants by Dr. Praminda Bhachu who is a specialist in ethnic studies in Britain, but they are studied under the term South Asian women also.

REFERENCES

1. Agnew, V., 1979, *Elite women in Indian Politics*, published by Vikas Publishing House Pvt. Ltd., Delhi, India.
2. Baig, T.A., 1976, *India's Women Power*, published by S. Chand Company Ltd., Delhi, India.
3. Baldwin James M (1897) 1906, *Social and Ethical interpretations in Mental development: A study in social Psychology*, 4th Edition, rev. and enl, Macmillan, New York.
4. Baxter Sandra and Lansing M.,—1980, *Women and Politics*, published by University of Michigan Press, USA.
5. Bertaux D., 1981, Biography and society-*The Life History Approach into Social Sciences*, Sage Publication, California, London.
6. Bhachu P, (1984-85), *Multicultural Educational Parental Views-New Community* Vol. XII, No. 1, Winter UK.
7. Bradney A.G.D., 1987, *Seprate schools, Ethnic Minorities and the Law'*, N. Community, Vol. XIII, No. 3, Spring, C.R.E. UK.
8. Brennan J, 1987 and McGreeror P, *Minorities Graduate Suffer in Search for Employment*, T.E.S. 8.5. 87 UK.
9. Burton Roger V., 1968, *International Encyclopedia of the Social Sciences*, Vol. 14. The Macmillan Company and the Free Press, Editor-David L Sills, USA.
10. Byrne Eileen M, 1978, *Women and Education*, Tavistock Publication, Britain.
11. Child Irvin L, 1954, *Socialisation*, Vol. 2, pp. 642-55, in Gardner Lindsey, *Handbook of Social Psychology*, Cambridge, Mass: Addison Wesley.
12. Child Irvin L, 1988, Storm Thomas, and Veroff Joseph, *Achievement Themes in Folk Tales Related to Socialization Practice.*, pp. 479-92 in John W. Atkinson, Motives in Fantasy, Action and Society, A method of Assessment and study, Princeton, N.J. Van Nostrand.
13. Delamont S, 1978, *Women and Schooling*, Routledge and Kegan Paul, London.
14. Delamont S, 1980, *Sex Role and the School*, Methun London.
15. Dale A, 1987, *Occupational Inequality, Gender and Life Cycle in the Journal Work, Employment and Society*-Vol. 2 UK.

16. Eggleston Report, 1986, *Education for Some*, edited by Dunn, Anjali, Cecil Wright. Published by Trentham Books, UK.

17. Erikson Erik H, (1950) 1964, *Childhood and Society*, 2nd Edition rev. and enl; New York, Norton.

18. Freud Sigmund, (1900) 1953, The standard edition of the complete Psychological works of Sigmund Freud, Vol. 4 and 5. The Interpretation of Dreams, London.

19. Gessell A, (1964) 1953, *The Ontogenesis of Infant Behaviour*, pp. 335-73 in Leonard Carmichael (ed.), *Manual of Child Psychology*, 2nd Edition, New York.

20. Giddens A., 1990, *Introductory Sociology*, Published by Macmillan Education Ltd., London.

21. Goffman E., 1968, *International Encyclopedia of the Social Sciences*; Vol. 14. The Macmillan Company and the Free Press, Editor-David L. Sills. USA.

22. Goslin David A. 1973, *Hand Book of Socialization Theory and Research*. Published by Rand McNally College Publishing Company Ltd., Chicago.

23. Greenstein Fred I 1965, *Children and Politics. Yale Studies in Political Science*, Vol. 12, New Haven, Yale University Press.

24. Gupta Y., 1989, *Educational and Vocational Aspiration of the Hindu Women who are settled in Britain*, M.A. Thesis, Sociology Department, Manchester University, UK.

25. Jaquette J.S, 1974, *Women and Politics, Published* by A. Wiley Inter Science Publications, Canada.

26. Jaros D., 1973, *Socialization to Politics*, Published by Thomas Nelson and Sons Ltd., Great Britain.

27. Jennings M.K. and 1981 Niemi Richard G., *Generations and Politics*, Published by Priceton University Press, Princeton, USA.

28. Juliet C and Watt S, 1987, *Racism, Women and Poverty* Chapter 3 in Glendinning's Women and Poverty, Published by Wheatsheaf Books Ltd., UK.

29. Kardiner A (1939) 1955, *The Individual and His Society: The Psychodynamics of Primitive Social Organization*, New York; Columbia University Press.

30. Kelly A., 1978, Girls and Science: *An International Study of Sex Differences in School, Science achievement*, Almquist and Wiksell, Sweden.

31. Kelly A, 1981, *The Missing Half,* Manchester University Press, Manchester, UK.

32. Kelly E, 1981, *Socialization in Patriarchal Society* in 'The Missing Half by Alison Kelly, Manchester University Press, Manchester, UK.

33. Kelly Rita Mae and Boutilier Mary, 1978, *The Making of Political Women: A study of Socialization and role conflict.* Published by Nelson Hall Publishers, Chicago.

34. Kenitkar H, 1979, *A School for Hindus,* New Community Journal, Vol. VII, No. 2, UK.

35. Lovenduski, 1986, *Women and European Politics Contemporary Feminism and Public Policy,* Published by Wheatsteaf Book Ltd.

36. Mackenzie W.J.M. 1978, *Political Identity,* Published by Penguin Books Ltd., England.

37. Mariamma A, Khanna G; and Verghese, 1979, *Indian Women Today,* Published by Vikas Publishing House Pvt. Ltd., N. Delhi, India.

38. Mead G.H. (1934) 1963, *Mind, Self and Society from the Stand Point of a Social Behaviourist,* Edited by Charles W. Morris, University of Chicago Press, Published Posthumously.

39. Mead Margaret (1928) 1961, *Coming of Age in Samoa—A Psychological Study of Primitive Youth of Western Civilisation,* Morrow.

40. Mies M, 1980, *Indian Women and Patriarchy* published by Navrang Rai Concept Publishing Company, Printed by Rajdhani Press, Delhi, India.

41. Pavlov Ivan P, (1927) 1969, *Conditioned Reflexes:* An Investigation of the Psychological Activity of the Cerebral Cortex, New York.

42. Phizacklea A, 1983, *One Way Ticket,* Published by Routledge and Kegan Paul Ltd., London, Boston, Melbourne and Henley.

43. Piaget J, (1923) 1959, *The Language and Thought of the Child;* 3rd Edition, Rev, New York, Humanities Press, First Published as Le Language et La Pensee ChezL' enfant.

44. Reingold Harriet L, 1968, *International Encyclopedia of the Social Sciences,* Vol. 14, The Macmillan Company and The Free Press; Editor-David L. Sills, USA.

45. Rex J. Tomlinson S., (1977—1978), *Housing Employment, Education and Race Relations in Birmingham N,* Community, Vol. VI 1 and 2, Winter, UK.

46. Sapir E. (1917) 1949, *Excerpts from a (book) Review of Oskar P Fista 'The Psychoanalytic Method,* pp. 522-25 in Edward Sapir, Selected Writings of Edward Sapir in Language, Culture and Personality, Berkeley and Los Angeles, University of California Press.

47. Scott R.A., 1968, *International Encyclopedia of the Social Sciences,* Vol. 14; The Macmillan Company and the Free Press; Editor David L Sills, USA.

48. Sears Robert R, Maccoby E.E. and Levin H., 1957, *'Patterns of Child Rearing',* Evanston III; Row Peterson.

49. Shaikh S, 1987, *The Education of Muslim Girls in British Schools,* M.A. Thesis, Manchester University, Sociology Department, UK.

50. Sills D.L., 1968, *International Encyclopedia of the Social Sciences,* Vol. 14. The Macmillan Company and the Free Press, Editor. USA.

51. Stacey B, 1978, *Political Socialization in Western Society: An Analysis from a Life Span* Perspective, Published by Edward Arnold Publishers Ltd., London.

52. Tomlinson S, 1980, *The Educational Performance of Children of Asian Origin,* New Community, Vol. VIII, Winter, UK.

53. Trapper T, 1976, *Political Education and Stability,* Elite Responses to Political Conflict. Published by John Wiley and Sons, London.

54. Verma G.K. And Bagley C., 1975, *'Race and Education Across Cultures',* Published by Heinemann, London.

55. Verma G.K. and Bagley C., 1979, *Race, Education and Identity.* Published by The Macmillan Press Ltd., London

56. Verma G.K., 1979, *Attitude Measurement in a Multi-ethnic Society; Bulletin of the British Psychological Society,* Printed in UK.

57. Verma G.K. Malik K. and Bagley C-1980, *Illusion and Reality in Indian Secondary Eduction Saxon House,* Farborough.

58. Verma G.K., 1980, *The Impact of Innovation* Edited by G. K. Verma etc. (Norwich) Centre for Applied Research in Education, University of East Anglia.

59. Verma G.K. and Bagley C., 1982, *Self Concept Achievement and Multicultural Education.* Published by Macmillan Press Ltd., London and Basingstoke.

60. Verma G.K. and Bagley C., 1984, *Race Relations and Cultural Differences* Edited, Published by Croom Helm Ltd., UK.

61. Verma G.K. and Bagley C., 1985, *Multicultural Childhood; Education, Ethnicity and Cognitive Styles,* Edited, Aldershot, Gower, UK.

62. Verma G.K., 1986, *The Swann Report and Ethnic Achievement—A comment, C.R.E. Journal N. Community*, Vol. XII, No. 3 Winter, UK.

63. Wadley S, 1977, *Women and the Hindu Tradition in Women in India* by Jacobson D and Wadley S. Published by Manchester Publication in N. Delhi, India.

64. Watson J.B. (1919) 1929, *Psychology from the Standpoint of a Behaviourist*, 3rd Edition rev. Philadelphia, London.

65. Westwood S, 1984, *All day Everyday*, Factory and Family in Making of Women's Lives; London, Pluto Press.

66. Whitting J.W.M., 1941, *Becoming a Kwoma; Teaching and Learning* in a New Guinea Tribe, New Haven, Yale University.

67. Whitting J.W.M. and Irvin Child, 1953, *Child Training and Personality, A Cross-Cultural Study, New Haven*; Yale University Press, A Paper Back Edition was Published in 1962.

BIBLIOGRAPHY

Barbara Arneil : "Politics and Feminisms, Blackwell Publishers, U.S. 1999".

Jane Lewis (ed.) : *Before the Vote was won Arguments for and Against Women's Suffrage,* Routtlege and Kagal Paul, New York and London, 1989.

Josefina Figueira CeMcdonough and Rosemarry Sarris (ed.) : *The Trapped Women,* Sage New Bury, Delhi, 1987.

Sandhy Venkatsaran : *Living on the Edge Women, Environment and Development, Delhi,* 1992.

INDEX

P

Q

R